The C

BLACKWELL READERS

In a number of disciplines, across a number of decades, and in a number of languages, writers and texts have emerged which require the attention of students and scholars around the world. United only by a concern with radical ideas, Blackwell Readers collect and introduce the works of pre-eminent theorists. Often translating works for the first time (Levinas, Irigaray, Lyotard, Blanchot, Kristeva) or presenting material previously inaccessible (C. L. R. James, Fanon, Elias), each volume in the series introduces and represents work which is now fundamental to study in the humanities and social sciences.

The Lyotard Reader
Edited by Andrew Benjamin

The Irigaray Reader
Edited by Margaret Whitford

The Kristeva Reader
Edited by Toril Moi

The Levinas Reader
Edited by Sean Hand

The C. L. R. James Reader
Edited by Anna Grimshaw

The Wittgenstein Reader
Edited by Anthony Kenny

The Blanchot Reader
Edited by Michael Holland

The Elias Reader
Edited by S. Mennell

The Lukács Reader
Edited by Arpad Kardakay

The Cavell Reader
Edited by Stephen Mulhall

The Guattari Reader
Edited by Garry Genosko

The Bataille Reader
Edited by Fred Botting and Scott Wilson

The Eagleton Reader
Edited by Stephen Regan

The Castoriadis Reader
Edited by David Ames Curtis

The Goffman Reader
Edited by Charles Lemert and Ann Branaman

The Hegel Reader
Edited by Stephen Houlgate

The Norbert Elias Reader
Edited by Johan Goudsblom and Stephen Mennell

The Frege Reader
Edited by Michael Beaney

The Virilio Reader
Edited by James Der Derian

The Angela Y. Davis Reader
Edited by Joy James

The Stanley Fish Reader
Edited by H. Aram Veeser

The Žižek Reader
Edited by Elizabeth Wright and Edmond Wright

The Talcott Parsons Reader
Edited by Bryan S. Turner

The Certeau Reader
Edited by Graham Ward

The Adorno Reader
Edited by Brian O'Connor

The Jameson Reader
Edited by Michael Hardt and Kathi Weeks

Forthcoming:

The Bakhtin Reader
Edited by Ken Hirschkop

The Kierkegaard Reader
Edited by Jonathan Rée and Jane Chamberlain

The Raymond Williams Reader
Edited by John Higgins

The Tocqueville Reader
Edited by Zunz

The Benjamin Reader
Edited by Drew Milne

The Fanon Reader
Edited by Homi Bhabha

The Bauman Reader
Edited by Peter Beilharz

The Castells Reader
Edited by Ida Susser

The Marcus Garvey Reader
Edited by Robert Hill

The Certeau Reader

Edited by

Graham Ward
University of Manchester

First published 2000

2 4 6 8 10 9 7 5 3 1

Blackwell Publishers Ltd
108 Cowley Road
Oxford OX4 1JF
UK

Blackwell Publishers Inc.
350 Main Street
Malden, Massachusetts 02148
USA

British Library Cataloguing in Publication Data

A CIP catalogue record for this book is available from the British Library.

Library of Congress Cataloging-in-Publication Data

Certeau, Michel de.
[Selections. 2000]
The Certeau reader/edited by Graham Ward.
p. cm.—(Blackwell readers)
Includes bibliographical references and index.
ISBN 0–631–21278–7 (hbk: alk. paper).—ISBN 0–631–21279–5 (pbk.: alk. paper)
1. Culture. 2. Historiography. 3. Ethnology. 4. Language and culture. 5. Religion and culture. I. Ward, Graham. II. Title.
III. Series.
HM621.C472 2000 306—dc21 99–33906 CIP

Typeset in 10½ on 12½ pt Bembo
by Kolam Information Services Pvt Ltd, Pondicherry, India
Printed in Great Britain by
TJ International Ltd, Padstow, Cornwall

This book is printed on acid-free paper

The origin of this book lies in
my long acquaintance with the Society of Jesus.
I dedicate this book to a whole line of Jesuits
who have been my friends, most particularly
Michael Barnes and John Montag

Contents

Notes on Contributors

Jeremy Ahearne is Lecturer in French Studies at the University of Warwick. He is author of *Michel de Certeau: Interpretation and Its Other* (Cambridge: Polity Press, 1995).

Frederick Christian Bauerschmidt is Assistant Professor at Loyola University, Baltimore. His essays have appeared in several journals, including *Modern Theology* and *New Blackfriars*.

Ian Buchanan is Lecturer in the Department of English, University of Tasmania. His essays have apeared in several journals, including *The South Atlantic Quarterly* and *New Blackfriars*, and he has edited two guest editions on Certeau's work, one for *Social Semiotics* and the other for *The South Atlantic Quarterly*.

Tom Conley is Professor of French at Harvard University. He is the author of several books, including *Film Hieroglyphics*, *The Graphic Unconscious* and *Self-made Map*, while also being the translator of Certeau's *The Writing of History*, *The Capture of Speech and Other Political Essays* and *Culture in the Plural* (all for the University of Minnesota Press).

Luce Giard is associated with the Centre de Recherches historiques at the Ecole des Hautes Etudes en Sciences Sociales, and regularly serves as visiting professor at the University of California, San Diego.

Graham Ward is Professor of Contextual Theology and Ethics at the University of Manchester. He is the author of *Barth, Derrida and the Language of Theology*, *Theology and Contemporary Critical Theory* and *Balthasar at the End of Modernity*, and editor of *The Postmodern God*. He has edited a special edition on Certeau's work for *New Blackfriars*.

Acknowledgments

The editor and publishers would like to thank the following for permission to reproduce the chapters contained in this book:

Excerpt from De Certeau, *The Mystic Fable* (The University of Chicago Press, Chicago, 1992).
De Certeau, 'The Social Architecture of Knowledge' from *Culture in the Plural* (trans. Tom Conley) (University of Minnesota Press, 1997. Copyright the Regents of the University of Minnesota).
De Certeau, 'The Symbolic Revolution' from *The Capture of Speech* (trans. Tom Conley) (University of Minnesota Press, 1997. Copyright the Regents of the University of Minnesota).
De Certeau, 'Le monde de la voyelle' from *Une Politique de la Langue* (Gallimard, 1975).
De Certeau, 'Writings and Histories' from *The Writing of History* (© 1988 Columbia University Press. Reprinted with the permission of the publisher).
De Certeau, 'Ethno-Graphy. Speech, or the Space of the Other: Jean de Léry' from *The Writing of History* (© 1988 Columbia University Press. Reprinted with permission of the publisher).
De Certeau, 'The Weakness of Believing. From the Body to Writing, a Christian Transit' from *La Faiblesse de croire* (Editions de Seuil, 1997).
De Certeau, 'The Scriptural Economy' from *The Practice of Everyday Life* (trans./ed. Steven Rendall) (The University of California Press. Copyright © 1984 The Regents of the University of California).

De Certeau, 'Mystic Speech' from *Heterologies* (trans. Brian Massumi) (University of Minnesota Press, 1987. Copyright the Regents of the University of Minnesota).
De Certeau, 'History: Science and Fiction' from *Heterologies* (trans. Brian Massumi) (University of Minnesota Press, 1987. Copyright the Regents of the University of Minnesota).
De Certeau, 'The Indian Long March' from *On Signs* (ed. Marshall Blonsky) (Blackwell Publishers, 1987).
De Certeau, 'Walking in the City' from *On Signs*, where it appears as 'Practices of Space' (ed. Marshall Blonsky) (Blackwell Publishers, 1987).
De Certeau, 'Believing and Making People Believe' from *On Signs*, where it appears as 'The Jabbering of Social Life' (ed. Marshall Blonsky) (Blackwell Publishers, 1987).

Every effort has been made to trace copyright holders. The editor and publishers apologize in advance for any inadvertent use of copyright material, and will be pleased to rectify any errors or omissions at the earliest opportunity.

Introduction

Graham Ward

Friedrich Munroe is a film director in a film by the German filmmaker Wim Wenders, entitled *The State of Things* (*Der Stand der Dinge*, 1982). Moving between Los Angeles and Portugal (where Friedrich's post-apocalyptic film *The Survivors* is being filmed), speaking German, Friedrich announces: "I'm at home now here, in no house, in no country." It is a statement which epitaphs Wenders's work to date: employing as he has, for many of his films, either the American road movie genre or the figure of the wanderer.

His most celebrated wanderer is Travis Henderson in a film awarded the Golden Palm at the Cannes Film Festival in 1984: *Paris, Texas*. Travis (pronounced, significantly, "traverse") emerges from the Mexican sierra like the survivor of some global catastrophe. He walks obsessively until, at a ramshackle bar, he collapses and his brother, Walt, is contacted to pick him up. Walt lives in Los Angeles and Travis hates flying, so the film tracks this first drive from Texas to Los Angeles. Travis has a son, significantly called Hunter, whom he abandoned. Hunter is now living with Walt and his wife (who are childless) as their son. Travis journeys back to LA to reclaim this son. Walt's Los Angeles home overlooks the runways of the airport. Together, Travis and Hunter go in search of their mother, Jane, who now lives in Houston and works in a porno palace. They discover her, and the haunting story of how Travis's love for the younger Jane turned into a jealous obsession is revealed in an astonishing dialogue between the two, which takes place in the palace between two booths, using a telephone connection and a two-way mirror. Travis had tied Jane to the stove and given up work, Hunter as a child was crying, Travis was drinking heavily. He woke up to find himself surrounded by flames. Jane had set fire to their trailer and left her husband in it as she escaped with Hunter. Now, four years later, Travis reunites Hunter and Jane. The pieces of the story of how he came to be in the desert are all in place and Travis has grown from a survivor in shock, unable to speak, to a man who has faced himself, his past and the knowledge that his relationship with Jane is over. From a parking lot Travis watches the meeting of Hunter and Jane, and the closing shots of the film are of Travis driving down the freeway from Houston, the city red-rimmed as the sun sets, Travis silent, watching the road.

For a man considerably interested in the practices of everyday life, in what constitutes the ordinary (in all its variety and complexity), it would not, I hope, come as a surprise to Michel de Certeau to find his work being brought into relation with a road movie. Among the 422 published items listed by Luce Giard in her definitive bibliography, it is interesting to note that Certeau wrote analyses of film for several journals: *Ça Cinéma*, *Les Novellas litteraires*, *Telerama*, and *Cinéma*. Certeau was a man for whom culture meant what the French sociologist Pierre Bourdieu defines as *habitus*. *Habitus* is the external practices produced by the unconscious internalization of certain structures and ways of seeing and acting that compose a specific society at a specific time.[1] These practices organize and structure a society; they express what that society takes to be "reality". It is an assumed reality, but the investigation into the production of that reality proceeds by way of investigating *habitus*, the practices of everyday life. And road movies? The theme of being at home nowhere, of walking, of wandering, of voyaging, of map-reading, of travelling, of time as living and living as changing complex relations, social, political, theological, psychological, is encountered again and again in Certeau's writings. A claustrophobic nightmare is associated with being in a place, like a railway car or Jules Verne's *Nautilus*, where one is forced to watch the inexorable march of history from a window. "A travelling incarceration. Immobile inside a train, seeing immobile things slip by. What is happening? Nothing is moving inside or outside the train. . . . The unchanging traveller is pigeonholed, numbered, and regulated in the grid of the railway car, which is a perfect actualisation of the rational utopia."[2] Furthermore, several Certeau scholars have characterized his *oeuvre* as a continual movement or journeying from one place to another, from one academic discipline to another, crossing, recrossing and confusing disciplinary boundaries. Some have compared this to an Abrahamic wandering which proceeds into ever-deepening exile and stands in contrast to the wanderings of Odysseus (made philosophically famous as a figure for the movement of Reasoning itself by Hegel). Odysseus sails from Ithaca to the Trojan Wars, leaving defeated Troy only to undergo years of embattled separation before returning home again to his wife Penelope, to his nurse Euryclea, to his son Telemachus, to his father Laertes, and to his ancient hound Argus. But

Certeau's journey, like Travis's in the Wenders adaptation of the road movie, is not circular. There is no return home. Certeau himself, who wanted to be a missionary in China, who joined an Order, the Jesuits, with a strong commitment to missionary activity, who travelled extensively through the Americas, North and South, lived for six years in California toward the end of his life. As a thinker, he moves out to question what we might mean by home; to question the fixity of place.[3] His was a search for somewhere else, another city, a heteropolis, another spatiality. His work inscribes the continual everyday movement toward the impossible other, the undomesticated, uncolonized other. It inscribes the economy of desire itself.[4] Therefore, by making an early acquaintance with Certeau via a road movie, we can perhaps situate this man's work with respect to West European and North American cultures of the late twentieth century. Further, the comparison enables us to raise the question (and maybe begin to answer it): why does Certeau's work resonate so clearly with our culture? Why is it important that account of Certeau's work is taken (and is being increasingly taken) today?

Of Wenders's work it is written: "Wenders, through his characters, their narratives, and his own acts as itinerant filmmaker, lives out the peculiarly Germanic state of post-war rootlessness. He makes homelessness a virtue, an aesthetic."[5] Wenders gives expression to a nameless desire that arises in the collapse of the German *Heimat*, which is simultaneously the collapse of belief in what George Steiner will call the civilizing of gentlemen;[6] that is, the *Bildung* tradition that founded Western European liberalism and humanism. Certeau was of a generation prior to Wenders (who was born in 1945), but shared the same disillusionment, the same sense of fragmentation and loss, as Wenders. Certeau was born in Chambéry in 1925, and his adolescence and youth had been torn apart by the Second World War. As Luce Giard, his close friend, colleague and later editor of his work, has so movingly written:

> What has specifically marked his generation was the common, painful experience of the shock, felt in his adolescence in 1940, when he had to witness – rage pulsating in his veins – the annihilation of the "old country" in resignation, fear, shame, and disorder. He retained its unforgettable lesson, which often returned through the detours of his conversation, to the effect that no place exists for children to obey their fathers and, even less, to accept the currency of their discourse of value or the code of honour whose celebration that these fathers, in their agreement with authorities, are forever ready to perpetuate. . . . He knew he was leading this labor of emancipation into a painful phase of sundering, of distance taken from earlier assurances, sometimes to the point of a break without possibility of return. . . . But the construction of his autonomy, the removal of the "obviously" received facts of a tradition, a milieu, a family, meant staying faithful to the inner violence of the adolescent of 1940 who had refused the resignation of the fathers (most of them in power), support for the old

Marshall [Petain], the moralizing discourse of the defeat that a sinful France really deserved.[7]

Studying classics and philosophy at the universities of Grenoble and Lyon, in the south-west of France, among its mountains, he entered the Society of Jesus at the age of 25, with, as I have said, the hope of being called to the missionary life. He was ordained to the Catholic priesthood in 1956 and began to develop his evident intellectual talents, taking a doctorate in religious science at the Sorbonne in 1960. This was a period of outstanding intellectual attainment for the Jesuits. Certeau was part of an Order which had nurtured the talents (and the theological controversies these talents provoked) of Hans Urs von Balthasar, Henri de Lubac, Karl Rahner and Pierre Teilhard de Chardin. What interested Certeau, with the encouragement of his Order, was the early history of the Jesuits. But this early history was also the dawn of modernity, when new sciences (of anthropology, of ethnography, of history, of technology) were emerging and changing the social, cultural and political landscape of Western Europe. In examining this period of history, then, he was examining questions concerning the power of institutions to produce new knowledges and discipline its subjects.

Two mystical writers in particular drew his attention: Bienheureux Pierre Favre and Jean-Joseph Surin. In the early 1960s he edited and introduced Favre's *Memorial* and Surin's *Guide spirituel pour la perfection*. He then teamed up with Henri de Lubac to edit and introduce the *Lettres à Leontine Zanta* of Pierre Teilhard de Chardin, who had died in 1955, before editing and introducing a definitive edition of Surin's *Correspondence*.[8] The year was 1966. The conservative government of France was in the hands of a one-time Resistance leader of fame and notoriety. Charles de Gaulle was in power. And then the student-led riots of May 1968 began:

> Something happened to us. Something began to stir us. Emerging from who knows where, suddenly filling the streets and the factories, circulating among us, becoming ours but no longer being the muffled noise of our solicitude, voices that had never been heard began to change us. At least that was what we felt. From this something unheard of was produced: we began to speak. It seemed as if it were for the first time. From everywhere emerged the treasures, either aslumber or tacit, of forever unspoken experiences.[9]

Even in English the very rhythms and wording attest to the dawning again, for Certeau, of an event that would change the course of history. It was as if the students-led riots of May 1968 released a French spirit trapped and disciplined by the North American and European settlements that brought to a close the Second World War. New possibilities were seen, and Certeau would not allow the French people to forget them.[10] Throughout the summer of 1968 he wrote feverishly, passionately. What does this revolutionary event mean for France, he asked. "We have to begin again from the phenomenon. It must, I believe, call into question our entire system of representation."[11] A new culture was making itself felt, a new reality, but it was hidden and repressed still beneath the remnants of modernity's unquestioned powers and disciplines. Certeau had found his vocation as a Jesuit, and as a missionary: it was to go out and excavate this other order, this other speaking going on beneath the civic-speak, this other place.

Back in 1964, Certeau had recognized the importance of a man overthrowing psychoanalytical practice as Freud had understood it. Jacques Lacan had opened his Ecole freudienne in Paris. Certeau was one of its first members.[12] There is, in this action, a glimpse of the revolutionary, the Resistance fighter who had not yet finished. Lacan had begun to rethink Freudian psychoanalysis along lines of thought opened up by Henri Wallon (who introduced the fundamental idea of the "mirror stage," the transit for Lacan between nature and culture) and the structuralism of the anthropologist Claude Lévi-Strauss. Lacan developed an understanding of the subject of desire in terms of the Real, the Imaginary and the Symbolic. The Real is the most primordial scene, which the subject can never face directly: it is dark, chaotic, amorphous, sublime, and horrific. The subject absorbs and stores various images and impressions of the world and his or her placing as a body within that world. The subject develops certain fantasies about himself or herself. All these impressions and intimations of experience constitute the Imaginary scene of the psyche. But it is only when the subject enters in the symbolic that he or she achieves a sense of identity. Identity is always fragile, mediated, and virtually real. The "mirror stage" was understood as the first step into the realm of the symbolic, ruled as it is by the Father. The Father (as the incarnation of the symbolic law) demands separation from the Mother for entry into the social and cultural. But, while having to take this step in order to give shape and articulation to the Imaginary sense of self, there is also (and the irruption of Real makes this evident) a sense of appalling loss. One is forever in mourning as a subject, forever seeking symbolic substitutions for the primary loss. One's life is a seeking for the final consummation of one's desire.

As Luce Giard, in her introduction to Certeau's historiography, points out, Certeau's interest in psychology and Lacan was not in terms of its therapeutic promises. More interesting to Certeau was – and here he links up with Herbert Marcuse, Wilhelm Reich and the Freud of *Civilization and Its Discontents* – the way it might be used to understand the cultural scene and study its other scene.[13] He is interested in the way Lacan's work is haunted by a monotheistic Otherness and how this otherness organizes a politics of speech. The riots of May 1968 were a rupturing "event" (an encounter with the Real). What they expressed was not a revolution in history; in fact, a social "normality" was resumed fairly quickly, but the events were, for him, a symbolic revolution. That is, they attested to what was lacking. Speech freed itself from a certain captivity to the status quo.

So although Certeau defined himself as a historian, even an ecclesiastical historian of sorts, we can see how his interests widened, developing into what today would often come under "cultural studies." He started to ask what makes us believe in the stability of the symbolic order or what makes any belief credible. In doing this he began to develop what he termed "an anthropology of credibility."[14] That is, it is impossible for we human beings to live without believing; to believe is an anthropological *a priori*. We believe because we desire and we desire because we lack the fulfilment, the *jouissance*, that forever we search out. What follows is an investigation, philosophical, psychological, sociological, semiotic, and theological, into what we believe in and how that belief is produced; the production, maintenance, and mutation of beliefs.

In a series of essays analysing cultural plurality in the early 1970s, Certeau explored this question in relation to the new secular space which had opened up following the collapse of two major belief systems: the religious and the political, Christianity and Marxism. What each of these belief systems had effected was a solidarity, a network of values that were shared. A form of participation and social cohesion was possible. This collapsed because people were unable to believe in these systems any more. Certeau asks why this could come about. His verdict is that, with the breakdown of ecclesial power, Christianity became privatized and this withdrew Christianity from politics, leaving a vacuum that the political as such filled. "Christianity had opened a gap in the interconnection of the visible objects of belief (the political authorities) and its invisible objects (the gods, spirits, etc.).... Christianity finally compromised the believability of the religiousness that it detached from the political,"[15] he writes. Political organizations became pseudo-ecclesias, often being invested with liturgies lifted from the religiousness they parodied. But then the social atomism that individualism and privatization of beliefs fostered brings about the collapse of political authority too.

What we have today is what he calls a "recited society." "Our society has become a recited society, in three senses; it is defined by *stories* (*récits*, the fables constituted by our advertising and informational media), by *citations* of stories, and by the interminable *recitation* of stories."[16] In a recited society people believe what they see and what they see is produced for them; hence simulacra created belief. "[T]he spectator-observer *knows* that they are merely 'semblances'... *but all the same* he assumes that these simulations are real."[17] This "objectless credibility" is based upon citing the authority of others. Thus the production of simulacrum involves making people believe that others

believe in it, but without providing any believable object. In a re
there is a multiplication of pseudo-believers promoted by a culture
and credit.

In his account of our contemporary believing, Certeau emp
aesthetics of absence. We are brought to believe in that which in itself is a representation of an object, not the object of belief itself. We defer the truth about the object to other experts, whom we have never met nor can substantiate. These hidden experts in whom we put our trust enable us to accept as credible that which *we are told* is true. The space we as believers inhabit then is a space of "consumable fictions."[18] Caught up in the endless traffic and exchange of signs – from billboards, through television, in newspapers, on film – we construct from this seductive public rhetoric versions of "reality" to which we give allegiance or in which we place our faith. These productions and exchanges organize what we take as our social reality.[19] But since the flow of signs is constantly changing in the practices which make up everyday living, since ideas are constantly being modified, disseminated, reexperienced, reexpressed and transplanted, what is believable changes too. What is constant is the gap between "what authorities *articulate* and what is *understood* by them, between the communication they allow and the legitimacy they presuppose, between what they make possible and what makes them credible."[20] It is this gap, negotiated and veiled by writing, that facilitates an aesthetics of absence and galvanizes Certeau's science of otherness.

Ian Buchanan, in his introduction to part III of this volume, outlines the nature of this science. One of the marked characteristics of post-structuralism is its concern with alterity. We find this concern in Lacan's understanding of the *réel*, with Levinas's construal of the subject being hostage to the other as both *autrui* and *autre*, with Derrida's work on *différance*, and with Irigaray's call to recognize the importance of sexual difference. But Certeau's heterological project is distinctive because of the way it is concerned with a variety of sites in which the other is silenced, erased and yet needed, constructed as other, in order to develop an understanding of those areas which consider themselves not-other. This volume is organized around an examination of five of the primary sites of Certeau's heterological project. We start with history – "Other Times: Historiography" – because, as Luce Giard, who introduces that section, points out, Certeau saw himself primarily as an historian. The pieces chosen for this part reflect, in the main, the impact Certeau's work has had upon the discipline. In the English-speaking world, his influence has predominantly been in terms of his reflections upon history as a discursive practice, its politics and its ethics. Both "Writings and Histories" (which forms the introduction to his seminal book *The Writing of History*) and "History: Science and Fiction" (taken from *Heterologies*) are essays on historiography. Had space permitted, I would have included extracts illustrating Certeau's work as a historian. His books *La Possession de Loudun* (1970) and *The Mystic Fable* (1982) furnish good examples and reveal the influence of structuralist methodology.

As Luce Giard points out, in his historiography Certeau was concerned to demonstrate connections between the writing of history, politics, anthropology, and theology. The second heterological site – "Other Cities: Politics" – focuses upon Certeau's explicit political writings. The three essays chosen point to the breadth of Certeau's concerns, and demonstrate, as Tom Conley's introduction notes, Certeau's complex blend of urban realism and visionary utopianisms. The first essay in this section, "The Symbolic Revolution," illustrates Certeau's early response to the May riots of 1968, the crisis that awoke Certeau to the politics of knowledge. "The Social Architecture of Knowledge" comes from Certeau's book *Culture in the Plural*. It is a later reflection on Marcuse's work in the light of the crisis of May 1968. But the essay is also an analysis of the contemporary cultural scene and an intellectual plea for interdisciplinary investigations in order to better understand the relationship between social structures and the variety of discourses which represent and police them. "The Indian Long March" illustrates Certeau's interest not only in the South American politics of the 1970s, but also in the continuing ideological exploitation which perpetuates colonialism. As Tom Conley points out, these essays are important for understanding Certeau's concern with space as distinct from place. The concept of space had been high on the French cultural agenda through the structuralist and phenomenological schools of thinking. Certeau joins other figures, such as Michel Foucault, Henri Lefebvre, and Louis Marin, who each, in his own distinctive way, gave geography back to the historians.

With "The Indian Long March" we begin to move from the political to the ethnographical and Certeau's analysis of micro-subversive tactics in the practice of everyday life. Part III takes up and develops these interests. "Walking in the City" and "Believing and Making People Believe" are taken from Certeau's volume *The Practice of Everyday Life* and demonstrate how he developed a means of analyzing the architecture of knowledge and its representation. "Ethno-graphy: Speech, or the space of the Other: Jean de Léry" is taken from *The Writing of History*. It not only returns us to Certeau's historical interests in the dawn of modernity (and the manner in which modernity colonized the other), but develops his investigation into how the identity of one culture is maintained through the representation of another. With its attention to how the voice of the other is transposed and translated into Léry's own writing, the essay also acts as a bridge between this part and the next. It is interesting to note how Certeau's concern with the writing up in a First World language of events and activities in a Third World country foreshadows the contemporary concerns of postcolonial and subaltern studies represented most forcefully in the work of Gayatri Chakravorty Spivak and Edward Said.[21]

Certeau's thinking continually returned to questions related to representation and the symbolic. Frequently, he explored such questions through the relationship between speech and writing. Part IV takes up this interest and Jeremy Ahearne explains why terms such as "scriptural economy," "voice," "utterance," and "speech act" are so important for Certeau's analyses of cultural politics. The three essays chosen move from a historical and theoretical examination of writing (in "The Scriptural Economy") to two specific case-studies (of French *patois* and the ecstatic utterance of the mystic). Had space been available, the cry of the mystic could have been supplemented by Certeau's interest in the cry of the possessed. Luce Giard refers to these cries and the manner in which they are colonized and mapped out by various intellectual sciences in her introduction to part I. "Mystic Speech" was chosen because of the way it rehearses many of the ideas which are given more detailed treatment in *The Mystic Fable* and introduces the theological Other, the absence of God. It is the very absence of God, understood in Christianity explicitly in terms of the empty tomb and the resurrection of Christ's body, which drives the production of a spiritual body substituting for and articulating the absence. Yet, in that very act of substitution, in that speech act, something is presenced.

As Frederick Christian Bauerschmidt states, in his introduction to part V, Certeau develops his ideas on the God who we are "not without" in an early essay entitled "How Is Christianity Thinkable Today?" The lost body of God, and the blend of mourning and desire this inaugurates for the Church, is a central idea in this essay, now available in Graham Ward (ed.), *The Postmodern God* (Oxford: Blackwell, 1997). The essay gave theological justification for a certain spiritual itinerary, an Abrahamic journey into deepening exile or the land of the other. Theologically, the idea of the infinite dispersal of Christianity, following the event of Christ, led Certeau into ways that the official Church would regard as heterodox – although some of Certeau's early articles were written for the conservative Catholic journal *Consilium*. This journal published, among others, the work of de Lubac, Hans Urs von Balthasar and Joseph Ratzinger. The latter are both still regarded as Catholic right-wingers. A story is told among the Jesuits that Certeau's Provincial commented: "I'm not sure Certeau died a Christian, but he certainly died a Jesuit." Luce Giard, in her introduction to a volume of his theological essays, entitled *La faiblesse de croire*, emphasizes that "Questions about God, faith and Christianity never ceased to preoccupy Michel de Certeau."[22] It is from that volume that his essay "From the Body to Writing, a Christian Transit" is taken. The text followed a radio debate between Certeau and Jean-Marie Domenach, broadcast in 1973, on "Christianity, a new mythology?" It is an amplified account of his responses to Domenach's own statement and questions to him. But as the opening to the essay shows, the movement from what was spoken on the radio to its present written form is itself a source for some reflection on the relationship between speech and writing. This essay, then, picks up concerns which have been evident throughout the volume. It gathers together concerns with the historical, political, sociological, symbolic, and theological. Although its focus is explicitly biblical and ecclesial, it nevertheless articulates a pastoral concern evident throughout Certeau's work: a concern with violence or the "distortion between what a discourse says and what a society does with it."[23]

Toward the end of October 1983 Certeau published a prose poem entitled "White Ecstasy." In it Certeau pictured two men meeting in the mountains: Simeon the monk and a visitor from the distant land of Panoptie. Simeon speaks of the "exorbitant goal of the millennial march . . . of travellers who have set out to see God."[24] The distant land of Panoptie sees everything and nothing; it is a shadowless plain. The visitor seeks to see God. Simeon describes the mystic journeying into "the final bedazzlement," in which there is "an absorption of objects and subjects in the act of seeing. No violence, only the unfolding of presence. Neither fold nor hole. Nothing hidden and thus nothing visible. A light without limits, without difference; neuter, in a sense, and continuous."[25] In the account the visitor recognizes the experience of "this silent ecstasy" as the experience of living in Panoptie: "I have known this in my country . . . The experience you speak of is commonplace there."[26] He returns home. Luce Giard comments that when she first read the piece she believed it announced the imminent arrival of the angel of death.[27] Michel de Certeau died, at the age of 61 and at the height of his intellectual powers, on January 9, 1986. He had fallen ill in the previous summer while engaged on the second volume of *The Mystic Fable*.

The journeying was over. It was always an impossible journey, an endless exile into alterity. In "White Ecstasy," which could almost have come from the pen of the Italian novelist Italo Calvino,[28] Simeon says, "How can I explain? . . . How to describe the exorbitant goal of the millennial march – many time millennial – of travellers who have set out to see God? . . . To see God is, in the end, to see *nothing*." As I said at the beginning of this introduction, this is not the journeying of Hegel or Odysseus. It is not the journeying either of the picaresque tradition or the journeying into self-knowledge of the *Bildungsroman*, although this journeying does share a certain romanticism, a certain climbing by the artist toward some summit of the sublime depicted in the famous paintings by Casper David Friedrich. For Certeau this entry into the seeing and knowing of nothing is a "white ecstasy." In the Lacanian terms so important for Certeau, in the moment of consummation, that impossible moment of *jouissance* as death, the symbolic (and the subject it constructs) collapses, the imaginary dissolves, and the real is recognized in the massive "absorption." It is this haunting of the sublime, this heterology, which brings together each of the academic disciplinary fields which Certeau crossed – his writings on the repressed in psychoanalysis, the other scene in historiography, the subversive in cultural politics, the subaltern in ethnography, the cries of the possessed and mystically illuminated in theology, and always the walking, the travelling which "no longer has foundation nor goal. Given over to a nameless desire . . . tracing itself out in silence, in writing."[29]

Let me return to road movies. For a question remains concerning why Certeau's work is significant today. I write "significant" because I am asking the question in the way Certeau himself might have asked it. Why do the signs and symbols of Certeau's own scriptural economies resonant in the contemporary cultural *Zeitgeist* and make a *Reader*, such as this one, important? The answer to that question is, I believe, because the character of his work voices, even anticipates, present preoccupations with "the social architecture of knowledge" and present possibilities for its subversion, for its being otherwise.

In 1991, Ridley Scott, the English director of American films often seen at the forefront of postmodern cinema, made his own famous version of the road movie, *Thelma and Louise*. It too traces an impossible journey: the travelling of two women towards freedom in a culture written for and organized by men. It is seen as impossible from very early on, when Louise (having escaped her domestic situation by not telling her husband she is taking a trip with Thelma) finds herself being raped simply because, in a bar, she "let her hair down". The rapist is shot by Thelma and their weekend holiday turns into a bid to live their own lives and discover their own vocations. Now on the run and heading for Mexico – the same Mexico from out of which Wenders's Travis emerged – their situation becomes accumulatively worse. They reach the edge of the Grand Canyon. In a moment of quiet, the reds, yellows, and golds of the scene stretch out beneath the blue of the sky. "It's beautiful," Louise says. "It's something else," Thelma replies. It is somewhere else, an other place. Suddenly the moment is violently broken by the intrusion of a police helicopter. Police surround them, they are hailed by megaphones to give up and "place your hands in plain view." In a reverse shot we see their faces and then see their heads through the telescopic lens of a rifle. "Oh my God!" Louise screams. "Looks like the army." "All this for us," Thelma replies. She starts looking for her revolver. "What are yer doin' now?" Louise asks. "I'm not giving up." The police give them another warning. The camera is placed hard and close to Louise's face.

Louise: Okay, then listen. Let's not get caught.
Thelma: What are you talking' about?"

Louise: Let's keep goin'."
Thelma: What d' y' mean?
Louise: (gesturing slightly, with both fear and awe, towards the canyon) Go. Go.
Thelma: Are you sure?
Louise: (breathlessly, eyes wide with adrenaline) Yeh. Yeh.

In another reverse shot we have a close up of the two women, who raise their joined hands into plain view, then from behind the detective is running wildly after them while the car proceeds to catapult over the edge. The frame freezes and fades with the car in mid-flight. There is no descent. The last glimpses of the women are of faces in silent ecstasy.

The ending to Ridley Scott's road movie is richly ambivalent. Is this suicide, sacrifice, or the consummation of a nameless desire? Is the somewhere else the illusion of utopia, psychological need, or the mystic's heaven? The horizon toward which Certeau's work points, the goal which drives and sings (with both delight and mourning) in Certeau's work, is also richly ambivalent. Is Certeau's project nihilistic? Does his work embrace a monism that would render his radical politics and his ethics of responsive acknowledgement of the other pragmatic, locally significant, but ultimately determined by a Nietzschean *amor fati*? Or is his work lit by a transcendent hope, an eschatological redemption of all things in a way no one culture can dream of or express? His figure of the nomadic wanderer finds a concluding focus in the seventeenth-century mystic Labadie, who was, in turn, "Jesuit, Jansenist, Calvinist, Pietist, Chiliast or Millenarian, and finally 'Labadist'."[30] But having following Labadie's footsteps, Certeau concludes: "Labadie has led us to the edge of a shore where there is nothing, formally, but the relation between defiance and loss." We are right at the centre of the problem facing Ridley Scott and postmodern culture. Certeau adds: "We must return to the 'finite' place, the body . . . and let Labadie pass by."[31]

There are academics who, similarly, stay with what Certeau has to say about the corporeal – the socially, politically, historically and culturally produced bodies and the practices of everyday life. They have investigated this work and employed it in analyses of their own. And there are scholars who push on to understand how what this man has written about psychology, anthropology, ethnography, history, and politics is related to the Jesuit and the metaphysician. In the bibliography the work of both groups is represented. And in the end the mystery remains. For Certeau himself remains other than himself, because he is now what he has written and excessive to all the ways we try to catalogue him. That is why his work will continue to be fruitful, and profoundly affect the academic disciplinary fields he traversed, bringing, in his own way, Paris to Texas.

Notes

1 See Certeau's essay "Foucault and Bourdieu," in his *Practices of Everyday Life*, pp. 45–60.
2 "Railway navigation and incarceration," in his *Practices of Everyday Life*, p. 111.
3 Certeau distinguishes between "place" (*lieu*), which is definable, limited, enclosed, and "space" (*espace*), which is that which is constantly being produced by the practices of living. One's own spacing may, then, transgress the boundaries of maps and cities that define places.
4 Wim Wenders's films have been read in a similar way. See Robert Phillip Kolker and Peter Beicken, *The Films of Wim Wenders: Cinema as Vision and Desire* (Cambridge: Cambridge University Press, 1993).
5 Ibid., p. 161.
6 *Language and Silence* (London: Faber and Faber, 1967), pp. 75–88.
7 From the Introduction to Tom Conley (tr.), *The Capture of Speech and Other Political Writings*, pp. x–xi.
8 De Lubac was the much older Catholic and academic statesman. Born in 1896, but also from the countryside around Lyon, his theology is concerned with returning to the patristic and medieval traditions. The theological movement he led through the 1940s in France with Jean Daniélou was known as the "New Theology". His book *Corpus Mysticum* was published in 1949, but because of an ecclesial controversy, which blew up in 1950, his books were banned and impounded. *Corpus Mysticum* was one such book. Certeau's indebtedness to de Lubac's work is footnoted in *The Mystic Fable*. Certeau's association with de Lubac is alluded to by Frederick Christian Bauerschmidt in his introduction to part V of this volume.
9 Conley, op. cit., n. 7, pp. 11–12.
10 To some extent, when figures such as Certi and Foucault went to lecture in California in the 1970s they encountered a situation similar to the one in Paris in May 1968. The political awakening of the American students was triggered by hostility to American involvement in Vietnam.
11 Op. cit., n. 8, p. 29.
12 For his views of Lacanian psychology see "Lacan: an ethics of speech," in *Heterologies*, pp. 47–64.
13 See the essays in *Heterologies*, part I, "The Return of the Repressed in Psychoanalysis," pp. 3–64; and *The* Writing of History, part IV, "Freudian Writing."
14 *Culture in the Plural*, p. viii.
15 *The Practice of Everyday Life*, pp. 181–2.
16 Ibid., p. 186.
17 Ibid., pp. 187–8.
18 *Culture in the Plural*, p. 25.
19 Again, this associates him profoundly with the work of Wim Wenders, whose films *Wings of Desire*, *Far Away, So Close*, and *The End of Violence* all pursue the theme of a culture caught up with the proliferation of seductive signs.

20 Ibid., p. 15.
21 Wlad Godzich draws an interesting comparison between Certeau's work and Said's in his foreword to *Heterologies*. For Spivak's analysis of cultural politics see her book *In Other Worlds: Essays in Cultural Politics* (London: Routledge, 1988).
22 *La faiblesse de croire*, p. i.
23 *Culture in the Plural*, p. 30.
24 "White Ecstasy," p. 155.
25 Ibid., p. 157.
26 Ibid., p. 158.
27 *La faiblesse de croire*, p. xix.
28 *Invisible Cities*, trans. William Weaver. Orlando, FL: Harcourt Brace and Company, 1974.
29 *The Mystic Fable*, p. 299.
30 *The Mystic Fable*, p. 271.
31 Ibid., p. 293.

Part I

Other Times: Historiography

1

Introduction: Michel de Certeau on Historiography

Luce Giard

When he was asked to declare a professional identity, his interlocutors being embarrassed by the variety of his works and the range of his expertise, Michel de Certeau used to answer that he was a historian, with religious history in early modern Europe as his main field. When his long-awaited book on mystics (*La Fable mystique*) was very favorably received, some friends suggested that he come back from the University of California at San Diego, where he was a full-time professor, and apply for a position at the Ecole des Hautes Etudes en Sciences Sociales. He successfully did it with a teaching programme on "the historical anthropology of beliefs (sixteenth to eighteenth centuries)" and was elected to a chair under this title. His self-understanding of his disciplinary locus and focus was neatly situated inside history, even if he inspired and directed innovative cross-disciplinary research projects, to which he owes some of his international influence.

Thus he was a historian, but of what kind? There are so many "houses" on the historian's territory and the word itself has so many different meanings and connotations, from entertaining popular books to strictly defined scholarly case studies, notwithstanding the major differences between national traditions and schools of thought. To appraise a pianist's art, one has to listen to him or her playing a sonata or some other piece. To appraise a historian's talent, to grasp the main features of his style of thought, one has to read a selection of his works. In that sense, a direct reading acquaintance with the author surpasses all commentaries and introductions. This text is no exception: it is intended to lead to Certeau's own works through some characteristics of his historical *oeuvre*.

Most musicians satisfy themselves with the practice and teaching of their instrument. They give performances, they take part in recording sessions of the best of their repertoire. They never think of writing a long treatise about their art's requirements. They leave this task to other kinds of professionals linked to the world of music. A similar divide can be encountered among historians. Most of them never find any spare time or strong motive for discussing methodology and historiography substantially at the theoretical level. Many historians would discard these problems as void of any interest to them, foreign to the very historical work, relevant only to philosophers of history. Nevertheless, the following selection from Certeau's texts shows that he professed the opposite opinion and could argue in favor of historiography convincingly and consistently.

Certeau belonged to this minority of historians who are not afraid of calling for a thorough rethinking of the prerequisites and presuppositions which rule the profession as a social body and guide its intellectual commitment. For followers of this line, historiography stands as an elucidatory activity which is inherent in any writing of history. They believe that the historiographical debate opens to historians a royal path toward clarification and validation of their craft. They also believe that this debate is to be renewed by every generation, in order for the discipline to stay alive, through the emergence of new research areas, new paradigms, new explanatory schemes, and the necessary criticism of previous methods, paradigms, and assumptions. Certeau's conception of the historian's task was far from the naive picture popularized by historical novels (and movies), which presents it as a retrospective criminal investigation, the result of which will be to tell what actually occurred, who murdered the victim or misled the credulous crowd.

Certeau's analysis of the famous Loudun Possession (in France, near Poitiers, 1632–5) is eloquent on this matter. It began with a bold statement: "History is never sure." It ended with another startling remark: "The possession has no 'true' explanation, since it is never possible to know who is *possessed* and by whom."[1] In other words, the historian does not exert police powers on past events. His mission is more humble; more subtle, too. With a light touch of irony, Certeau remarks that the historian is not in charge of "speaking the truth," but in charge of "diagnosing the false."[2] Surveying the varied treatments given to the possessed nuns in Loudun, in which priests, physicians, and judges intervened (and competed against one another), Certeau notices that the historian "too has received from society an exorcist's task. He is asked to eliminate the danger of the *other*."[3] Here is seen Certeau's broader understanding of past and present societies. At different historical moments, in diverse social and cultural settings, "the poison of the other" presents itself under varied forms and guises. It is the responsibility of the historian to identify "the new social figures of the other," so that his or her contemporaries can understand that no society is totally homogeneous and unified, that there will be new irruptions of a troubling otherness. Studying the past, the historian allows the future to come and bears a political responsibility of his own; that is the reason why he needs historiographical awareness, ethical inspiration and critical epistemology. Certeau placed history among these "sciences of the other," which were dear to him and which he called "heterologies."[4] Here he singled out ethnography and psychoanalysis with history itself. Nowadays, we are less familiar with demons' uncanny visitations than the Loudun crowds, judges, and nuns, but we do have our horrible paroxysms of otherness, operating on unprecedented scales, with relentless brutality, through mass murder, genocide, totalitarianism, political violence. Who could forget it? Who could ignore it?

Two of Certeau's books specifically concern historiography, one under the sign of "the absent", the other focused on the problem of "writing."[5] Both books will disappoint readers in search of a general handbook for would-be historians. They do not belong to the familiar literary genre of those loosely arranged booklets, where an old scholar indulges in a miscellany of reminiscences, anecdotes, commonplaces, and inoffensive advice amid the universal benevolence which may grace one's old age. Certeau died too early to face the temptation of avuncular historiography. Besides, he never accepted the parallel illusions linked to the mastery of knowledge and the convenience of didactic simplification. He respected his readers' intellectual autonomy, had a very high opinion of their needs and demands, and would never give them a simplified version of his reflections and scholarly hesitations. As a result, he did not compose user-friendly texts; his books ask for close reading and sustained attention. But his readers are rewarded in a deeper way, by the force and breadth of the thought, by the poetical beauty of the style, and by the intellectual generosity which flows through his texts.

With regular new reprints in French, and five or six translations into other languages, *The Writing of History* has gained the status of a classic. It attests to the range and richness of Certeau's reflections on historiography. The first part addresses the ambiguous social role of the historian. He chronicles the deeds of the Prince, the State, the Nation. He stands too close to authorities, leaders, institutions, too far from individuals, subjects, minorities. He thinks about power, he does not exert it. He "does work in history," he "does not make history."[6] Certeau goes further in his critical sociology of the profession: he details the implicit and explicit rules a historian follows in order to be legitimized and accredited to the milieu. Certeau does not call for an institutional revolution, he pleads for some epistemological self-awareness and ethical commitment from historians. "The historiographical operation" is presented "as the relation between a *place* (a recruitment, a milieu, a profession, etc.), analytical *procedures* (a discipline), and the construction of a *text* (a literature)."[7] Each operation must be well determined: its results are to be put to the test, first by the author, then by readers. This means that the final narrative accounts for all steps of the operation, explains the decisions made, discusses the interpretative hypotheses preferred. Readers must be allowed the means to disagree, even if the author's scholarship and intellectual integrity are faultless. Any interpretation carries more falseness than truth.

The second part concerns religious history, in which the historian accounts for beliefs and commitments he does not share or even finds meaningless. He has to keep himself respectful, fair, generous toward believers, dissenters, prophets, reformers whose logic sounds illogical to him. In a brilliant chapter, "The formality of [religious] practices", Certeau shows how in seventeenth- and eighteenth-century France the Christian faith, its religious system, its complacent authorities, were skilfully used by the political power to control its subjects. Everything was done formally "in the name of God," but really in the service of the King. Certeau here develops an original hypothesis backed by a complex argumentation in which he deftly intertwines elements from theology, political history, anthropology, cultural history.

Then the book focuses on the other and its sciences. First comes a comparison between "written" and "oral" narratives. Jean de Léry's *récit de voyage* to Brazil (first edition 1578) gives Certeau the opportunity of visiting America and trying on early modern Europe his conception of "scriptural economies": when God stops to speak directly, financial and political scriptures of many kinds take the lead. A shorter essay returns to the possessed nuns of Loudun and follows their efforts to resist the questioning of judges who tried hard to make demons accept their mental categories. The judiciary proceedings started in an oral form, and were then recorded by clerks in written legal documents. Finally, the "diabolical phenomena," which passed the judges' understanding, were narrated in legal language, but the records convey some traces of the "double [linguistic] play" maintained by nuns and demons.[8] In the fourth part of his book, Certeau presents an original reading of two historical studies written by Freud, the first one on a demonological neurosis in seventeenth-century Austria, the second one about the biblical Moses, founding father of the Jewish people and in whom Freud thought he saw an Egyptian. Certeau was extremely interested in Freud's works, which he read in German, and in psychoanalytical interpretation. In it, he expected to find an instrument for the study of otherness and of its mobile repertoire of corporal, intellectual and social expressions. His relation with Freud and with Lacan's Ecole freudienne was more anthropological and historically interpretative than therapeutic. Moreover, he did not think much of the type of retrospective psychoanalysis produced by some historians to explain the individual achievements and shortcomings of political leaders, religious reformers, serial killers, etc.[9]

Michel de Certeau believed in the Christian God. From 1950 to his death, he was a member of the Society of Jesus, a religious Catholic Order. His first historical studies concerned early Jesuits Pierre Favre (a contemporary of Ignatius of Loyola) and Jean-Joseph Surin (the exorcist who saved Jeanne des Anges in Loudun, but was afterwards mentally ill for many years). His religious commitment and affiliation did not limit his intellectual quest, and did not lead him to ready-made answers. On the contrary, his theological studies and religious milieu acted on his mind as strong incentives. Past and present both required from him more thinking and inquirying, more knowing and believing. The core of his historical work concerned mystics and mystical literature. He did not look for a universal theory of "mystical experience," he did not trust ahistorical generalizations. He did not wish to prove the preeminence of Christian mystics over other religious traditions. He followed the common historical path with a few case studies, documented and contextualized in the sixteenth and seventeenth centuries. *The Mystic Fable* was his life labour and a labour of love. In the "disenchanted world" of early modern Europe, God turned silent for the majority of people. Some believers in a few social circles tried to restore a communication with God, they let their hearts and minds tell their desire of Him in strange narratives which report the secret events of their inner lives. Certeau read hundreds of those texts, and regarded them as precious documents and valuable literary sources. He analyzed them with sophisticated linguistic procedures, paid them all due respect, made their original content and poetic power visible. He was careful to begin his book with an insistent denial. The author studies mysticism, but he has no "special jurisdiction over its domain," "no insider's knowledge" of it, his book is written in the name of an Absent, "it stands exiled from its subject-matter."[10] On this point, readers can make their own judgement, after reading and comparing a few other texts from Certeau.[11] Let us say with Shakespeare that "the rest is silence."

Notes

1 *La Possession de Loudun*, translation by Michael B. Smith published by the University of Chicago Press in late 1999. Quotations come from the introductory and concluding chapters of this translation.

2 *Heterologies: Discourse on the Other*, p. 200.
3 *La Possession de Loudun*, concluding chapter.
4 *Heterologies*.
5 *L'Absent de l'histoire* and *The Writing of History*.
6 *The Writing of History*, chapter 1; *Heterologies*, p. 213. The French text is more effective: "il fait de l'histoire," "il ne fait pas l'histoire."
7 *The Writing of History*, p. 57.
8 Ibid., pp. 263–4.
9 The limits of space made it impossible to include any of Certeau's Freudian studies in this volume, although they constitute an essential part of his innovative historical work.
10 *The Mystic Fable*, pp. 1–2.
11 See *La Faiblesse de croire*. Its last piece, "White Ecstasy," translated by Frederick C. Bauerschmidt and Catriona Hanley, is included in Graham Ward (ed.), *The Postmodern God* (Oxford: Blackwell, 1997), pp. 155–8.

2

Writings and Histories

"Studious and charitable, tender as I am for the dead of the world . . . thus I roamed, from age to age, always young and never tired, for thousands of years." The open road – "my road" – seems to take hold of the text of this traveler on foot: "I went, I wandered . . . I ran along my path . . . I went . . . as a bold voyager." Walking and/or writing is a labor knowing no rest, "by the force of desire, pricked by an ardent curiosity that nothing could restrain." Michelet multiplies his meetings, with "indulgence" and "filial fear" in respect to the dead who are the inheritors of a "strange dialogue," but also with the assurance "that never could anyone ever stir up again what life has left behind." In the sepulcher which the historian inhabits, only "emptiness remains."[1] Hence this "intimacy with the other world poses no threat":[2] "This security made me all the more charitable toward those who were unable to harm me." Every day he even becomes "younger" by getting acquainted over and over again with this world that is dead, and definitely other.

After having successively passed through the *History of France*, the shadows "have returned less saddened to their tombs."[3] Discourse drives them back into the dark. It is a deposition. It turns them into *severed souls*. It honors them with a ritual of which they had been deprived. It "bemoans" them by fulfilling the duty of filial piety enjoined upon Freud through a dream in which he saw written on the wall of a railway station, "Please close the eyes."[4] Michelet's "tenderness" seeks one after another of the dead in order to insert every one of them into time, "this omnipotent decorator of ruins: O Time beautifying of things!"[5] The dear departed find a haven in the text *because* they can neither speak nor do harm anymore. These ghosts find access through *writing* on the condition that they remain *forever silent*.

Another, graver mourning is added to the first. The People are also the separated. "I was born of the people. I had the people in my heart. . . . But I found their language inaccessible. I was unable to make it speak."[6] It is also silent, in order to become the object of this poem that speaks of it. Surely, only this language "authorizes" the historian's writing, but, for the same reason, it becomes history's absent figure. An *Infans*, this Voice does not speak. It exists only outside of itself, in Michelet's discourse, but it allows him to become a "popular" writer, to "jettison" pride and, becoming "rough and barbaric," to "lose . . . what I had owned of literary subtlety."[7]

The other is the phantasm of historiography, the object that it seeks, honors, and buries. A labor of separation concerning this uncanny and fascinating proximity is effected. Michelet stakes himself at this border where, from Virgil to Dante, *fictions* were erected that were not yet *history*. This place points to the question that scientific practices have been articulating ever since, and that a discipline has assigned itself to solve. Alphonse Dupront has said, "The sole historical quest for 'meaning' remains indeed a quest for the Other,"[8] but, however contradictory it may be, this project aims at "understanding" and, through "meaning," at hiding the alterity of this foreigner; or, in what amounts to the same thing, it aims at calming the dead who still haunt the present, and at offering them scriptural tombs.

The Discourse of Separation: Writing

Modern Western history essentially begins with differentiation between the *present* and the *past*. In this way it is unlike tradition (religious tradition), though it never succeeds in being entirely dissociated from this archeology, maintaining with it a relation of indebtedness and rejection. This rupture also organizes the content of history within the relations between *labor* and *nature*; and finally, as its third form, it ubiquitously takes for granted a rift between *discourse* and the *body* (the social body). It forces the silent body to speak. It assumes a gap to exist between the silent opacity of the "reality" that it seeks to express and the place where it produces its own speech, protected by the distance established between itself and its object (*Gegen-stand*). The violence of the body reaches the written page only through absence, through the intermediary of documents that the historian has been able to see on the sands from which a presence has since been washed away, and through a murmur that lets us hear – but from afar – the unknown immensity that seduces and menaces our knowledge.

A structure belonging to modern Western culture can doubtless be seen in this historiography: *intelligibility is established through a relation with the other*; it moves (or "progresses") by changing what it makes of its "other" – the Indian, the past, the people, the mad, the child, the Third World. Through these variants that are all heteronomous – ethnology, history, psychiatry, pedagogy, etc. – unfolds a problematic form basing its mastery of expression upon what the other keeps silent, and guaranteeing the interpretive work of a science (a "human" science) by the frontier that separates it from an area awaiting this work in order to be known. Here modern medicine is a decisive figure, from the moment when the body becomes a *legible* picture that can in turn be translated into that which can be *written* within a space of language. Thanks to the unfolding of the body before the doctor's eyes, what is seen and what is known of it can be superimposed or exchanged (be translated from one to the other). The body is a cipher that awaits deciphering. Between the seventeenth and the eighteenth century, what allows the seen body to be converted into the known body, or what turns the spatial organization of the body into a semantic organization of a vocabulary – and vice versa – is the transformation of the body into extension, into open interiority like a book, or like a silent corpse placed under our eyes. An analogous change takes place when tradition, a lived body, is revealed to erudite curiosity through a corpus of texts. Modern medicine and historiography are born almost simultaneously from the rift between a subject that is supposedly literate, and an object that is supposedly written in an unknown language. The latter always remains to be decoded. These two "heterologies" (discourses on the other) are built upon a division between the body of knowledge that utters a discourse and the mute body that nourishes it.

First of all, historiography separates its present time from a past. But everywhere it repeats the initial act of division. Thus its chronology is composed of "periods" (for example, the Middle Ages, modern history, contemporary history) between which, in every instance, is traced the *decision* to become different or no longer to be such as one had been up to that time (the Renaissance, the French Revolution). In their respective turns, each "new" time provides the *place* for a discourse considering whatever preceded it to be "dead," but welcoming a "past" that had already been specified by former ruptures. Breakage is therefore the postulate of interpretation (which is constructed as of the present time) and its object (divisions organizing representations that must be reinterpreted). The labor designated by this breakage is self-motivated. In the past from which it is distinguished, it promotes a selection between what can be *understood* and what must be *forgotten* in order to obtain the representation of a present intelligibility. But whatever this new understanding of the past holds to be irrelevant – shards created by the selection of materials, remainders left aside by an explication – comes back, despite everything, on the edges of discourse or in its rifts and crannies: "resistances," "survivals," or delays discreetly perturb the pretty order of a line of "progress" or a system of interpretation. These are lapses in the syntax constructed by the law of a place. Therein they symbolize a return of the repressed, that is, a return of what, at a given moment, has *become* unthinkable in order for a new identity to *become* thinkable.

Far from being self-evident, this construction is a uniquely Western trait. In India, for example, "new forms never drive the older ones away." Rather, there exists a "stratified stockpiling," Louis Dumont has noted. The march of time no more needs to be certified by distances taken from various "pasts" than a position needs to establish itself by being sectioned off from "heresies." A "process of coexistence and reabsorption" is, on the contrary, the "cardinal fact" of Indian history.[9] And, too, among the Merina of Madagascar, the *tetiarana* (former genealogical lists), then the *tantara* (past history) form a "legacy of ears" (*lovantsofina*) or a "memory by mouth" (*tadidivava*): far from being an "ob-ject" thrown behind so that an autonomous present will be possible, the past is a treasure placed in the *midst* of the society that is its memorial, a food intended to be chewed and memorized. History is the "privilege" (*tantara*) that must be remembered so that one shall not oneself be forgotten. In its own midst it places the people who stretch from a past to a future. Among the Fô of Dahomey, history is *remuho*, "the speech of these past times" – speech (*ho*), or presence, which comes from upriver and carries downstream. It has nothing in common with the conception (apparently close to it, but actually of ethnographical and museological origin) that, in *dissociating* current time from tradition, in thus imposing a break between a present and a past, and in actually upholding the Western relation whose terms it simply reverses, defines identity through a return to a past or marginalized "negritude."

It would be senseless to multiply the examples, beyond our historiography, that bear witness to another relation with time or, in what amounts to the same thing, another relation with death. In the West, the group (or the individual) is legitimized by what it excludes (this is the creation of its own space), and it discovers its faith in the confession that it extracts from a dominated being (thus is established the *knowledge* based upon, or of, the other: human science). It comes of realizing how ephemeral is every victory over death: inevitably, the raper returns and cuts his swath. Death obsesses the West. In this respect, the discourse of the human sciences is pathological: a discourse of *pathos* – misfortune and passionate action – in a confrontation with this death that our society can no longer conceive of as a way of living one's life. On its own account, historiography takes for granted the fact that it has become impossible to believe in this presence of the dead that has organized (or organizes) the experience of entire civilizations; and the fact too that it is nonetheless impossible "to get over it," to accept the loss of a living solidarity with what is gone, or to confirm an irreducible limit. What is *perishable* is its data; *progress* is its motto. The one is the experience which the other must both compensate for and struggle against. Historiography tends to prove that the site of its production can encompass the past: it is an odd procedure that posits death, a breakage everywhere reiterated in discourse, and that yet denies loss by appropriating to the present the privilege of recapitulating the past as a form of knowledge. A labor of death and a labor against death.

This paradoxical procedure is symbolized and performed in a gesture which has at once the value of myth and of ritual: *writing*. Indeed, writing replaces the traditional representations that gave authority to the present with a representative labor that places both absence and production in the same area. In its most elementary form, writing is equivalent to constructing a sentence by going over an apparently blank surface, a page. But isn't historiography also an activity that recommences from the point of a new time, which is separated from the ancients, and which takes charge of the construction of a rationality within this new time? It appears to me that in the West, for the last four centuries, "the making of history" has referred to writing. Little by little it has replaced the myths of yesterday with a practice of meaning. As a practice (and not by virtue of the discourses that are its result) it symbolizes a society capable of managing the space that it provides for itself, of replacing the obscurity of the lived body with the expression of a "will to know" or a "will to dominate" the body, of changing inherited traditions into a textual product or, in short, of being turned into a blank page that it should itself be able to write. This practice of history is an ambitious, progressive, also utopian practice that is linked to the endless institution of areas "proper," where a will to power can be inscribed in terms of reason. It has the value of a scientific model. It is not content with a hidden "truth" that needs to be discovered; it *produces* a symbol through the very relation between a space newly designated within time and a *modus operandi* that fabricates "scenarios" capable of organizing practices into a currently intelligible discourse – namely, the task of "the making of history." Indissociable from the destiny of writing in the modern and contemporary West until now, historiography nonetheless has the qualities of grasping scriptural invention in its relation with the elements it inherits, of operating right where the *given* must be transformed into a *construct*, of building representations with past materials, of being situated, finally, on this frontier of the present where, simultaneously, a past must be made from a tradition (by exclusion) and where nothing must be lost in the process (exploitation by means of new methods).

History and Politics: a Place

By taking for granted its distancing from tradition and the social body, in the last resort historiography is based upon a power that in effect distinguishes it from the past and from the whole of society. "The making of history" is buttressed by a political power which creates a space proper (a walled city, a nation, etc.) where a will can and must write (construct) a system (a reason articulating practices). In the sixteenth and seventeenth centuries, by being established spatially and by being distinguished by virtue of an autonomous will, political power also occasions restriction of thought. Two tasks are necessary and especially important from the standpoint of the historiography that they are going to transform through the intermediary of jurists and "politicists." On the one hand, power must be legitimized, it must attribute to its grounding force an authority which in turn makes this very power credible. On the other hand, the relation between a "will to produce history" (a subject of the political operation) and the "environment" (into which is carved a power of decision and action) calls for an analysis of the variables thrown into play through any intervention that might influence this relation of forces – that is, an art of manipulating complexity as a function of objectives, hence a calculus of possible relations between a will (that of the prince) and a set of coordinates (the givens of a situation).

These are two features of the "science" constructed between the sixteenth and the eighteenth century by "historiographers." Mostly jurists and magistrates, they were provided by the prince – and in his service – with a privileged "place" whence it was necessary, for the "utility" of the state and "the common good," to bring into accord the truth of the letter and the efficacy of power – "the first dignity of literature" and the capacity of a "man of government." On the one hand, this discourse "legitimizes" the force that power exerts; it provides this force with a familial, political, or moral genealogy; it accredits the prince's current "utility" while transforming it into "values" that organize the representation of the past. On the other hand, the picture that is drawn from this past, which is the equivalent of current prospective "scenarios," formulates *praxeological* models and, through a series of situations, a typology of feasible relations between a concrete will and conjunctural variants; by analyzing the failures and successes, this discourse sketches a science of the practices of power. In this way, it is not satisfied with historical justification of the prince through offering him a genealogical blazon. The prince receives a "lesson" provided by a technician of political management.

Since the sixteenth century – or, to take up clearly marked signs, since Machiavelli and Guichardin – historiography has ceased to be the representation of a providential time, that is, of a history decided by an inaccessible Subject who can be deciphered only in the signs that he gives of his wishes. Historiography takes the position of the subject of action – of the prince, whose objective is to "make history." The historiography gives intelligence the function of mobilizing possible moves between a power and the realities from which it is distinguished. Its very definition is furnished through a policy of the state; in brief, its purpose is to construct a coherent discourse that specifies the "shots" that a power is capable of making in relation to given facts, by virtue of an art of dealing with the elements imposed by an environment. This science is strategic because of its object, political history; on other grounds, it is equally strategic through the method it uses in handling given facts, archives, or documents.

It is through a sort of fiction, however, that the historian is accorded this place. In fact, the historians are not the agents of the operation for which they are technicians. They do not make history, they can only engage in the making of histories: the partitive usage indicates the role they play in a position that does not belong to them, but without which a new kind of historiographical analysis would not have been possible.[10] They are solely "around" power. Thus they receive the directives, in more or less explicit form, that in every modern country burden history – from theses to textbooks – with the task of educating and mobilizing. Its discourse will be magisterial without being that of the master, in the same way that historians will be teaching lessons of government without knowing either its responsibilities or its risks. They reflect on the power that they lack. Their analysis is therefore deployed "next to" the present time, in a staging of the past which is analogous to that which, drawn also through a relation to the present, the prospectivist produces in terms of the future.

Thus located in the vicinity of political problems – but not in the place where political power is exercised – historiography is given an ambivalent status which shows forth most visibly in its modern archeology. It is in a strange situation, at once critical and fictive. The fact is evident with particular clarity in Machiavelli's *Discorsi* and *Istorie fiorentine*. When the historian seeks to establish, for the place of power, the rules of political conduct and the best political institutions, he *plays the role* of the prince that he is not; he analyzes what the prince *ought* to do. Such is the fiction that gives his discourse an access to the space in which it is written. Indeed, a fiction, for it is at once the discourse of the master and that of the servant – it is legitimized through power and drawn from it, in a position where, withdrawn from the scene, as a master thinker, the technician can replay the problems facing the prince.[11] The historiographer depends on "the prince in fact," and he produces "the virtual prince."[12] Therefore he must act *as if* effective power fell under the jurisdiction of his teaching even while, against all probability, his teaching expects the prince to insert himself into a democratic organization. In this way his fiction puts in question – and makes chimerical – the possibility that political *analysis* would find its extension in the effective *practice* of power. Never will the "virtual prince," a construct of discourse, be the "prince in fact." Never will the gap separating reality from discourse be filled; to the very degree that this discourse is rigorous, it will be destined for futility.

An originary frustration that will make the effectiveness of political life a fascinating question for historians (just as, inversely, the political man will be led to take the historian's position and to play back what he has done, in order to reflect upon it and accredit it), this fiction is also betrayed in the fact that the historian analyzes *situations* whereas, for a power, it was at the time a question of *objectives* to be sought. The historian receives, as already realized by another, what the political man should do. Here the past is the consequence of a lack of articulation over "making history." The unreal is insinuated into this science of action, with the fiction which consists of acting as if one were the subject of the operation – or with this activity which reproduces politics in laboratory conditions, and substitutes the subject of a historiographical operation for the subject of a historical action. Archives make up the world of this technical game, a world in which complexity is found, but sifted through and miniaturized, therefore made capable of being formalized. A precious space in every sense of the term: I would see in it the professionalized and scriptural equivalent of what games represent in everyone's common experience; that is, practices by which every society makes explicit, puts in miniature, and formalizes its most fundamental strategies, and thus acts itself out without the risks or responsibilities of having to make history.

In the case of historiography, fiction can be found at the end of the process, in the product of the manipulation and the analysis. Its story is given as a staging of the past, and not as the circumscribed area in which is effected an operation characterized by its gap in respect to power. Such was already the case of the *Discorsi:* Machiavelli offers them as a commentary on Livy. In fact, the historical figure is only a dummy. The author knows that the principles in whose name he is erecting the model of Roman institutions "fragment" the tradition and that his enterprise is "without precedent."[13] Roman history, a common reference and an agreeable subject in Florentine discussions, furnishes him with a public arena where he can deal with politics instead of the prince. The past is the area of *interest* and *pleasure* that situates beyond the current problems the prince is facing – within the field of "opinion" or public "curiosity" – the scene where the historian can play his role as the prince's technician-substitute. The gap in respect to present events delimits the space where historiography is manufactured, around the prince and near the public.

It plays between what one *does* and what *pleases* the other, yet it can be identified neither with the one nor the other. Thus the past is the fiction of the present. The same holds true for all veritable historiographical labors. The explication of the past endlessly marks distinctions between the analytical apparatus, which is present, and the materials analyzed, the documents concerning curiosities about the dead. A rationalization of practices and the pleasure of telling legends of former days ("the charm of history," Marbeau used to say)[14] – the techniques that allow the complexity of current times to be managed, and the poignant curiosity surrounding the dead members of the "family" – are combined within the same text in order to produce both scientific "reduction" and narrative techniques turning the strategies of power into metaphors belonging to current times.

The real which is written in historiographical discourse originates from the determinations of a place. A *dependency* in respect to a power established from elsewhere, a *mastery* of techniques dealing with social strategies, a *play* with symbols and references that represent public authority: such are the effective relations that appear to characterize this space of writing. Placed next to power, based upon it, yet held at a critical distance; holding in its hands – mimicked by writing itself – the rational instruments of operations modifying the balance of forces in the name of a conquering will; rejoining the masses from afar (from behind political and social separation, which "distinguishes" it from them) by reinterpreting the traditional references that are invested in them: in its near totality, modern French historiography is bourgeois and – not astonishingly – rationalist.[15]

This given situation is written into the text. The more or less discreet dedication (the fiction of the past must be upheld so that the scholarly play of history can "take place") bestows upon discourse its status of being *indebted* in respect to the power that, beforehand, belonged to the prince, and that today, by the way of delegation, characterizes the scientific institution of the state or its eponym, the *patron* (or thesis director). This "envoy" designates the legitimizing place, the referent of an organized force, inside of which and through which analysis has its place. But the *story* itself, a body of fiction, through the methods it uses and the content it takes up, also marks on the one hand a distance in respect to this debt, and on the other, the two foundations that allow for this deviation: through a technical labor and a public interest historians receive from current events the means for their research and the context for their interests.

By virtue of this triangular structuring, historiography therefore cannot be thought of in terms of an opposition or an adequacy between a subject and an object; that is nothing more than the play of the fiction that it constructs. Nor could anyone believe, as much as historiography might tend to have us believe, that a "beginning" situated in a former time might explain the present: each historian situates elsewhere the inaugural rupture, at the point where his or her investigations stop; that is, at the borders demarcating a specialization within the disciplines to which he or she belongs. In fact, historians begin from present determinations. Current events are their real beginning. Lucien Febvre already noted this fact in his own style: "The Past," he wrote, "is a reconstitution of societies and human beings engaged in the network of human realities of today."[16] That this place prohibits the historian from speaking in the name of Man is what Febvre would never have admitted. He felt historical work to be exempt from the law that would submit it to the logic of a *site* of production, and not just to the "mentality" of a period in a "progress" of time. . . . But, like all historians, he knew that *to write* is to meet the death that inhabits this site, to make death manifest through a representation of the relations that current time keeps with its other, and to struggle against death through the work of intellectually controlling the connection of a particular will to the forces facing it. Through all of these aspects, historiography stages the conditions of possibility of production, and it is itself the subject on which it endlessly writes.

Production and/or Archeology

Production is indeed historiography's quasi-universal principal of explanation, since historical research grasps every document as the symptom of whatever produced it. Clearly, it is not so easy to do as Jean Desanti has said, to "learn from the very product to be deciphered and to read the concatenation of its generative acts."[17] On a first level of analysis, we can state that production names a question that appeared in the West with the mythic practice of writing. Up until then, history was developed by introducing a cleavage everywhere between *materia* (facts, the *simplex historia*) and *ornamentum* (presentation, staging, commentary). It aimed at recovering a truth of facts under the proliferation of "legends," and in thus instituting a discourse conforming to the "natural order" of things, at the point where mixtures of illusion and truth were proliferating. The problem is no longer advanced in the same way from the time when the "fact" ceases to function as the "sign" of a truth, when "truth" changes its status, slowly ceasing to be what is manifest in order to become what is produced, thereby acquiring a scriptural form. The idea of production transposes the ancient conception of a "causality" and separates two kinds of problems: on the one hand, reference of the "fact" to what *made it possible*; on the other, a *coherence* or a "concatenation" among observed phenomena. The first question is translated in terms of genesis, and endlessly bestows privilege upon what occurs "before"; the second is expressed in the form of series whose makeup calls for an almost obsessive worry on the part of historians over filling lacunae and maintaining, more or less metaphorically, an order of structure. Often reduced to being no more than a filiation and an order, the two elements are combined in the quasi-concept of temporality. In this respect, it is true, as Desanti says, that it is "solely at the time when a specific concept of temporality is at hand and fully elaborated that the problem of *History* can be approached."[18] Meanwhile, temporality can designate the necessary linkage of the two problems, and expose or represent in the same text the ways by which the historian meets the double demand of expressing what existed before hand and filling lacunae with facts. History furnishes the empty frame of a linear succession which formally answers to questions on *beginnings* and to the need for *order*. It is thus less the result obtained from research than its condition: the web woven a priori by the two threads with which the historical loom moves forward in the single gesture of filling holes. For lack of being able to transform the postulate of their study into its object, historians, Gérard Mairet says, "replace an acquaintance with time with the knowledge of *what* exists within time."[19]

In this respect, historiography would simply be a philosophical discourse that is unaware of itself; it would obfuscate the formidable questions that it bears by replacing them with the infinite labor of doing "as if" it were responding to them. In fact, this repressed dimension returns endlessly in its labors; it can be seen, among other signs, in that which inscribes into it the reference to a "production" and/or in the questioning that can be placed under the sign of an "archeology."

So that, through "production," we will not be limited to naming a necessary but unknown relation among known terms – in other words, to designating what supports historical discourse but which is not the object of analysis – we must recall what Marx noted in his *Theses on Feuerbach*, to the effect that "the thing, reality, sensuousness" must be grasped "*as a human sensuous activity*," as a "*practice*."[20] A return to fundamentals: "Life involves, before everything else, eating and drinking, habitation, and many other things. The first historical fact [*die erste geschichtliche Tat*] is thus the production [*die Erzeugung*] of the means to satisfy these needs, the production [*die Produktion*] of material life itself. And this is a historical fact [*geschichtliche Tat*], a fundamental condition [*Grundbedingung*] of all history, which today, as thousands of years ago, must daily and hourly be fulfilled."[21] From this base, production diversifies according to needs that are or are not easily satisfied, and according to the conditions under which they are satisfied. Production is everywhere, but "*production in general* is an abstraction": "When we speak of production, we always have in mind production at a definite stage of social development, of the production by individuals in society. . . . For example, no production is possible without an instrument of production. . . . It is not possible without past, accumulated labors. . . . Production is always a particular branch of production." "Finally, not only is production particular production, but it is invariably only a definite social corpus, a social subject, that is engaged in a wider or narrower totality of production spheres."[22] Thus the analysis returns to needs, to technical organizations, to social places and institutions in which, as Marx notes of the piano manufacturer, only that labor which produces capital is productive.[23]

I emphasize and underscore these classical texts because they specify the interrogation that I have encountered by beginning from a so-called history of ideas or mentalities: what relation can be established among definite *places* and the *discourses* that are produced therein? Here it has seemed to me that it might be possible to transpose what Marx calls productive labor in the economical sense of the term to the extent that "labor is productive only if it produces its opposite," that is, capital.[24] Discourse is doubtless a form of capital, invested in symbols; it can be transmitted, displaced, accrued, or lost. Clearly this perspective also holds for the historian's "labor" that uses discourse as its tool; and in this respect, historiography also clearly pertains to what it must study: the relation among a *place*, a *labor*, and this "increase of capital" that can constitute *discourse*. That for Marx discourse falls into the category of what is generated by "improductive labor" does not impede us from envisaging the *possibility* of treating in these terms the questions placed before historiography, and the questions posed by it.

Perhaps it is a question of giving a specific content already to the "archeology" that Michel Fourcault has surrounded with new prestige. For my part, born as a historian within religious history, and formed by the dialect of that discipline, I asked myself what role religious productions and institutions might have had in the organization of the modern "scriptural" society that has replaced them by transforming them. Archeology was the way by which I sought to specify the return of a repressed, a system of Scriptures which modernity has *made* into an absent body, without being able to eliminate it. This "analysis" allowed me also to recognize in current labors a "past, accumulated" and still-influential labor. In this fashion, which made continuities and distortions appear within systems of *practice*, I was also the subject of my own analysis. That analysis has no autobiographical interest, yet by restoring in a new form the relation of production that a place keeps with a product, it led me to a study of historiography itself. The subject appears within his own text: not with the marvelous liberty that allows Martin Duberman to become in his discourse the interlocutor of his absent characters and to tell of himself by telling of them,[25] but in the manner of an unassailable lacuna that brings to light a lack within the text and ceaselessly moves and misleads him, or indeed *writes*.

This lacuna, a mark of the place within the text and the questioning of the place through the text, ultimately refers to what archeology designates without being able to put in words: the relation of the *logos* to an *archè*, a "principle" or "beginning" which is its other. This other on which it is based, which makes it possible, is what historiography can place always "earlier," go further and further back to, or designate as what it is within the "real" that legitimizes representation but is not identical to it. The *archè* is *nothing* of what can be said. It is only insinuated into the text through the labor of division, or with the evocation of death.

Thus historians can write only by combining within their practice the "other" that moves and misleads them and the real that they can represent only through fiction. They are historiographers. Indebted to the experience I have had of the field, I should like to render homage to this writing of history.

Notes

1 Jules Michelet, "L'Héroïsme de l'esprit," unpublished project from the preface to *L'Histoire de France*, 1869, in *L'Arc* (1973), no. 52, pp. 7, 5, and 8. [Unless otherwise indicated, all translations from the French are my own. – TR.]
2 Jules Michelet, *Préface à l'Histoire de France*, Morazé, ed. (Paris: Colin, 1962), p. 175.
3 Michelet, "L'Héroïsme de l'esprit," p. 8.
4 [De Certeau refers to a passage in Freud's *Moses and Monotheism* which is crucial for the relations of historiography and psychoanalysis. – TR.]
5 Michelet, "L'Héroïsme de l'esprit," p. 8.
6 Michelet, quoted by Roland Barthes in "Aujourd'hui Michelet," *L'Arc* (1973), no. 52, p. 26.
7 Michelet, "L'Héroïsme de l'esprit," pp. 12–13.
8 Alphonse Dupront, "Language et histoire," in *XIII'e Congrès international des sciences historiques* (Moscow: 1970).
9 Louis Dumont, "Le Problème de l'histoire," in *La Civilization indienne et nous* (Paris: Colin, Coll. Cahiers des Annales, 1964), pp. 31–54.
10 [The author distinguishes between *faire de l'histoire*, what is tantamount to the task by which rhetoric is used to make an illusion of posterity, and *faire l'histoire*, the making of a limited number of material effects in a given time. – TR.]
11 See Claude Lefort, *Le Travail de l'oeuvre Machiavel* (Paris: Gallimard, 1972), pp. 447–9.
12 See *ibid.*, p. 456.
13 See Lefort, *Le Travail*, pp. 453–66.
14 Eugène Marbeau, *Le Charme de l'histoire* (Paris: Picard, 1902).
15 See for example Jean-Yves Guiomar's remarks in *L'Idéologie nationale* (Paris: Champ Libre, 1974), pp. 17 and 45–65.

16 Lucien Febvre, preface to Charles Morazé, *Trois essais sur histoire et culture* (Paris: Colin, Coll. Cahiers des Annales, 1948), p. viii.
17 Jean T. Desanti, *Les Idéalités mathématiques* (Paris: Seuil, 1968), p. 8.
18 Desanti, *Les Idéalités mathématiques*, p. 29.
19 Gérard Mairet, *Les Discours et Phistorique: Essai sur la représentation historienne du temps* (Paris: Mame, 1974), p. 168.
20 Karl Marx, *These on Feuerbach*, Thesis I, in Karl Marx and Friedrich Engels, *Basic Writings on Politics and Philosophy*, L. S. Feuer, ed. (New York: Doubleday, 1959), p. 243. On the same topic, see also "Marginal Gloss to the Program of the German Workers' Party," paragraph 1, Marx and Engels, *Critique of the Gotha Erfurt Program*, in *Basic Writings*, pp. 112–32.
21 Karl Marx and Friedrich Engels, *The German Ideology*, in *Basic Writings*, p. 249; and Karl Marx, *Die Fruhschriften*, S. Landshut, ed. (Stuttgart: A. Kroner, 1853), p. 354.
22 Karl Marx, *Introduction to a Critique of Political Economy*, in *The German Ideology*, C. S. Arthur, ed. (New York: International Publishers, 1978), pp. 125–26.
23 Karl Marx, *Critique of Political Economy*, in *The German Ideology*, pp. 127ff.
24 *Ibid.*
25 See Martin Duberman, *Black Mountain: An Exploration in Community* (New York: Dutton, 1973).

3

History: Science and Fiction

1 Fiction

"Fiction" is a perilous word, much like its correlative, "science." Having discussed the fictive aspects of historical discourse elsewhere,[1] I should like here only to specify, in the form of a preliminary note, four possible ways in which fiction operates in the historian's discourse.

1.1 Fiction and history

Western historiography struggles against fiction. This internecine strife between history and storytelling is very old. Like an old family quarrel, positions and opinions are often fixed. In its struggle against genealogical storytelling, the myths and legends of the collective memory, and the meanderings of the oral tradition, historiography establishes a certain distance between itself and common assertion and belief; it locates itself in this difference, which gives it the accreditation of erudition because it is separated from ordinary discourse.

Not that it speaks the truth; never has the historian pretended to do that! Rather, with his apparatus for the critical reading of documents, the scholar effaces error from the "fables" of the past. The territory that he occupies is acquired through a diagnosis of the false. He hollows out a place for his discipline in the terrain of received tradition. In this way, installed in the midst of a given society's stratified and interconnected modes of narrative (that is to say, all that this society tells or told of itself), he spends his time in pursuing the false rather than in the construction of the true, as though truth could be produced only by means of determining error.... From this viewpoint, "fiction" is that which the historiographer constitutes as erroneous; thereby, he delimits his proper territory.

1.2 Fiction and reality

At the level of analytic procedures (the examination and comparison of documents), as at the level of interpretations (the products of the historiographical operation), the technical discourse capable of determining the errors characteristic of fiction has come to be authorized to speak in the name of the "real." By distinguishing between the two discourses – the one scientific, the other fictive – according to its own criteria, historiography credits itself with having a special relationship to the "real" because its contrary is posited as "false."

This reciprocal determination operates elsewhere as well, although by other means and with other aims. It involves a double displacement, which renders a concept plausible or true by pointing to an error and, at the same time, by enforcing belief in something real through a denunciation of the false. The assumption is made that what is not held to be false must be real.... By demonstrating the presence of errors historiographic discourse must pass off as "real" whatever is placed in opposition to the errors. Even though this is logically questionable, it works, and it fools people. Consequently, fiction is deported to the land of the unreal, but the discourse that is armed with the technical "know-how" to discern errors is given the supplementary privilege of prepresenting something "real."

1.3 Fiction and science

Through a rather logical reversal, fiction may have the same position in the realm of science. In place of the metaphysician's and theologian's discourse, which once deciphered the order of all things and the will of their author, a slow revolution constitutive of our "modernity" has substituted writings ("écritures" or scientific languages) capable of establishing coherences that could produce an order, a progress, a history. Detached from their epiphanic function of representing things, these "formal" languages in their various applications give rise to scenarios whose relevance no longer depends on what they express but on what they render possible. These scenarios constitute a new species of fiction, scientific artifacts, which are not judged in terms of reality – which they are said to lack – but in terms of the possibilities they generate for producing or transforming reality....

Historiography also utilizes fictions of this type when it constructs systems of correlation among unities defined as distinct and stable – for example, when it investigates the past, but applies hypotheses and scientific rules of the present; or in the case of historical econometrics, when it analyzes the probable consequences of counterfactual hypotheses (for example, the fate of slavery if the Civil War had not taken place). However, historians are no less suspicious of this particular fiction cum scientific artifact. They accuse it of "destroying" historiography, as the debates over econometrics have demonstrated. Their resistance appeals once again to that method which, while supporting itself by "facts," reveals errors. But, again, the method is founded on the relationship that historians' discourse is presumed to have with the "real." In fiction, even of this kind, historians struggle against a lack of referentiality, an injury to "realist" discourse, a break in the marriage they suppose exists between words and things.

1.4 Fiction and "univocity"

Fiction is accused, finally, of not being a "univocal" discourse or, to put it another way, of lacking scientific "univocity." In effect, fiction plays on the stratification of meaning: it narrates one thing in order to tell something else; it delineates itself in a language from which it continuously draws effects of meaning that cannot be circumscribed or checked. In contrast to an artificial language which is "univocal" in principle, fiction has no proper place of its own. It is "metaphoric"; it moves elusively in the domain of the other. Knowledge is insecure when dealing with the problem of fiction; consequently, its effort consists in analysis (of a sort) that reduces or translates the elusive language of fiction into stable and easily combined elements. From this point of view, fiction violates one of the rules of scientificity....

In fact, however, despite the quid pro quo of its different statues, fiction, in any of its modalities – mythic, literary, scientific, or metaphorical – is a discourse that "informs" the "real" without pretending either to represent it or to credit itself with the capacity for such a representation. In this way, it is fundamentally opposed to a historiography that is always attached to an ambition to speak the "real." This ambition contains the trace of a primitive global representation of the world. It is a mythic structure whose opaque presence haunts our scientific, historical discipline. In any case, it remains essential.

This then is the obscure center around which revolve a number of considerations that I should like to introduce concerning the interplay of science and fiction. I shall break these down into three propositions as follows: (1) the "real" produced by historiography is also the orthodox legend of the institution of history; (2) scientific apparatus – for example, computer technology – also have a certain fictive quality in the work of historians; and (3) considering the relationship of discourse to that which produces it, that is, a relationship with a professional institution and with a scientific methodology, one can regard historiography as something of a mix of science and fiction or as a field of knowledge where questions of time and tense regain a central importance.

2 The Epic of the Institution

In general, every story that relates what is happening or what has happened constitutes something real to the extent that it pretends to be the representation of a past reality. It takes on authority by passing itself off as the witness of what is or of what has been. . . . In effect, every authority bases itself on the notion of the "real," which it is supposed to recount. It is always in the name of the "real" that one produces and moves the faithful. Historiography acquires this power in so far as it presents and interprets the "facts." How can readers resist discourse that tells them what is or what has been? They must agree to the law, which expresses itself in terms of events.

However, the "real" as represented by historiography does not correspond to the "real" that determines its production. It hides behind the picture of a past the present that produces and organizes it. Expressed bluntly, the problem is as follows: a *mise en scène* of a (past) actuality, that is, the historiographical discourse itself, occults the social and technical apparatus of the professional institution that produces it. . . . Representation thus disguises the praxis that organizes it.

2.1 The discourse and/of the institution

The historian's discourse does not escape the constraint of those socioeconomic structures that determine the representations of a society. Indeed, by isolating itself, a specalized social group has attempted to shield this discourse from the politicization and the commercialization of those daily news stories which recount our contemporary actuality to us. This separation, which sometimes takes on an official form (a *corps d'état*), sometimes a corporate form (a profession), enables the circumscribing of more ancient objects (a past), the setting aside of especially rare materials (that is, archives) and the codifying of procedures by the profession (that is, techniques). But all this happens as though the general procedures for making our common "histories" or our everyday news stories (television, newspapers) had not been eliminated from their laboratories but, rather, as though they were put to the test there, criticized, and verified by the historians in their experimental setting. It becomes necessary, therefore, prior to analyzing the specific techniques proper to scholarly historical research, to recall what these procedures have in common with the daily production of news stories by the media. The institutional apparatus of history itself, in supporting the researches of its members, blinds them to the ordinary practices from which they pretend to be detached.

Except in marginal cases, erudition is no longer an individual phenomenon. It is a collective enterprise. For Popper, the scientific community corrects any effects of the researcher's subjectivity. But this community is also a factory, its members distributed along assembly lines, subject to budgetary pressures, hence, dependent on political decisions and bound by the growing constraints of a sophisticated machinery (archival infrastructures, computers, publishers' demands, etc.). Its operations are determined by a rather narrow and homogeneous segment of society from which its members are recruited. Its general orientation is governed by sociocultural assumptions and postulates imposed through recruitment, through the existing and established fields of research, through the demands stemming from the personal interests of a boss, through the modes and fashions of the moment, etc. Moreover, its interior organization follows a division of labor: it has its bosses, its aristocracy....

The books that are the products of this factory say nothing about how they are made or so little as to amount to nothing. They conceal their relationship to this hierarchical, socioeconomic apparatus....

To be sure, this historian's representation has its necessary role in a society or a group. It constantly mends the rents in the fabric that joins past and present. It assures a "meaning," which surmounts the violence and the divisions of time. It creates a theater of references and of common values, which guarantee a sense of unity and a "symbolic" communicability to the group. Finally, as Michelet once said, it is the work of the living in order to "quiet the dead"[2] and to reunite all sorts of separated things and people into the semblance of a unity and a presence that constitutes representation itself. It is a discourse based on conjunction, which fights against all the disjunctions produced by competition, labor, time, and death. But this social task calls precisely for the occultation of everything that would particularize the representation. It leads to an avoidance in the unifying representation of all traces of the division which organizes its production. Thus, the text substitutes a representation of a past for elucidation of present institutional operation that manufactures the historian's text. It puts an appearance of the real (past) in place of the praxis (present) that produces it, thus developing an actual case of quid pro quo.

2.2 From scholarly product to the media: general historiography

From this viewpoint, scholarly discourse is no longer distinguishable from that prolix and fundamental narrativity that is our everyday historiography. Scholarship is an integral part of the system that organizes by means of "histories" all social communication and everything that makes the present habitable. The book or the professional article, on the one hand, and the magazine or the television news, on the other, are distinguishable from one another only within the same historiographical field which is constituted by the innumerable narratives that recount and interpret events. Of course, the "specialist" in history will persist in denying this compromising solidarity. But the disavowal is in vain. . . .

Without ceasing, morning, noon, and night, history, in effect, "tells" its story. It gives privileged position to whatever goes badly (the event is first and foremost an accident, a misfortune, a crisis) because of an urgent need to mend these holes immediately with the thread of a language that makes sense. In a reciprocal fashion, such misfortunes generate stories; they authorize the historian's or newsmaker's tireless production of them. . . . These informational discourses furnish a common referent to all those who are otherwise separated. In the name of the "real," they institute a symbol-creating language that generates belief in the process of communication and in what is communicated, thereby forming the tangled web of "our" history.

With regard to this general historiography, I would note three traits common to the entire genus, even though these are likely to be more visible in the species of the "media" and better controlled (or ordered in different modalities) in the "scientific" species.

2.2.1

The representation of historical realities is itself the means by which the real conditions of its own production are camouflaged. The "documentary" fails to show that it is the result, in the first place, of a selective socioeconomic institution and of a technical encoding apparatus – newspapers or television. . . . The clarity and simplicity of the information conceal the complex laws of production that govern its fabrication. It is a sort of *trompe l'oeil*, but different from the *trompe l'oeil* of old in that it no longer furnishes any visible sign of its theatrical nature or of the code whereby it is fabricated. . . .

2.2.2

The story which speaks in the name of the real is injunctive. It "signifies" in the way a command is issued. . . . It consists in endless dictation, in the name of the "real," of what must be said, what must be believed, and what must be done. . . . The law, which is given in numbers and in data (that is, in terms fabricated by technicians) but presented as the manifestation of the ultimate authority, the "real," constitutes our new orthodoxy, an immense discourse of the order of things. We know that the same holds true for historigraphical literature; many recent analyses show that it has always been a pedagogical discourse, and a normative and militantly nationalist one at that. But in setting forth what must be thought and what must be done, this dogmatic discourse does not have to justify itself because it speaks in the name of the "real."

2.2.3
Furthermore, this storytelling has a pragmatic efficacy. In pretending to recount the real, it manufactures it. It is performative. It renders believable what it says, and it generates appropriate action. In making believers, it produces an active-body of practitioners. . . . The bewitching voices of the narration transform, reorient, and regulate the space of social relations. They exercise an immense power, but a power that eludes control because it presents itself as the only representation of what is happening or of what happened in the past. Professional history operates in an analogous way through the subjects it selects, through the problematics that it privileges, through the documents and the models that it employs. Under the name of science, it too arms and mobilizes a clientele of the faithful. . . .

3 Scientificity and History: the Computer

In order to establish its own setting and base of power, discourse binds itself to the institutional structure that legitimates it in the eyes of the public and, at the same time, makes it dependent on the play of social forces. Corporate bodies underwrite the text or the image, providing a guarantee to readers or spectators that it is a discourse of the "real" while, simultaneously, by its internal functioning, the institution articulates the mode of production upon the ensemble of social practices. But there is a reciprocal exchange in the parts played by these two aspects. Representations are authorized to speak in the name of the "real" only if they are successful in obliterating any memory of the conditions under which they were produced. Now, it is again the institution that manages to achieve an amalgam of these contraries. Drawing on common social conflicts, rules, and procedures, the institution constrains the activity of production, and it authorizes the occultation of this process by the very discourse that is produced. Carried out by the professional milieu, these practices can then by hidden by the representation. But is this situation really so paradoxical? After all, the exclusion from the discourse of reference to the conditions that produced it is precisely what actually binds the group (of scholars).

Of course, this practice cannot simply be reduced to everything that makes it be part of the category of general historiography. As a "scientific" practice, it has certain specific characteristics. I shall take as an example the functioning of the computer in the field of professional historiography. The computer opens up the possibility of quantitative, serial analysis of variable relationships among stable units over an extended period of time. For the historian, it is tantamount to discovering the Island of the Blessed. At last he will be able to sever historiography from its compromising relations with rhetoric, with all its metonymic and metaphorical uses of details that are supposed to be the signifying elements of the ensemble and with all its cunning devices of oratory and persuasion. At last he is going to be able to disengage historiography from its dependence on the surrounding culture, out of which prejudgments and expectancies determine in advance certain postulates, units of study, and interpretations. Thanks to the computer, he becomes capable of mastering numbers, of constructing regularities, and of determining periodicities according to correlation curves – three frequent distress points in the strategy of his work. . . .

3.1

Nothing seems more extraneous to the avatars through which the historian's discipline has passed than this mathematician's scientificity. . . . Three circumstantial conditions connect this idea with a particular historical conjuncture. First is progress in the techniques of mathematics (the calculus of probabilities, etc.), which cannot be dissociated from the quantitative approach to nature and to the deduction of universal laws that are characteristics of eighteenth century science;[3] then the sociopolitical organization of an administration for rationalizing territory, centralizing information, and furnishing the model for the general management of citizens; and, finally, the establishment of a bourgeois elite ideologically persuaded that its own power and the wealth of the nation would be assured by the rationalization of society.

This triple historical determination, one technical, another sociopolitical, and a third ideological and social, was – and remains – the necessary condition for all statistical operations. In addition is the fact that today scientific progress, a national or international institutional apparatus, and a technocratic milieu combine to support the computer industry.[4] In other words, the mathematization of society does not escape history. On the contrary, it depends on new knowledge and on institutional structures and social formations, the historical implications of which are developed across the entire field of this ahistorical methodology.

3.2

Furthermore, mathematical rigor pays the price of restricting the domain in which it can be employed. . . . Today only drastic restrictions permit the use of statistics, which is still an elementary form of mathematics, in historical studies. So, from the very outset of the statistical operation, one can retain only so much of the material being studied as is susceptible to arrangement in a linear series; and this kind of data favors, for example, electoral history or the history of urban planning, to the detriment of other histories, which are left to lie fallow or are relegated to amateurs. One must define the units to be treated in such a way that the statistical sign (the numbered object) must never be identified with things or words, in which case historical or semantic variations would compromise the stability of the sign and, thereby, the validity of calculations. . . .

3.3

To the degree that they are honored in the actual practice of the historian, these constraints produce a technical and methodological auditing of sorts. They make some effects of scientificity. . . . [But] Computation proves nothing. It increases the number of legitimate formal relations among abstractly defined elements, and it designates the hypotheses to be rejected on the grounds that they are poorly formulated, unexaminable, or contrary to the results of the analysis.

But this being so, computation ceases to be fundamentally concerned with the "real." It amounts to no more than a managing of formal units. Actual history is, in fact, thrown out of its laboratories. Consequently, the reaction that the computer produces in historians is extremely ambiguous. Simultaneously, they want it and they don't want it. They are at once seduced by it and rebel against it. . . .

3.3.1

In distinguishing, as one must, among the computer sciences (where statistics plays a lesser role), probability theory, statistics itself (and applied statistics), and the analysis of data, it could be said that, in general, historians confined themselves to the last sector, the quantitative treatment of data. In the field of history, the computer is used essentially to build new archives. These archives, public or private, duplicate and then eventually replace the older archives. . . .

3.3.2

Rather than employing the computer for the sake of the formal operations that it sets in motion, historians use it as a source of more solid and extensive data. The computer appears in their work in its current image of technocratic power. It is introduced into historiography by virtue of a socio-economic reality rather than by virtue of a system of rules and hypotheses proper to a scientific field. This is the reaction of a historian, not of a mathematician. . . .

Consequently, each book of history must include a minimal base of statistics, which both guarantees the seriousness of the study and renders homage to the power that reorganizes our productive apparatus. The two gestures, one of conformity to a contemporary technical method and the other of dedication to the reigning authority, are inseparable from each other. They are one and the same.

3.3.3

[The historian's] dedication to this scientificity accredits his text. It plays the role of the authoritative citation. Among all the authorities to which the historiographical discourse may refer, it is this one that lends it the utmost legitimacy. In the final analysis, what always accredits the discourse is power because power functions as a guarantee of the "real," in the manner in which gold bullion validates bank notes and paper money. This motive, which draws the representational discourse toward the center of power, is more fundamental than psychological or political motivations. Power today takes on the technocratic form of the computer. Therefore, to cite its operations is, thanks to this "authority," to bestow credibility on the representation. By the tribute it pays the computer, historiography produces the belief that it is not fiction. Its scientific proceedings express once again something unscientific: the homage rendered to the computer sustains an old hope of making historical discourse pass for discourse on the "real."

A corollary to this problematic of compelling belief by citing a source of power is the more general problematic of the "belief" that is bound to a citation of the other. . . .

The use of the computer in the field of historiography cannot be dissociated from what it enables the historian to make others believe, nor from what it presupposes he believes himself. This superabundance (this superstition) of the past plays a part in the way historians employ modern techniques of investigation. So it is that in this very relation to scientificity, to mathematics, to the computer, historiography is "historical" – no longer in the sense that it produces an interpretation of previous epochs but in the sense that it is reproducing and recounting what modern sciences have rejected or lost and constituted as "past" – a finite, separate entity.

4 Science-Fiction, or the Place of Time

This combination may be what constitutes the essence of the historical: a return of the past in the present discourse. In broader terms, this mixture (science and fiction) obscures the neat dichotomy that established modern historiography as a relation between a "present" and a "past" distinct from each other, one being the producer of the discourse and the other being what is represented by it, one the "subject," the other the "object" of a certain knowledge. This object, presumed to be exterior to the work of the laboratory, in fact determines its operations from within.

The presence of this combination is frequently treated as the effect of an archaeology that must be gradually eliminated from any true science or as a "necessary evil" to be tolerated like an incurable malady. But I believe it can also be understood as the index of a peculiar epistemological status and, therefore, of a function and a scientificity to be reckoned with in its own right. If this is the case, then we must bring to light those "shameful" aspects that historiography believes it must keep hidden. The discursive formation which will then appear is an interspace (between science and fiction). It has its own norms and these do not correspond to the usual model which is always being transgressed but which one might like to believe, or to make others believe, it obeys. This science fiction, science and fiction, like other "heterologies," operates at the juncture of scientific discourse and ordinary language, in the same place where the past is conjugated in the present, and where questions that are not amenable to a technical approach reappear in the form of narrative metaphors. In concluding, I would like to specify a number of questions which an elucidation of this mixture of science and fiction must consider.

4.1 A repoliticization

Our sciences were born with that "modern" historical act that depoliticized research by establishing "disinterested" and "neutral" fields of study supported by scientific institutions. This act of neutralization continues in many instances to be organizing the ideology proclaimed in certain scientific communities. But the further development of what this act made possible has tended to invert its neutralizing effects. Having become actual seats of logistic power, scientific institutions have fitted themselves into the system they serve to rationalize, a system that links them to each other, fixes the direction of their research, and assures their integration into the existing socioeconomic framework. These effects of assimilation naturally weigh most heavily on those disciplines which are the least technologically developed. And this is the case with historiography.

It is therefore necessary today to "repoliticize" the sciences, that is to focus their technical apparatus on the fields of force within which they operate and produce their discourse. This task is preeminently that of the historian.... Historical elucidation unfolds under the domination of what it treats. It must make explicit its internal and prevailing relationship to power (as was the case in the past for the relation to the prince).... Technically, this "repoliticization" will consist in "historicizing" historiography itself. By a professional reflex, the historian refers any discourse to the socioeconomic or mental conditions that produced it. He needs to apply this kind of analysis to his own discourse in a manner that will make it pertinent to the elucidation of those forces that presently organize representations of the past. His very work will then become a laboratory in which to test how a symbolic system articulates itself in a political one.

4.2 The Coming back of time

In this way the epistemology that would differentiate an object from the subject and, consequently, reduce time to the function of classifying objects will be modified. In historiography, the two causalities, that of the object and that of time, are connected. For three centuries maybe the objectification of the past has made of time the unrelflected category of a discipline that never ceases to use it as an instrument of classification.... In other words, the "past" is the object from which a mode of production distinguishes itself in order to transform it. Historical acts transform contemporary documents into archives, or make the countryside into a museum of memorable and/or superstitious traditions. Such acts determine an opposition which circumscribes a "past" within a given society.... In this typical conception of the expansionist "bourgeois" economy, it is striking that time is exterior, is considered "other".... Time continues to be experienced within the productive process; but, now, transformed from within into a rational series of operations and objectified from without into a metric system of chronological units, this experience has only one language: an ethical language which expresses the imperative to produce.

Perhaps in restoring the ambiguity that characterizes relationships between object and subject or past and present, historiography could return to its traditional task – which is both a philosophical and a technical one – of articulating time as the ambivalence that affects the place from which it speaks and, thus, of reflecting upon the ambiguity of place as the work of time within the space of knowledge itself. . . . A "past" reappears through the very activity of historiographical production. That the "other" is already there, in place, is the very mode through which time insinuates itself. . . .

4.3 Subjects and affects

That the particularity of the place where discourse is produced is relevant will be naturally more apparent where historiographical discourse treats matters that put the subject-producer of history into question: the history of women, of blacks, of Jews, of cultural minorities, etc. In these fields one can, of course, either maintain that the personal status of the author is a matter of indifference (in relation to the objectivity of his or her work) or that he or she alone authorizes or invalidates the discourse (according to whether he or she is "of it" or not). But this debate requires what has been concealed by an epistemology, namely, the impact of subject-to-subject relationships (women and men, blacks and whites, etc.) on the use of apparently "neutral" techniques and in the organization of discourses that are, perhaps, equally scientific. For example, from the fact of the differentiation of the sexes, must one conclude that a woman produces a different historiography from that of a man? Of course, I do not answer this question, but I do assert that this interrogation puts the place of the subject in question and requires a treatment of it unlike the epistemology that constructed the "truth" of the work on the foundation of the speaker's irrelevance. Questioning the subject of knowledge demands that one rethink the concept of time, if it is true that the subject is constructed as a stratification of heterogeneous moments and that whether the scholar is woman, black, or Basque, it is structured by relations to the other. Time is precisely the impossibility of an identity fixed by a place. Thus begins a reflection on time. The problem of history is inscribed in the place of this subject, which is in itself a play of difference, the historicity of a nonidentity with itself. . . .

4.4 A scientific myth as ethical discourse

The fact that identities of time, place, subject, and object assumed by classical historiography do not hold, that they have been stirred by forces that trouble them, has been for a long time underscored by the proliferation of fiction. But this is a part of historiography which is held to be shameful and illegitimate – a disreputable family member that the discipline disavows. . . . [I]mprovements in its technique and the general evolution of knowledge have increasingly led it to camouflage its links, inadmissible to scientific thought, with what had been identified during the same period of time as "literature." This camouflage is precisely what introduces into contemporary historiography the simulacrum that it refuses to be.

In order to grant legitimacy to the fiction that haunts the field of historiography, we must first "recognize" the repressed, which takes the form of "literature," within the discourse that is legitimated as scientific. The ruses that the discourse must employ in its relationship to power in the hope of using that power without serving it, the manifestations of the object as a "fantastic" actor in the very place of the "subject of knowledge," the repetitions and returns of time that are supposed to be irrevocably past, the disguises of passion under the mask of reason, etc. – all concern fiction in the "literary" sense of the term. And fiction is hardly a stranger to the "real." On the contrary, as Jeremy Bentham already noted in the eighteenth century, "fictitious" discourse may be closer to the real than objective discourse.[5] But another logic comes into play here, which is not that of the positive sciences. It began to re-emerge with Freud. Its elucidation will be one of the tasks of historiography. Under this aspect, fiction is recognizable where there is no fixed, "univocal" position proper to itself, that is, where the other insinuates itself in the place of the "subject of knowledge." The central role of rhetoric in the field of historiography is precisely an important symptom of this different logic.

Envisaged then as a "discipline," historiography is a science which lacks the means of being one. Its discourse undertakes to deal with what is most resistant to scientificity (the relation of the social to the event, to violence, to the past, to death), that is, those matters each scientific discipline must eliminate in order to be constituted as a science. But in this tenuous position, historiography seeks to maintain the possibility of a scientific explanation through the textual globalization produced by a narrative synthesis. The "verisimilitude" that characterizes this discourse is its defense of a principle of explanation and of the right to a meaning. The "as if" of its reasoning (the enthymematic style of historiographical demonstration) has the value of a scientific project. It maintains a belief in the intelligibility of things that resist it the most. Thus, historiography juxtaposes elements that are inconsistent and even contradictory and often appears to "explain" them; it is through historiography that scientific models are reconnected with what is missing from them. This relating of systems to what displaces them, or metaphorically transforms them, corresponds as well to the way time appears to us and is experienced by us. From this perspective, historiographical discourse is, in itself, the struggle of reason with time, but of reason which does not renounce what it is as yet incapable of comprehending, a reason which is, in its fundamental workings, *ethical*. Thus it will be, in the vanguard of the sciences as the present fiction of what they are only partially able to achieve. An affirmation of scientificity rules this discourse, which conjoins the explicable with the not yet explicable. What is recounted there is a fiction of science itself.

Continuing to maintain its traditional function of "conjunction," historiography links the cultural, legendary manifestations of a time to what, in these legends, is already controllable, correctible, or prohibited by technical practices. It cannot be identified with its practices, but it is produced by what those practices trace, erase, or confirm in the received language of a given milieu. The traditional model of a global, symbolizing, and legitimating discourse is thus still in evidence here but worked by instruments and controls that belong specifically to the productive apparatus of our society. Furthermore, neither the totalizing narrativity of our culture's legends nor its technical and critical operations can be assumed to be absent or eliminated, except arbitrarily, from what finally results in a representation – the historical book or article. From this point of view, each of these representations, or the mass they form taken together, could be compared to myth if we define myth as a story permeated by social practices – that is, a global discourse articulating practices which it does not talk about but which it must respect, practices that are at once absent from its narrative and yet oversee it. Our technical practices are often as silent, as circumscribed, and as essential as were the initiation rites of the past, but henceforth they are of a scientific nature. It is in relation to these technical practices that historical discourse is elaborated, assuring them as a symbolic legitimacy and at the same time, "respecting" them. They depend on historical discourse for their social articulation, and yet they retain control over it. Thus, historical discourse becomes the one possible myth of a scientific society that rejects myths – the fiction of a social relationship between specified practices and general legends, between techniques that produce and demacrate places in society and legends that propose a symbolical ambiguity as an effect of time. I shall conclude with a formula. The very place established by procedures of control is itself historicized by time, past or future; time is inscribed there as the return of the "other" (a relationship to power, to precedents, or to ambitions), and while "metaphorizing" the discourse of a science, it turns it into the discourse of a social reciprocity and of an ethical project. While place is dogmatic, the coming back of time restores an ethics.

Notes

1 Michel de Certeau, "La fiction de l'histoire," *L'écriture de l'histoire*, 2nd edn (Paris: Gallimard, 1978), pp. 312–58.

2 Jules Michelet, "L'heroisme de l'esprit" (1869), in *L'Arc*, no. 52, pp. 7–13.

3 See Morris Kline, *Mathematics in Western Culture* (New York: Oxford University Press, 1972), pp. 190–286.

4 See, for example, "IBM ou l'émergence d'une nouvelle dictature," *Les temps modernes*, no. 351, October 1975.

5 Jeremy Bentham's theory of linguistic fictions and of "incomplete symbols" enables him to analyze the effective operations connected with a logic of "as if." See C. K. Ogden, *Bentham's Theory of Fictions* (London: Kegan Paul, 1932).

Part II

Other Cities: Cultural Politics

4

Introduction

Tom Conley

What can an other city be? Were Michel de Certeau to ponder the question today he would no doubt begin by contrasting the maps given to show the formal design of cities of our time to the ways that people circulate within them. He would set into a relation of tension an overlay of printed iconographic views with oral tales relating the challenge of living within these often squalid and dystopic spaces. He would recall how much the life of an *other* city, of a time less crushing than our own, would be tied to the ways its inhabitants govern their lives within it. Study of an other city would begin from historical relation of various modes of *police*, understood in the historical depth of the term, to ways of living in the *polis*.[1] Time and again in his writings on space and praxis Certeau returns to the political basis of life defined by the relation of the one to the other. Were he to write in the style of a Brillat-Savarin reflecting on a physiology of everyday life in the twenty-first century, one of his reigning aphorisms might be turned as "Tell me how you spatialize and I'll tell you who you are."

At the same time, as Graham Ward has already suggested in the title of this part of the *Certeau Reader*, he would have pluralized the city in order to provide groundings for a variety of political practices. Their plurality constitutes an "art of the possible," in other words a politics, that appeals to models of utopias both past and present. In Certeau's world what is possible is best understood in terms of extension that can be felt and fathomed. Activity "takes place" when speech and dialogue produces consciousness of relations that define social ecologies of space in given milieus. His politics are entrenched in the belief that exchange is vital to the workings in and of any place. These places must be known and sensed in terms of the physical matter that comprises them, their geographies, and the broader reach of their histories. How various styles or modes of exchange are invented to cope with these places is what energizes the spirits of the political animal that we are.

The conception of space that prevails in all his writings, as the title of this part rightly insists, is born of the history of urban experience. All over the world city planners who are coping with urban sprawl know that demographic concentration follows a development, beginning in the thirteenth century, that has gone unabated since the Industrial Revolution. Following the model that Balzac makes clear in many of the novels of the *Human Comedy*, masses of disenfranchised peasants emigrate to urban areas in search of remunerative labor. What they find is usually as oppressive or unyielding as what they flee. Herein the city is a site of uneven economic development, but also a point where centralization of power is made manifest. Paris, a locus for many of Certeau's political writings, is an emblem of a political elite that reigns over the provinces. Since the great development of postal roads in the eighteenth century, railways in the nineteenth century, and the automotive highway in our age, the city has been defined as might a hub with spokes extending to the hexagonal circumference of the provinces. In this sense, a dialectical principle of the difference of the city and the country, vital in the writings of both Marx and Engels and Henri Lefebvre for the detection of social contradiction, bears a strong presence in the utopian aura of "other cities."[2] The point is driven home to today's tourists, who wander about the streets and who bump into maroon-colored escutcheons on posts that bear, beneath the emblem of the ship of the city, informative but highly inflected textual histories that show the passers-by who have stopped in their tracks and taken time enough to read the prose the wealth of the history on which they are walking.

The tensions of pragmatic thinking in Certeau's political writings run against the utopian grain of a city that riddles its streets and squares with hagiographies of its community. Paradoxically, they have a deep and rich grounding in medieval history. One of the conceptual origins of his work on city spaces begins with Isidore of Seville's enduring distinction of *civitas* and *urbs*. For the seventh-century polymath bearing the name of the great Iberian city an *urbs* is a mapped or architecturally conceived concept of the city, whereas a *civitas* is a space defined as a community, a living assembly that bears resemblance to a *polis*.[3] Historians of the representations of cities have shown that the two concepts do not frequently overlap. When they do, they give rise to what Barbara Mundy has called "communocentric" maps or images of towns, cities, and locally populated spaces. A communocentric plan bears strong resemblance to an *urbs* but inflects it with the presence of communal activities. They give reason to space by thematizing the ways that life is lived within its confines. As a result they tend to be charged with ideology in their role of producing for the reader and viewer of their chorography imaginary, and often seductively compelling and conflicting, views about how life is said to be led in a given place.[4]

Communocentrism is a useful standard of measure for any study of the politics of Certeau's writing. In the work on cities, whether in his treatment of the World Trade Tower of Manhattan or the streets of Paris in May and June 1968, prevail signs bearing a double valence. On the one hand, his analyses of published or official views of assembled groups, such as a thematic map of a town in which are inserted notable buildings, places, and vignettes of daily life, bear the trace of practices that may have been invented by people who had sought to materialize new and other ways of living. Yet, in their given form they are almost inevitably signs of cooptation and control. On the other hand, there exist networks of exchange, relay, invention, and passage of knowledge that are forever on the margins of communocentric representations. Maps of this variety attest not to a community but to its own possibility of being *unstated* or unavowed in the ways it constructs areas of habitation. They come from persistently internalized modes of resistance. They may indeed be constructed from shards of memory that infuse the present with affective forces that resist commodification. A celebrated passage from *The Practice of Everyday Life* recalls a study by Charlotte Linde and William Labove about how New Yorkers led their lives in their apartments. In one register they could produce an image of an *urbs*, a memory map of the layout of rooms and the number of square feet allotted to them, while in another they described how they distributed personal objects in the space and how they moved about the area. From the study Certeau deduced the concept of "space-acts," or bodily performances based on often unconscious choices that citizens of given areas are prone to make in the way they live and, literally, the way they work through and about what is in their midst.

The choices are not arbitrary. They belong to an indiscernible and immemorial time informed by generations of subjectivity. Practitioners of space do fail to respect ghosts that inhabit certain places; they are attracted to others for reasons of fantasy and delight gained by recall of singular pleasures that no authority can ever control.[5] They cannot easily be semiotized. Their cultural locations are at once historical, mental, physical, but especially mobile. They are often mantled in silence and shared only by the fleeting recognition of imperceptible signs their users exchange with each other. In the literature of religion the sites would be part of popular hagiographies that mix together imposed narratives of official saints with others that pass through oral traditions or that are born of events in the affective lives of individuals. In its most stenographic definition, a *space* amounts to a *practiced place*.

As Certeau states in the paragraph ending "The Long Indian March," a space of exchange and sharing is founded through ostensively silent movements of communities. Around such silences, "keystones" of the community, "gestures, groups and federations of Indians form networks." He calls the work of the Chiaps Indians a labor that is also born in ourselves through their example, in the attention they give to others, but in which we are also, in reanimating the narrative of their resistance, invited to play a renewing and vital part in our time and space. As is the case elsewhere, the reader is pulled into an ongoing politics whose patterns, rhythms, and stakes change according to given contexts of geography and history.

Crucial to the politics of the two essays that follow is a style of analysis that continually summons the authority of both elite – that is, "urban" – and popular – or democratically correct, "civic" – culture. In "A Symbolic Revolution," an essay written in the ashes of the revolts of May 1968, a politics of language emerges from an implicit and guiding distinction demarcating an authority from an other, visibly urban (but not entirely "popular") culture. The latter is at odds about how to formulate a mode of address that will not reproduce the style of the reigning orders, while it must appeal to them in the words that only they will recognize. In the double bind of this *politics of language* the oppressed culture faces the challenge of inventing discourses that "deterritorialize" the markers that establish common fields of meaning. One of the enthusing anomalies of 1968, he argues, is that elite culture could not even think of the possibility of students and workers sharing common concerns. Through speech that they "captured" together, as might have been the Bastille in 1789 or Paris of the Commune of 1870 in the memory they constructed to suit the instant, the students and workers made of their words a symbolic site. It was a gap opened in the distance "that separates those being represented from their representations." In the new space there was, all of a sudden, born a consciousness about how much the discourse of republican democracy was riddled with lies and built over exploitation.

"The Social Architecture of Knowledge" extends the history of the struggle of May 1968 into a broader picture of elite and mass culture. Included in the purview are secondary education and the historical geography of the centralized state, the latter hanging in the shape of maps in practically every classroom in the nation. A spatial apparatus designed to channel speech according to hierarchies of accepted rhetoric and to institute silences reaches back to the classical regime. Yet since the classical age is also a chapter in the history of France taught in French schools, its authority eternally returns. Its memory is constructed to redraw a line of demarcation between two alternately profane and sacred entities. On the one hand, the *ancien régime* is represented for its sin of holding to a tiered order of classes, but it is also championed for bequeathing a tradition of elite and popular culture that supposedly made democracy possible. On the other hand, the Revolution and the creation of Republican

France are praised for demolishing the difference but are also taken to task for reifying the idea of community. Given in the transmission of the images of the past is the project of what Certeau calls the institution of "a museum, not a society." The former would be the *place* in which gaps need to be opened for other *practices of space*.

The essays chosen to convey the political dimension of Michel de Certeau's writings are roughly of the same vintage. "The Indian Long March" first appeared in 1977, in a book entitled *Le réveil indien en Amérique latine* (*The Indian Awakening in Latin America*). In being displaced into *La prise de parole et autres écrits politiques.* (*The Capture of Speech and Other Political Writings*) as the eighth chapter and second unit of a central section entitled "Amériques: le réveil politique" ("Latin America: Political Awakening"), the essay is both an effect of an itinerary and the central point of convergence of Certeau's work on politics. It follows the ample work on Paris in 1968 and thus in the form of its arrangement mimes the configuration of a centralized regime. Paris, the origin of the "capture of speech," would be seen transported to the Americas. But seen from another angle, that of what in *The Writing of History* he calls specular narration, this vital essay stands at a vanishing point and intersection of both old and new worlds. Its own practice of space in the overall cartography of Certeau's writings cannot be underestimated.

Nor can "A Symbolic Revolution." The essay carries a poetic charge that inaugurates and inspires the monograph entitled *La prise de parole*, first published in October 1968, but that, thanks to the work of Luce Giard, effectively "returns" in the same name but in an expanded and annotated edition in 1994.

Notes

1 In *The Writing of History* (New York: Columbia University Press, 1992), he notes that "In the eighteenth century the French word *police* designates both the culture (one is *policé* if civilized) and the order that it takes for granted" (p. 188). The sentence betrays a compelling irony. It implies that governance works where suppositions have been internalized by way of ideology (in the context, that of centralized education). He goes on to show that subjects in eighteenth-century France were often left to negotiate in silence or by imperceptible practices imposed models of practice ordained by science and religion. Nicholas Delamare's *Traité de la police* (1705) locates governance in the area of the latter, the category of *sin* being used by the political order to locate "where an obstacle or a deviation appears with respect to a governance of mores" (p. 191). Notwithstanding the pertinence of the observation for what preoccupied elected officials in the United States Congress in 1998–9, the willed confusion of religion and politics that Certeau locates in the Enlightenment fails to control a dimension of popular culture, "no matter how

fragile it may be" (p. 191), that draws on "ancestral experience" and *savoir vivre*. It is a paradoxically communal and personal area of popular practices that uses vulgarized science and religion for ends other than those proclaimed, and that mixes "tacit" ways of doing things in "the language of gestures and utensils" (scythes, pitchforks, hoes) made audible only in revolts or *jacqueries*.

2 Raymond Williams's seminal work, *The Country and the City* (New York: Oxford University Press, 1973), offers a literary and social history that bears strong affiliation with Certeau's concept of "politics of language." In *Une politique de la langue*, co-written with Dominique Julia and Jacques Revel (Paris: Gallimard, 1975), a study of the Abbé Grégoire's questionnaire of 1793 about the status of patois in the provinces, concerns the sudden "discovery" on the part of the city of the rich variety of French popular cultures. At the point where the country was about to be put under the administrative control of Paris, the responses to the questionnaire reveal a wealth of practices and ways of doing things unknown to the urban elite. For Henri Lefebvre urban space follows a parabola of development similar to what obtains in Marx and Engels. But he adds that "use-value" tends to be what the city-dwellers are compelled to invent with urban space in a practice of everyday life. "Exchange-value" would be what the city commodifies and sends to provinces in order to make clear a process of uneven economic development it controls. What he notes in *The Production of Space* (translated by Donald Nicholson-Smith, Oxford, Blackwell, 1991) about power, that "aspires to control space in its entirety," to maintain in in "a 'disjointed unity', as at once fragmentary and homogenous" (p. 388), has affinity with the observations in *Une politique de la langue* about how the post-Revolutionary city in 1793 imposed French to divide the nation in order better to control it. The development of roads and lines of division went parallel with that of the dissemination of French, I have tried to situate the politics of the treatment of this historical moment in Certeau's work at large in "The Savage Country," *South Atlantic Quarterly*, 1999.

3 Isidore's definition follows that of Aristotle in the *Politics*, notes Richard Kagan in "*Urbs* and *Civitas* in Sixteenth-and Seventeenth-Century Spain," in David Buisseret (ed.), *Envisioning the City: Six Studies in Urban Cartography* (Chicago: University of Chicago Press, 1998), pp. 75 and 104n1.

4 Mundy's view is developed in *The Mapping of New Spain* (Chicago: University of Chicago Press, 1996) and summarized in Kagan (no. 3 above), p. 77. Mundy's study provides a background of images that inform Certeau's essay "The Long Indian March" (in *Heterdogies*).

5 Marc Augé, a student of Michel de Certeau, notes in his short masterpiece of spatial practice, *An Ethnologist in the Metro* (in English, University of Minnesota Press, 1999; in French as *Un ethnologue dans le métro*, Paris: Seuil, 1986), that a subway rider in his or her middle age is wont to associate subway stations with past life in the way that art historians study the "periods" or "phases" of a painter's career. To a "blue period" in Picasso's life there would correspond a "Delancy Street" or "103rd Street" phase in the life of a New Yorker.

5

A Symbolic Revolution

The rains of August seem to have doused the fires of May and flushed their ashes down the sewers. With Paris emptied, the streets, then the walls have been cleaned. This cleansing has also washed our brains and erased our memories. As a wave laps over a sandy beach, the great silence of midsummer has passed over the many speeches and protests of spring. Here we are, back to the "law and order" that a *Walkout of Yesterday* (the announced title of a German film) was supposed to have suppressed and that soon appeared either uniquely compromised or intolerable. The *after* recommences the *before*. Here we are back where we were.

Impossible to Forget

Even if the waste of a failed revolution is thrown into the dumpsters, it still cannot be said that the revolution has been forgotten. Something in us is caught up in it, something we cannot eliminate so easily. The event cannot be dissociated from the options to which it *gave place*; it is that space constituted by often surprising choices that have modified customary divisions, groups, parties, and communities, following an unforeseen division. A new topography has transformed (at least, let's say, a moment), as a function of this place surging up like an island, the official map of ideological, political, or religious constituencies.

Can this past, which is *our* past, also be "cleansed"? Was it merely a dream, or have we fallen back into the sleep from which we awakened last May? Where is the fiction? Where is the real? The link between the "events" and "order" engages the relation that we have with ourselves, both individually and collectively. To let go means choosing and selecting once again, but a choice made in secret. It is tantamount to pronouncing a judgment, but without a trial, cutting into our history in order to make a division between truth on one side and illusion on the other. No, in the aftermath we cannot accept the blind simplicity of a dividing line that would withdraw all meaning from one side of the country and from one side of ourselves. We have to come back to this "thing" that happened and understand what the unpredictable taught us about ourselves, that is, what, since then, we have become.

An abundant literature on the subject has responded to our need to situate ourselves in regard to the events. It attests to very divergent approaches and contrary interpretations, but in that very way it comprises a rich and incoherent dossier for a new debate about what we are and the methods we have for analyzing it. At stake are both nations and human sciences. A disquiet is resurgent everywhere, even in the most categorical affirmations, as soon as we tire of fingering a rosary of facts and documents: what, after all, do we know about a society and the mute agreements on which the contracts of language are based? What does it mean to understand that society? As the wise Épistémon puts it, "with what concepts can this revolt be thought?"[1] Something that had been tacit began to stir, something that invalidates the mental hardware built for stability. Its instruments were also part of what shifted, went awry. They referred to something *unthinkable*, which, last May, was unveiled while being contested: values taken to be self-evident; social exchanges, the progress of which was enough to define their success; commodities, the possession of which represented happiness.

An idea of man inhabited the immense organizational apparatus of society at large. Implicitly recognized or accepted, this secret rule was pulled out of the shadows in which it was keeping an order. From André Glucksmann to Raymond Aron, from Claude Lefort to Épistémon, every one of the authors who reflected on the events has taken up, in his or her own way, what Lenin formerly stated: "What is important in these crises is that they make manifest what had until then remained latent."[2] But, today, what had been made manifest as latent is not a *force* more powerful than the ideological or political powers (from the Marxist perspective, it would be the proletariat), but a sum of principles, essential to the established order, that have *become* an issue. Where, in order to restore this order, can reasons be found that justify what its reason was? Conversely, what references can be substituted that are fundamental for another order? *"In the name of what?"* Pierre Emmanuel had asked long ago. The irruption of the unthinkable is as dangerous for any "specialist" as it is for the entire nation. The survival of the tree is at risk when its roots become exposed.

It therefore no longer suffices to *say* that the "evident truths" of earlier times must become evident once again or that social life becomes impossible from the moment when its roots are exposed to critical view. It does not suffice to live *as if* nothing had happened, as if one had not *viewed*, beneath the assurance of the country, a system of conventions that had become fragile (because they were becoming subject to debate) and the lack of other recourses (capable of upholding or replacing the shaken order). This hole, opened by a society that calls itself into question, cannot be covered over with the massive and normal reaction that has merely refused the void, cast aside a question that was still without an answer, and hastily replaced the need for a better division of goods on the demand, indicated by the crisis, for a restoration or for a veracity in social relations.

It was a question of redefining a social *code*, at the end of a period that had slowly brought about a distortion between a rationalization of society and the system of values that had animated this labor in the nineteenth century, but that is now imposed upon it. Beyond an always unforeseen threshold (because it is always linked to accidents), such a distortion is no longer tolerable. It does not mean that this system can be replaced, much less that it *is* replaced. This system is perhaps so intimately linked to a civilization that it will not survive being scrutinized. Perhaps too, the country, being forced into redefining itself while existing as it is, will no longer have the strength to do so. No matter what happens, if we face these recent "events" that oblige us to interrogate ourselves and that open up an uncertain future, I do not believe (and who indeed could believe?) that it is possible to speak of a revolution said and done. But it is the symptom of a global problem, one that quite possibly characterizes a society on the road to technical rationalization and in which the tensions are all the more searing in that it bears an older tradition and its relation to its past is less frankly elucidated.

A *symbolic* revolution, therefore, either because it *signifies* more than it effectuates, or because of the fact that it contests given social and historical *relations* in order to create authentic ones. After all, the "symbol" is the indication that affects the entire movement, in practice as well as in theory. From the beginning to the end, speech is what has played the decisive role, from that of Daniel Cohn-Bendit to that of Charles de Gaulle. I have lingered on this strange fact (it is a way of approaching it) by believing that it was fundamental and that it engaged the entire structuring of our culture (it is an option).

Symbolic Action

The revolution of May was not explained by any hostility to odious characters or by the destruction of instruments and products of labor. Neither professors nor bosses were directly threatened, and a sort of respect protected machinery and laboratories (in truth, more in the factories than in the universities): workers spent entire nights in keeping their material functioning during the strike; students maintained a defense guard.

The damages – beyond those that inevitably came with the disorder – seemed to have the allure of sacrifices necessary for the *expression* of a demand. Thus, the history of May–June was written in terms of cars, of overturning or maintaining the autonomous machine, at once possessed and possessive, a symbolic vocabulary of a human conduct.

People were killed, but only in spite of extraordinary precautions taken to avoid a loss of life.[3] A return to order was necessary and essential for, suddenly, at the beginning of June, the number of dead victims (who were then considered "normal") to be known and for a newspaper to publish, at the end of the summer holidays, this hallucinating headline: "10,000 deaths predicted..." The May protesters were struggling against helmetted black Martians, an irruption and a sign of power in the streets, whereas, in contrast, the police violence was provoked less by the students – even the "insurgents" – than by their color and, especially, by the red flag (to the point where this reaction extended to everything red!) or by black banners, ultimately visible signs of a threat whose horrific image had been carefully cultivated by the anticommunist training given to armed troops. Were these struggles shadow-boxing in which all the players were clashing with their phantoms? Not at all, but they were struggles that were not taken literally. It was a spiritual war or, if one prefers, a *ritual* struggle (not that it was any less real), before being harnessed for political, social, or simply individual ends. The revolt was opposed to a system; it "demonstrated" signs contrary to other signs. It ultimately attacked the *credibility* of a social language. In that way it was already a symbolic action.

It was no less so in its topography, which renewed the classical geography of strikes and riots. First the Sorbonne and, turned toward the Left Bank, the parade toward Denfert-Rochereau, the Arc de Triomphe, the Odéon, the Stock Exchange ("the temple of profit," as one poster proclaimed), the pilgrimage led to Billancourt, and so on (not to mention those that failed to take place, such as the plan to go to the ORTF [French Radio and Television Service], which Alain Geismar called "one of the symbolic places of power") – all these gestures aimed at an effect of language. They were subversive because they were chosen or, in the national idiom, because they took the signs of its articulation *against the grain*. The site of knowledge passed into the hands of its "objects"; a sacred linkage overcame the partition between university students and workers; "blasphemy" desacralized a patriotism; a theater (all of society is one) changed spectators into actors, and the spectacle into a collective creation;

the fireworks (always associated with spending beyond calculation) were celebrated right where accounts had measured exchanges according to their monetary worth, and so on. The protests created a network of symbols by taking the signs of a society in order to invert their meaning. This scheme of a vocabulary did not convey, but rather *represented*, a "qualitative" change.

As one sign among many, the barricades also had little meaning in terms of their logistic value. They clearly played a political role in that they drove the enormous governmental machine into taking the dangerous alternative of capitulating in front of these curtains of pebbles, or turning the "insurgents" into innocent martyrs – two ways of losing face. But, on a deeper level, they transformed the fear of the cop into a collective action; they broke the spell of an authority; from a paralyzing atomization they produced the joyous experience of a creatively communal transgression; they disenchanted a social organization by revealing a fragility in the space where force was supposed to reign, and by making possible a power at the very site where the feeling of powerlessness held sway.

No doubt this symbolic weapon is the converse of a strongly anchored ideological power; it threatens by demystifying the "aura" with which that power is credited. It would function less well in a more pragmatic organization, of an American type, for example. If realism is no less in Paris or in Moscow than in New York, it is nonetheless necessary to refer the successive – indeed, contradictory – choices to monolithic doctrinal positions imposed by politics. Hence the impact of gestures that affect the system in the cloudy heavens from which it claims to receive a sense of history. At the outer limit, it was a revolution of humor. Laughter can kill power that plays the role of Jupiter and that thus cannot tolerate it. The Czechs used this weapon masterfully: the heaviest tanks in all of Europe rumbled down the streets of Prague, but the banners inserted in the muzzles of their cannon barrels made a mockery of them.[4] In France, the same humor did not prevail, for there was neither the same assurance nor the same unanimity. Instead of expressing what an entire nation surely knew, the symbolic action was aimed at opening perspectives that, until then, had been forbidden. It was a way out of a heretofore ineffable malaise and of a "repressed voice."

The central place of the symbol in the events has resulted not merely from an analysis of what happened. It has been the object of a reflection that is perhaps, in the style of a tactic, the most original theoretical contribution of this period. In fact, this tactic is defined as a function of what a society *does not state* and of what it tacitly admits to be *impossible*. It therefore has the effect of a dissuasion in respect to an organization of possibilities: the creation of a "symbolic site" is also an action. That students *can* sit in professors' chairs, that a common language *can* assail the division between intellectuals and manual laborers, or that a collective initiative *can* respond to the representatives of an omnipotent system – thus is modified the tacitly "received" code that separates the possible from the impossible, the licit from the illicit. The *exemplary action* "opens a breach," not because of its own efficacity, but because it displaces a law that was all the more powerful in that it had not been brought to mind; it unveils what was latent and makes it contestable. It is decisive, contagious, and dangerous because it touches this obscure zone that every system takes for granted and that it cannot justify. It remains no less "a symbolic place," as the March 22d Movement put it.[5] The exemplary action changes nothing; it creates *possibilities* relative to *impossibilities* that had until then been admitted but not clarified. I see a new and important sociocultural phenomenon in the impact of the expression that demonstrates a disarticulation between what is *said* and what is *unsaid*, that deprives a social practice of its tacit foundations, that ultimately refers, I believe, to a displacement of "values" on which an architecture of powers and exchanges had been constructed and that was still assumed to be a solid base. From this point of view, symbolic action also opens a breach in our conception of society.

It leads us to what might be the essential and most enigmatic quality of a "revolution" characterized by a desire, articulated in terms of "places of speech" that contest silent acceptances. Speech and action become identical in the repetition of the same type of gesture: "Contestation-revolution," declared the March 22d Movement, "the unmasking of something untenable, light shed on the mechanism responsible for this untenable condition, the creation of a place where a mode of speech that rejects and refuses is made possible."

A Revolution of Words

Two quotations among thousands can state precisely the nature of this strange "revolution." Both are taken from the important dossier that Philippe Labro assembled.[6] A young elevator operator from the Samaritaine department store who was being interviewed by a journalist stated: "I really don't know what to say, I don't have any education." A friend who was on strike interrupted him: "Don't say that! Knowledge is finished. *Today, education, well, it's all in what we say!*" For his part, Jacques Sauvageot declared, "Everybody wanted to express themselves, to take matters into their own hands. That's what socialism is all about."

Did speech really redefine education and culture? Is there an equivalence between "taking speech" and "taking matters into one's own hands"? By June 1968 the facts proved the contrary. But the problem became even more serious. Speech that appeals to a change of culture or for socialism surges forth from the untrained world or from those who had been assumed to be irresponsible. What was no longer being stated in the text became a margin. The nonparticipation in the social mechanisms that ought to have assured communication took the form of an exteriority. A contestatory interrogation, aiming at this public institution that is language and that unveils the fragility of its foundations, had as a safety valve nothing more than an *aside* of language.

Speech that had become a "symbolic place" designates the space created through the distance that separates the represented from their representations, the members of a society and the modalities of their association. It is at once everything and nothing because it announces an unpacking in the density of exchange and a void, a disagreement, exactly where the mechanisms ought to be built upon what they claim to express. It escapes outside of structures, but in order to indicate what is *lacking* in them, namely, solidarity and the participation of those who are subjected to them.

No more than becoming conscious, taking speech is neither an effective occupation nor the seizure of a power. By denouncing a lack, speech refers to a labor. It is a symbolic action par excellence that reveals a task that today concerns the totality of our system. To believe it effective on its own would be to take it for granted and, as if by magic, to claim to control forces with words, to substitute words for work. But then to conclude that it is meaningless would be to lose meaning, to put a mechanism in the place of a system of relations, and to suppose, ultimately, that a society can function without human beings.

The reflections that follow are born of the conviction that the "revolutionary" speech of May 1968, a symbolic action, puts language on trial and calls for a global revision of our cultural system. The question posed by my experience as a historian, a traveler, and a Christian, I recognize, and I also discover, in the movement that stirred the inner workings of the country. I needed to clarify it. Not in the first instance for others. Rather, because of a need for veracity. A partisan of what such a fundamental "speech" meant and what it was teaching me, I could neither think nor believe that it could have been exiled to the borders of the country, a prisoner of itself at the same time as it was imprisoned; its absence promised also the death of the society that sought to expel it. A schism between the irreducibility of consciousness and the objectivity of social institutions appeared to me at once as the denounced and unacceptable fact, that is, as the current problem of thought and action. To the challenge that, in May 1968, made clear the givens of an *illegitimate* situation, a wager to be won responds today.

Notes

1 Épistémon, *Ces idées qui ont ébranlé la France (Nanterre, novembre 1967–juin 1968)* (Paris: Fayard, 1968). The author borrows his pseudonym from Rabelais's *Pantagruel*, from which he drew a quotation in epigraph (but a second epigraph is drawn from Erasmus's *In Praise of Folly*). Épistémon was in fact Didier Anzieu, a former student of the École Normale Supérieure (at the rue d'Ulm), a professor of philosophy in what was then the college of liberal arts at Nanterre, a university known for its many works on group and adolescent psychology and on psychoanalysis [L. G.].

2 A detailed bibliography of the works on May 1968 will be found in chapters 5 and 6 [L. G.].

3 In the Paris that was brimming with rumors in May – and elsewhere, of course – much was made about deaths caused by the "events," but the news of them was kept secret by the political authorities. There was in fact the death of Gilles Tautin near the Renault factory at Flins: this high-school student drowned while attempting to flee a police attack on June 10, 1968 (see Alain Schnapp and Pierre Vidal-Naquet, *Journal de la Commune étudiante*, rev. ed. [Paris: Seuil, 1988], 521–3). There were also, it appears, a very small number of deaths that were more accidental than the result of violence by or against the police, in the provinces (Sochaux, Lyons), during this period [L. G.].

4 Allusion is made here to the bare-handed resistance, founded on free and open discussion and humor, that the Czech population, at the end of the "Prague Spring" in 1968, tried in vain to oppose to the advance of the Soviet army, charged with reestablishing order and orthodoxy in the Eastern bloc [L. G.].

5 The name given to the active kernel of students at Nanterre, where the first strike of the university year (November 17–25, 1967) began, and whose agitation mounted from January to March 1968. On this topic, see Schnapp and Vidal-Naquet, *Journal de la Commune étudiante*, 101ff. and 415ff., who termed the Movement an "anti-groupuscule." Épistémon gives his account of the facts and offers his own analysis of the Movement's actions in *Ces idées qui ont ébranlé la France* [L. G.].

6 Philippe Labro, *Ce n'est qu'un début* (Paris: Éditions Premières, 1968) [L. G.].

6

The Social Architecture of Knowledge

We must provide the practical and theoretical afterthoughts to the request for a democratic creativity, or for everyone's active participation in common representations. Practical *and* theoretical: the linkage is crucial if current crises challenge the bond of power and representation, after having begun with a challenge to the disciplines that provide social life with an operative apparatus and an interpretation, a tool and and an image (psychology, sociology, etc.).

A dangerous gap between what is said and what is done calls for a labor that will not set aside either theory – political science, the study of society, economy – or conceptions of history and culture. The symbolic revolution of May 1968 has called into question the relation of theory to action,[1] whence its global character: at stake is a *totality* when the *relation of a society to its own system of representation* is put in doubt. May 1968 is not a ghost story, an image that would for a moment flicker on the screen of everyday life. A problem of structure has been revealed with a gap opened up between knowing [*savoir*] and doing [*faire*]. We are all being examined about our *conceptions*, which are suddenly covered, as if under a shadow, by the reality that they felt they were designating; a *functioning* seems to command the disciplines that until now were considered stable and determinative; a cultural *organization* is at issue with the divisions we use to develop disciplines and the divisions in which production is made – a broadening of critical scope that in May 1968 aimed at the division between students and workers. Now a new "disquiet" sends tremors through the foundation of our society.

The slippage that puts the latent and explicit layers of the nation out of touch with each other requires us to ask some global questions for which we have to muster the courage to debate; for the phenomenon that has been produced is, perhaps, telling civilization that a point of maturity has been reached, one in which the fruit bursts and is scattered, in which meaning appears to be exiled from structures, in which the quest for identity leads us far from home. Thus an ending would be heralded, and so would the beginning of something else . . . It also might be that the requirement leading so many people to protest against a society and institutions that *refuse to speak the truth* is vain, either because *no* society can satisfy the requirements of this complaint, or because it can no longer be so through the one in which *we* belong, if the confidence that it had in itself and in its language disappears in order to leave only one remainder: the security owed to the commodities it produces. It is still important to distinguish between these two hypotheses.[2]

From a historical point of view, it is striking to observe once again the alternation of brief ideological revolutions that contrast with the long duration of identification with a central power. It may be a specifically French condition. The centralized "model" of Louis XIV would have been indefinitely reused later on (though in the name of different principles); France, "the land of a state tradition" – in which reign a worry over the definition of status and an (egalitarian) suspicion about "savage" initiatives, hence an establishment of strict hierarchies that favors bureaucratic centralization – would only know abrupt ruptures, of a nature too ideological and too absolute not to be compensated for and destined to failure.[3] Or else does it point to a Latin mentality, as might be suggested at once by the origins and development of democracy, which are typically northern (?), and the conflicts that underpin our modern societies, between "Roman" hierarchies and Protestant communities?

In a more sociopolitical perspective, the timeworn distinction between the "explicit" function and the "latent" function of social institutions gains a growing importance.[4] It will thus be necessary to analyze why and how their divergence develops and what it means. In the same way, the history of ideas invites reflection on the process that now reduces so many rich theories or representations to mere surface effects, deceptive signs of a reality that carries them off at the moment when they are supposed to represent it. In these methodologies of every discipline, a gap is opened up between their theory and their action. The net effect is that parties, unions, and often churches are no longer where they say they are. Recent events and facts bring all these questions forward.

A Conception of Culture: the Elite and the Mass

As an example, I would like only to envisage a conception of culture that we are also led to reexamine – one of those that determine our analysis of situations: the connection between the elite and the mass. Insofar as the event resists being sifted through this conceptual grid, it requires us to revise that connection and is thus brought into our representation of the real by reorganizing it. Thus a suture can work, already mending in this particular area the tear between "what is happening" and "what is being thought."

At the beginning, one sign among thousands. For many it seems obvious that the events of May 1968 can be understood only through the intervention of *groupuscules*, that is, through a dangerous "elite" capable of training many of the protesters and circulating subversive ideas; an active and reflective minority alone would thus be able to account for a massive movement. This interpretation is resurgent at many points on the political or scientific horizon. It is not the fact of an interest group. And too, I would prefer not to consider whether it is accompanied by either praise or damnation of these *groupuscules*. Here I retain only a cultural "model": the idea, assumed to be an *evidence* of the mind and a *normal* procedure of comprehension, that a *mass* phenomenon is explained through the actions of an *elite*; that the crowd is by definition passive, thus ravished or victimized according to how the "leaders" want what is good for it or take their distance from it. From this one would conclude that the mass must be protected by a containing frame fashioned for its own good, and that good "directors" must be substituted for "bad" ones.

The recent events have given a better definition of this assumption because they subjected any explanation to a process of enlargement that revealed its organization. But the assumption was already dwelling in our conceptions of culture, political parties, or social structures. It commanded the implicit "philosophy" of labors that *see* in popular culture of the past nothing more than a delayed diffusion and degradation of ideas originally expressed by researchers or centrers of learning.[5] This idea inspired the institution that has nonetheless worked the most for cultural promotion, but by assigning cadres to it. Since 1880, primary education has provided the structure for national cohesion and has indelibly marked French culture and society. In disseminating teaching (that is, a knowledge: what must be learned) and education (a civic morality: what must be done), has it not accelerated the destruction of local cultures? Has not cultural imperialism, which was the underside of a great social and centralizing ambition, created this "incapacity" that consists in the failure to conform to the criteria of disciplines distributed from above, intellectualized culture to the detriment of other kinds of experience, and thus impoverished local areas through what fortified centralization?[6]

The process becomes even clearer in the examinations. Here, a selection establishes scholarly itineraries on the model of a social hierarchy and filters intelligence according to the norms or mental habits of a sociocultural group. The "inept" are excluded not only from *a* culture, but also from *the* culture (since the system that eliminates them from an "instruction" also deprives them of their own traditions); and, being judged only as a function of the unique criterion imposed through the secondary school (but also through the family and through the milieu), they marginalize themselves, becoming these "self-dropouts" whom Pierre Bourdieu has studied,[7] and who, despite themselves, ultimately remain in complicity with the system that tends to perpetuate the existing relations of force.

Since then, the politics of the mass media appear to amplify – but not modify – this social conception of the relation between the elite and the public. It furnishes an immense mass with images and information manufactured in a laboratory. The organization of labor unions, political parties, or the Catholic Action Movement bears witness to an analogous structuring; it tends to turn the "base" into a receptacle of ideas or programs developed higher up, in the "centers" of thought and in the offices of the "directors."

Is it astonishing that revolutions or independence movements have been thought of in higher places only along the lines of this model, and hence as the result of an acting minority? According to this principle, it was enough to destroy the minority to suppress these movements. Many calculations or policies have been based on this cultural "evidence." It could only lead them to failure, but the social reflex is so powerful that the failure does not seem to affect it. It seems henceforth to have become – and today it is probably second nature – constitutive of a civilization of Latin and medieval origin whose oligopoly and monopoly have consolidated the endlessly leftover structure. Through a process of concentration, the modern "bourgeois" technocracy would constantly reinforce it, such that all our Western conceptions of culture would be secreting the same substance in different forms, imposing on everyone our technologies and our notorious "values" as well as our chronology and our intellectual paradigms.

Closer to home, how could the silence of the peasantry in French history be explained otherwise? How to know what were these millions of "little people," not only in the Middle Ages, but more recently, if not through what scholars and lawyers have filtered and retained? A massive unawareness consigns the "masses" to oblivion, probably because of the privilege enjoyed by written culture, because of its repression of oral culture and of *different* expressions that then became types of "folklore" along the borderlines of an empire.

But this privilege belongs to scholars. It grounds the certainty, born with them and assumed by their position, that one gets to know a society as a whole by knowing what it thinks. That the learned class can change the world is the assumption of the learned class. It is also what they are doomed to *repeat* in myriad ways. A culture of teachers, professors, and readers will silence "the remainder" because it wants to be and calls itself the origin of all things. A *theoretical interpretation* is thus tied to the *power of a group* and to the structure of the society in which it conquered this position.

Without seeking sources and causes in the past, we can merely add that similar "evidence" argues for the *transmissibility* of "values" (so to speak) in a *centrifugal* way. Everything originates in the center. Everything comes down from on high. Moreover, the law that would like everything to depend on an "elite" also attaches to the transmission of culture a descending and *hierarchical* path: culture trickles down from the father to his children, from the professor to his or her students, from administrative offices to those being administrated and, in an admirable technical word, to those being "subjugated."

"The Number Began to Live"

In this framework, reality nevertheless shifted. Not long ago, Oscar Lewis remarked that, contrary to the "comfortable stereotype" according to which "it has commonly been held that peasants are a stabilizing and conservative force in human history," they have "had an important, if not crucial, role in at least four revolutions," as Pedro Martinez had shown him, because they "actively participated" in the Revolution in order to be "identified with its ideals."[8] In the American system of interpretation, this was a surprise. The words of an Aztec peasant reached back to the immense country of silent people. And for Oscar Lewis, the sociologist who hoped to let the peasant speak on his own terms, it awakened a criticism of his own North American *society* and, at the same time, it brought him to revise a *theoretical* position advanced by that society. A representation of culture was modified through this first form of a "capture of speech."

An analogous displacement is outlined in other areas, even in the arts. Thus a new theory of theater will, for example, accompany the shift that turns spectators into actors. One conception wears away whenever a theatrical (symbolic) experiment breaks the barrier between "players" and a "public," and when the latter also becomes a player by participating in a common symbolic action. But that remains an action carried out in a laboratory, or under cellophane. In a broader and less common way, this shift modifies the balance of families or universities that are "disorganized" or reorganized by the *autonomy* of "children." It affects the filiations of memory and those of patriotism. The very possibility of a "transmission" becomes problematic. What has every generation – that of the Liberation, of Algeria, and so on – taught the next generation? The relation between generations changes according to the same rhythm as the relation between contemporary cultures or nations. Something new begins to stir in history with the political independence of cultures that until now were subject to a Western intellectual grid, and even in our own country with the social autonomy of youth, which brings about the disappearance of *our* children or *our* students.

According to Philippe Ariès, since the *child* was born as a social and cultural category in the sixteenth and seventeenth centuries,[9] the *young man* could have appeared in the nineteenth century with the spread of secondary schools, the growing needs of technical training, the universalization of military service, and the beginnings of the literary figure of the "adolescent" poet. In the nineteenth century, the boy slowly withdraws from direct participation in professional structures. Apprenticeship is detached from specialized careers and is set in another time and space. But it remains a space of privilege.

Today, by overextending this space, *youth* takes on another meaning. While young people see the time of intellectual training lengthen, their irresponsibility grows along the same lines, and also (?) the game (including delinquency), the occupation of professional positions by adults hardens and emphasizes the severity of selections, a compensatory phenomenon confers on them another role: knowledge changes hands; professional training loses its prestige; permanent education becomes a collective necessity; the authority of age is devalorized. In the gap opened by the nineteenth-century adolescent, the youth of the first half of the twentieth century enters and creates an empire, but of a different order. There is a new category in the nation, and it displaces the hierarchical coordination of those that preceded it. Youth imposes itself at once on business (as a clientele of consumers) and on production (by virtue of its adaptability, etc.).[10] It suffers the nostalgic adulation of adults who then begin to depend on it. Because it carries their dreams, it formulates the demands that it can level against them. Have they not often turned it into their precious and closeted "reserve"? They themselves need this "reduction" (which, once thrust into the future, is their lost paradise), and they are afraid of it (therefore they protect their present against it). A reciprocity thus replaces "transmission" or the "integration" of the past.[11] A new organization is inaugurated. But it is not yet *recognized* for what it is. It is folded into older structures as if it were a vice, whereas in reality it invents a new structure, that is, *different* relations among categories that have changed. Rather than a rejection of the preceding generation by the following one, in terms of a conflict, mutation aims at a new type of relation between the two. It is not a rupture, but communication that is sought whenever a social and mental displacement is already written into the condition of things.

Brutal and progressive, this movement calls into question the characteristic privilege of a society and of the conception that it mirrored of "the" culture. It has irrupted in our country. It was "incomprehensible," but why? Was it because it could no longer correspond to systems of analysis built on another model? Or was it "grasped" only insofar as it was recuperated in this former model? The event thus shakes the structure of *knowledge* just as it shakes that of *society*. Clearly, it is normal that this threatened society will use its knowledge for self-defense (which also means in order to "comprehend" the crisis, but to comprehend it so that "nothing will rock the boat"). In conformity with the law of their thinking, it is normal that the "scholars" are now reducing innovation to nothing more than the repetition of their own cultural past, but devalued by its popularization, or by the action of a competing "elite." It is normal that they classify things in that way, following mental habits inhering in their "position," the massive fact that they neither wish nor are able to "know." That is all very normal. But . . . it is no longer true. As has been observed elsewhere, an irreducible experience has taken place. "The number began to live, to destroy, individual by individual, the myth of their abstract inertia."[12]

But would the number also have changed? Only heaven knows if the human sciences use and abuse it in the form of "quantitative" things. An indispensable instrument, thus necessary, the number perhaps still contains, beneath the methods that exclude the event and that eliminate all particularities, the argument for an "abstract inertia" of the multitude. Perhaps it is the extreme case of what allowed the cultural and technical expansionism of *one* society, but at the cost of a choice that this development implies and everywhere makes clear: the anonymity of the masses, the inertia of the number. We know that the same does not hold in other civilizations in which other types of thinking developed. At the origin of a science, there are always ethical and cultural options. Today, the historical and social a prioris of our knowledge are best revealed through the event itself.[13]

Not that one "piece of evidence" *needs* to be replaced by another. It is a matter of a critical question. No longer can we assume evidence to be what had been so up to now. Experiences have changed our assurance; no theory can escape that fact. Every human science has to introduce doubt into its own development in order to investigate where it stands in its historical relation to a social type. It has a stake in *one* form of culture. In order to redefine itself, it has to proceed to an analysis that challenges the civilization for which it argues.

Between a society and its scientific models, between a historical situation and the intellectual tools that belong to it, there exists a relation that constitutes a cultural system. The event can change it, thus calling for the readjustment of cultural representations and social institutions. In knowledge, it will be translated *either* by a refusal – but so too the new and concealed role hereafter assigned to conceptions that have become archaic – *or* by a displacement that is explained by the appearance of theories corresponding to a different cultural experience. Seen from this angle, and from this angle alone, Herbert Marcuse's writings can help us to state this problem precisely, for they assemble under the rubric of a single problematic the development of our civilization and that of the so-called human sciences.

The Function of Knowledge in Consumer Society (Herbert Marcuse)

Marcuse seems to have retained from his revolutionary past the taste for concepts sculpted like bricks.[14] His intellectual instruments are unwieldy but because they would like to be pervasively engaging. He reads like a news writer for *Time* magazine, probably because he wants to make his model visible. In his view, our society has become so victimized by the law of "profit" that any opposition – political, social, or religious – is assimilated into the system and can offer hardly a trace, other than some "ideological" leftovers, of the resistance needed for a social dynamism. One wants to refer to – or believes one still is referring to – *another* dimension of humanity; but, in reality, it is eliminated by the development of civilization that catches every activity in the tightly knit web of production and consumption. In Heideggerian terms (that do not belong to Marcuse), we might say that the thinking that counts, that calculates, and that is infinitely absorbed by its productive operation causes meditation, a mode of reflection that "is in pursuit of meaning that dominates in everything that is," to vanish or be forgotten.[15] For Marcuse, this "meditating" reflection is contestatory, essential to people who refuse to be reduced to instruments of labor or commodities of commercialization. But this refusal can only be a fiction.

In fact, a social logic unwittingly displaces primitively autonomous sectors and sets them under its purview, but without their theory accounting for this tacit functioning. Thus social demands are turned into sources of *profit* (the enrichment of poorer classes assuring sales to a clientele); spiritual protests into therapies *useful* to the establishment (an "adaptation" endlessly adjusts ideals to "reality" and thus suppresses the interrogative resistance of an absolute); "negative" thinking, the symptom of an irreducible alterity, into a functionalism that metamorphoses the intellectual and social criterion of rational "operations" into things "operative" and hence *efficacious* (the way in which general interests direct private research toward what can be commercialized).

Thus the oppositions that drew their origin from a needed contestation begin, slowly, with an often static doctrine, to play a role contrary to what they had announced. They fly under a new flag but are conscripted into the service of an anonymous necessity. They are effectively put to uses other than what their theory dictates. They become *ideologies* that deceive, that are satisfied with offering to liberty an alibi that masks their real docility with respect to a "capitalism" that has become, in the words of Max Weber, "a system of slavery without a master."

This form of discrete "repression" organized by American civilization corresponds to a present situation. It is historical in nature. It would be built over a more structural repression of a psychosocial type: the "pleasure principle" is always repressed by society. "Our civilization is founded on the repression of instincts." Thus Marcuse takes up Freud's words. But these *repressed* instincts are also, through a "return of the repressed," *represented* in the language that censors them. Individual and collective lapses alike, dysfunctionings and traces of every kind, allow this endlessly leftover and masked "repressed" to appear in the very expressions of repression. Marcuse's thinking can thus certainly be broadened.

From time to time, a volcanic rift opens up a submerged violence with an abrupt explosion of language. A verbal lava, already metamorphosed in its irruption into daylight, attests to what repression has done to the repressed; for if human history is the history of repression, "the return of what was repressed" nonetheless constitutes a permanently dangerous underground, a secret and resurgent life in every civilization that takes the form of an instinct forever obliterated by law but that always threatens. A revolution would be simmering beneath the feet of every society, as witnessed by the very repetition of its failures. Every piece of speech would signify the violence of an irrepressible *desire*, but in the social language that represses and "betrays" it (in the double sense of the term: to deceive and to reveal) with *needs* to satisfy or that are satisfied.

Thus, two kinds of "repression" are collapsed into one. The former is inherent in all societies, and the latter characterizes a present situation. Marcuse designates the latter as "surrepression" and esteems it to be a repetition of the first. This architecture attempts to superimpose the one on the other, that is, both the historical (in economy) and the structural (in psychology).

Now we have to take leave of Marcuse if we want to seriously consider the dilemma that he is positing; for right where he believes he is speaking of (economic and psychological) *realities* for the sake of demonstrating the new conflation, he is really confronting the two great *systems of interpretation* to which each are referred in order to understand what is happening: Marxism and Freudianism. These systems both date from the second half of the nineteenth century and the first half of the twentieth century. They are themselves inscribed in history. Now, in analyzing the recent development of society, Marcuse shows a displacement not only in the "ideologies" he examines but in the sciences to which he makes reference. In his work, a cross-fire is produced in which the role that was originally given to each is inverted. Marxism, the theoretical instrument of a revolution based on the critical examination of relations of production, becomes a force deployed by the consumer society. Inversely, Freudianism, which was passed off as a method facilitating or restoring the integration of individuals into society, becomes sign of the irreducibility of whatever the "pleasure principle" constitutes as something left over or repressed.

Marcuse is led to draw this chiasm by using two currently cardinal "human sciences" simply because he wants to analyze the "monstrous" development of American consumer society. He is unable to account for *what civilization has become* unless his demonstration also involves *what these two sciences have become.* Described as the emergence of a new social system, a history (or a becoming) is legible in the reployment of the two scientific systems, that is, in the distance that separates their current functioning from their primitive use. Knowledge and society simultaneously "budge."

What Marcuse *does with* these sciences (when he wants to describe this global evolution on his own account) he also *states*, but only obliquely. He notes the displacement of social categories on which these sciences had founded a type of investigation: for Marxism, the creative and revolutionary role of *labor*; in Freudianism, the repressive and dominating function of the *father.* In his view, labor ceased to be creative once it was integrated into the system of production; furthermore, it is especially hard labor, pain and fatigue, whose compensation is the alienated liberty of leisure. In this configuration, as a social figure the father vanishes in order to be replaced by the anonymity of a society whose law becomes more imposing in that no single character can figure at the head of collective revolt.

No matter how inexact Marcusian analysis may be, the procedure it follows and the theoretical questions it raises are capital: on the one hand, the *method* that makes possible the examination of civilization consists in exhuming the *social* assumptions of psychoanalysis (the role of the father being linked to a type of civilization), at the same time that it takes up Marxian categories in the name of *psychological* structures of society (labor being inscribed in a more fundamental repression). In other words, Marcuse exceeds the framework of "specializations" – or a former classification of the sciences – in order to grasp the global extent of a new system. But if it is true that consideration of a different *totality* is formulated with the reciprocal critique of the sciences developed in the context of another time, what instrument do we have to analyze our own time? It seems that a new stage of civilization can be grasped only along a fault line (in this space that is the residual trace of the movement of intellectual constellations), or rather through the crisscrossing of sciences proportioned to a moment in the past.

That too is the *theoretical question* opened by *Eros and Civilization* and *One Dimensional Man*, if we admit – as these two works aim to prove – that "class conflict" (determined by the relations of labor in capitalism) and rivalry with the father (in a strongly hierarchized family and social structure) tend to become concepts inadequate to the real. Although he rejects the easy category of a "culturalism" that is really only a sloppy empiricism, Marcuse offers us the spectacle of a new social logic that corresponds only to a disarmed logic.[16] He says as much (perhaps more than he would wish) through the type of conflation he makes between Marxism and Freudianism: in order to revise and coordinate the instruments at his disposal, in order to adjust them to the reality he wishes to take account of, he nails them together in an unconvincing intellectual carpentry.

For example, he wants to determine *where* a resistance can be found that might invigorate humans in industrial society with a second "dimension." He has to find *somewhere* a truth or an innocence in which a society of happiness can be born. In that way he might even further resemble his two masters. Freud scoured history in muttering to himself, "There's got to be a cadaver somewhere or other!" But for him everything was the sign of something missing, of the murdered father. Marx, for his part, everywhere discerned an organizing force of society, the birth of the proletariat. Marcuse flaccidly mimicks both of them. He attaches an identical role to the opposition that is born with the social outcasts and to the one that is always resurgent with the return of repressed pleasure: the lumpen proletariat and art share a similar function of "rejection" in respect to the one-dimensional universe. The idea is interesting. It is adjusted to the fact that the alliance to which social unrest now attests associates misery and poetry. Like a label, the idea designates the fact rather than its analysis. It too hastily marries a shard of Marxism to a shard of Freudianism in order to force both to say that "truth" or salvation are found in the same place.

To be sure, these two systems share this resemblance of being geologies that explain the configuration of the earth by its relation to fundamental infrastructures. But in this relation they are not placing "reality" in the same spot. The former locates it somewhere in the economic infrastructure; the latter refuses to establish a site for it, or rather keeps it as something endlessly both represented *and* lost in the reciprocal relation of resistance and repression. By crossing the two, Marcuse constructs hybrid concepts with notions that are elaborated as functions of different analytical procedures. Furthermore, he assigns them the role of plugging up the same hole, of filling the lacuna of a "second dimension."

For him, it is enough to know if indeed, yes or no, social "truth" has a place; if human destinies can be localized; and, as a consequence, if the resistance or the "great refusal" somewhere owns a principle on which the future would depend. He *wants* to point his finger at the axis of a future revolution, and he *knows* that it cannot be what Marxism had indicated. He thus explains through a Freudian analysis of social repression the failure of "Marxist" revolutions, and he buys into an instinctual liberation, the source of an "erotic" accomplishment of man in nature, the Marxist dream of a classless society.

When, with his weapons and his intellectual baggage, he passes from the Marxist to the Freudian revolution, he keeps from the first the "model" of a topography of the opposition and perhaps finds in the second what he needs to justify his disillusionment or his skepticism.[17] What, in the guise of a Marxist, he had considered as the site of the revolution and the force of history from an economic and social perspective – the proletariat – he then retains as a place hereafter "co-opted" and integrated into the civilization of the present day; but he conserves the idea of somewhere nailing down the resistance whose failure Freudianism will allow him to explain. His reading of Freud remains staunchly Marxist insofar as it unduly transposes onto the field of psychoanalysis a cast of roles or forces that had meaning only in economy or sociology. His work takes on the fascinating but partially deceptive allure of a tragic epic.

It is an *Iliad*. The epic portrays a war of the gods, the struggle of Eros and Thanatos, of the "pleasure instinct" and of the "profit principle," and other abstractions. A lucid revolutionary who is increasingly disillusioned. In this respect, *One Dimensional Man* marks a clear withdrawal in relation to the (purely "prophetic") optimism of *Eros and Civilization*, a work that opened the hypothesis of a liberation as a sort of deus ex machina. But his thinking has continued to vacillate between a miracle to come – that he would renounce only in ceasing to be himself – and the totalitarian *functioning* whose new and repressive character he analyzes. A resident of La Jolla, as if on an Olympus over San Diego that dominates opposing superpowers, he follows their endless battles. Victory no longer goes from one side to the other and could never be final. In truth, identified with the "poor" or with artists, David is always slain by Goliath. His revolt, by protesting a repressed truth, emits only sterile and impoverished words.

But at least Marcuse has the courage – which prompts "specialists" to smile – to put society at large on trial.[18] That is the genre of his essay, in which he proportions a *method* to the *object* of the examination, since his study of the possibility of revolution in the current system is tied to an attempt to overcome the compartmentalization of the human sciences. In that way, he shows – and the point is fundamental – that a shift reaches both social divisions and scientific classifications; that it concerns a praxis and its theory; and that, finally, it can be *lived* only if it can be *thought* in the wake of a shift in thinking. He also carries out his analysis in a way that *designates* (or symbolizes) a *global* problem, but without being able to give it an adequate conceptual apparatus. May less whoever can do better cast the first stone! Through this double aspect of his work, Marcuse indicates a task to be done. He also connects to the questions opened up since May 1968, even if we were to assume that on the topic of Marcuse the words of Talleyrand after the fall of Villèle could be recalled: he leaves behind an emptiness that is greater than the place he occupied.

Social Structures and Systems of Representation

A putative grandfather of the "extremists" of Nanterre (which in fact is not true), Marcuse conflates two current types of interrogation on the future and on the meaning of our society. With him we can be led to think that they are indissociable and, by extracting them from his work, we can bind them in the following way.

1. A same contestatory opposition is offered in two different forms (at least according to the former classifications) that have in common being the effects of a sociocultural repression: the one, "bourgeois," of an intelligentsia (frustrated by the benefits it expected from university privileges, or lucid about the nature of the "service" that society asks of it); the other, "proletarian," of the socially excluded, the culturally homeless – foreigners, subcultures of "paupers," the lumpen proletariat, and so on. Here is the beginning of a *social reorganization* if a *same* force were able to be constituted from places that, today, social organization is *separating*.

2. At stake also is a *reorganization of the human sciences*. Born of a history (that of the nineteenth and early twentieth centuries), Marxist economy and Freudian psychology were displaced by later events, but this slippage has not yet received the theoretical status of another taxonomy of sciences; it intervenes only surreptitiously, in the name of their new functioning. The order of reason already obeys a law that continues to escape it. But it must represent it through its own reorganization. The objects defined and labeled by sciences born only yesterday (the "proletariat," for example, or the "unconscious") corresponded to methods of investigation; they cannot be taken as immutable realities; they are linked to the scientific organization that had to produce reason and permit the analysis of *a* human situation. A past is invested in a scientific theory and in its "objects." A more recent history thus appeals to a new structuration for the categories of knowledge, and in that way it will gain meaning.

We find these two aspects of cultural change expressed during the crisis of May 1968 in the form of an interrogation (but one that remained marginal to the system that was brought back to reality by the resurgence in June). This is not surprising, since the protests were dealing with an *organization* of society *and* of its representations. A few examples demonstrate that the questioning of "*order*" was a throwback to the mutation of a *reason*.

1. The association of "bourgeois" students and the "sleaze" is only one indication of a much more basic attempt to *overcome*, as "laborers," the *division* between workers and students. A division was becoming archaic because of a movement that had already arisen; but the fact was not yet recognized by conceptual modes and theories that shouldered the weight of their historical origins. It was translated only by what students and workers had *become*, and by the homologous lag of conceptions that were supposed to "represent" them.

A revision of structures is also implied by the movement that now envisions culture in the name of a solidarity with "excluded" groups. It wishes to overcome a classification and thus shift a type of organization. The demarcation itself becomes the "tactical" site of a *global* revision. Thus Pierre Bourdieu and Jean-Claude Passeron begin with the "eliminated" in order to study schooling or national examinations[19] – not that those who are eliminated can themselves define what true culture must be (as if "truth" were in their hands)! But the problem of a culture that could be everyone's language is posed beyond the divisions that are assumed by a demarcation based on social criteria. In the same way, many works contest a *general* division of civilization when they *reject the boundary* created through the isolation of a "workers'" culture, of a "poor France," or of "another America."[20] Even if their authors merely become the explorers of an "other" region, they must not be interpreted as if one side had to gain preference over the other. In fact, their studies challenge the dividing line, and in that way they call into question a sociocultural system. Everywhere "contestation is 'negative' insofar as it is outside of the divisions and the disciplines of established society."[21]

2. The revision of the compartmentalization between disciplines is also part of a structural shift. The theoretical status of each discipline holds less to the definition that it ascribes to itself than to its relation with others, that is, its inscription in a network of reciprocal determinations.[22] A renewal is therefore not possible if one is pigeonholded inside of a (or each) discipline: one thus necessarily confirms the system that is implied by its specific place in the constellation of an epistemological classification – or, in the more immediate sense, in the organization of this universe of knowledge called the "university." Structural innovation takes place only in interdisciplinarity, wherever *relations* can be grasped and debated, wherever boundaries and significant divisions of a system can be challenged.

In a "savage" form, such were the discussions and the procedures of the educational reforms of May 1968. For example, the relation between general assemblies and commissions showed how, simultaneously, social groups and divisions of disciplines were being shifted. The role of the assembly as a witness to a certain "universality" consisted less in developing projects than criticizing situations put forward through the work of a commission and in explaining its theoretical consequences for the sake of structuring. In a sense, this criticism unveiled in a *discipline* its relation with a historical *situation*. It made possible a revision of knowledge through the clarification of an axiomatic datum: relations among sciences and a position vis-à-vis students were implied through the very localization of a reformist project. A discipline needed to be examined from a global point of view, in a general assembly, in order for its unspoken function or its forgotten history to be brought into view and then modified.

In other words, a *theoretical* revision of disciplines could only call into question the connections that held them together and reveal an entire system of historical and social relations – which also amounts to a combination of places occupied and of powers held. Inversely, the specific *action* of students to get out of their isolation (which they saw as an encirclement, or a "ghetto") and to demonstrate their solidarity with the workers could not fail to be related to the structures of thought that were defining the relation of the elite to the masses or the transmission of knowledge (by fathers, priests, or directors) – a thought that was located in the apparatus of the "opposition" merely replacing a hierarchy of a party with a hierarchy of classes (contrary forces or doctrines are ultimately indifferent; they are reciprocally devoted to homologous mental organizations through the sole force of the system that holds them together).

In the first case, a theoretical discussion referred to a conflation of powers; in the second, a praxis contradicted a "division" (what is known as a division of sciences) and appealed to another conceptualization, one that might provide the category of "workers" with a determining role in a different social combination.

The effect and the meaning of a crisis are revealed in the connections and latent cohesions, especially because a profound shift makes them evident only when they are uprooted. Can one, from that point, splinter the problem and redivide it into questions proportioned to the compartments that an order constituted – or a social reason – that has since been displaced? That is the option of a narrow reformism. It wishes to account for a *global* shift only inside of the division or as a function of categories that are specifically linked to the social architecture in question. In that way, it censures the question itself. It refuses it. It has an excuse or a justification that is also a fact: the "poverty" of concepts or actions that attempted to signify a modification of the entire system. People conclude with assurance that it is nothing more than a psychodrama or an outlet, and that we have to be "realistic," that is, reform each sector in isolation so as to respond to each of the ills bandied about by the rhetoric of a few common places. This conclusion is hastily drawn and, I believe, erroneous, as would be one that challenged the question posed by Marcuse by arguing that he had not produced a theory of his vision.

In an established order, every deeper movement can be *symbolized* only through a different use of methods or conceptions developed as a function of procedures that are themselves epistemologically linked to earlier constructions of knowledge. This new use is thus *incorrect* with respect to past definitions, and *imprecise* with respect to determinations that would make another organization possible. Understood in this way, the symbol is a joke. It amuses, it irritates specialists or directors who sit in worlds of the past that can now be exploited. They may be right about novelties. Despite the myriad emergence of its symptoms, every beginning is fragile, and no necessity will mirror it in order to assure its success. The inheritors of established forms of knowledge are not, however, correct. The shifts are running through their own disciplines; they are already perceptible in the distortions of their system, in the same way that their own concepts are being recaptured by protesting groups.

A myopic politics is one that refuses what is translated *both* by these distortions in the inner function and by outer irruptions that still lack new and "correct" definitions. It is aimed at preparing museums, not a society. More audacious and, ultimately, more lucid in matters of knowledge, is the politics that discerns in the diversity of signs the symbol of a general movement and thus the indication of a reorganization that needs to be undertaken. But, whereas intellectual courage no more suffices than does lucidity alone, here a choice is needed, one linked to the ambition of beginning over again, that is, of living.

Notes

1 See Michel de Certeau, *The Capture of Speech and Other Political Writings*, ed. and introd. Luce Giard, trans. and Afterword Tom Conley (Minneapolis: University of Minnesota Press, 1997), chap. 5.

2 To finally make *true* statements was what was asked through so many accusations leveled against the "lies" of institutions. But Julien Freund argued, even recently, that "sincerity is a private, not a public, virtue" (in *L'Essence du politique* [Paris: Sirey, 1965], 161; cf. 199). However, even if they are utopian (in part because they are born outside of the sites of political responsibility), these demands at the very least attest to a displacement of *ethical* conscience, which has henceforth become a *political* requirement. The restoration or the innovation of a "truth" of representa-

tions and communications must correspond to the suspicion that bores into "values" invested in social exchanges.

3 Cf. Andrew Schonfield, *Modern Capitalism: The Changing Balance of Public and Private Power* (New York and London: Oxford University Press, 1965), 71–87.

4 Cf. Robert K. Merton, *Social Theory and Social Structure* (Glencoe, III.: Free Press, 1949), 120–52.

5 That is clearly what Robert Mandrou himself "states" in his inventory of the "bibliothèque bleue" of Troyes, a collection of popular editions sold by itinerant merchants in eighteenth-century France (*De la culture populaire aux XVIIe et XVIIIe siècles* [Paris: Stock, 1964]). There are, unfortunately, few equivalents of this exemplary work. Nonetheless, its conclusions, or rather its assumptions, seem debatable. Robert Montrou betrays why: the booklets edited in Troyes draw off older material and simplify conceptions that reach back to the sciences of astrology or medicine in the sixteenth century. But can we conclude that they show us the rural culture in which they are diffused? They represent a *leftover* of elite culture, and this leftover is exactly what the authors ("squires," theologians, etc.) and the editors of Troyes *produce for the use* of the villagers and what they sell to them. It is a commercial production that "trickles down" from the learned class to people through the intermediary of these local printers and that attests, rather, to the conception that the *manufacturers* make for popular culture. That the literature is sold and read does not prove that it renders an account of the language of the rural people of the period. It might prove that they lived outside of the "literary" circles, from whose tables the crumbs fell into their midst. Geneviève Bollème notes, furthermore: "Made for the people, this literature nonetheless speaks neither of it nor for it. The people are absent from these works that are intended to be written for it" and by specialists ("Littérature populaire et littérature de colportage au XVIIIe siècle," in *Livre et Société dans la France du XVIIIe siècle* [The Hague: Mouton, 1965], 66–67). Similarly, would it now be a worthwhile method to assimilate the culture of television viewers to the tenor of the programs aimed at them? It would mean confusing the expression of a local (and no doubt *different*) experience for the cultural system that is imposed on it from above and that tends either to eliminate or to marginalize it further. Here too, up to the analysis of a "popular culture," the intellectual paradigm of an elite *postulates* in advance the result that will justify it. The fact is all the more noteworthy in that the book is remarkable.

6 I especially refer to the very nuanced report by Pierre Vilar, "Enseignement primaire et culture populaire sous la IIIe République," in *Niveaux de culture et groupes sociaux* (The Hague: Mouton, 1968), 267–76.

7 See in particular Pierre Bourdieu and Jean-Claude Passeron, *Les Héritiers*, rev. ed. (Paris: Minuit, 1966); Pierre Bourdieu, "La transmission de l'héritage culturel," in *Darras. Le partage des bénéfices* (Paris: Minuit, 1966), 387–405; and Pierre Bourdieu, "L'École conservatrice. Les inégalités devant l'École et devant la culture," *Revue française de sociologie* 6 (1966): 325–47. From a methodological point of view, Pierre Bourdieu has pointed out the danger among sociologists of a certain "class ethnocentrism": "Among all the cultural presuppositions in which researchers risk

engaging in their interpretations, the 'ethos' of class, a principle on which the acquisition of other unconscious models are organized, acts in the most systematic and obsequious of ways" (Pierre Bourdieu, Jean-Claude Chamboredon, and Jean-Claude Passeron, *Le Métier de sociologue* [Paris: Mouton-Bordas, 1968], 108, a page that should be cited in entirety).

8 Oscar Lewis, *Pedro Martinez: A Mexican Peasant and His Family* (New York: Random House, 1964).

9 Philippe Ariès, *L'Enfant et la Vie familiale sous l'Ancien Régime* (Paris: Plon, 1960).

10 On this topic, see Henri Lefebvre, *Introduction à la modernité* (Paris: Minuit, 1962), 159–68.

11 Michel de Certeau, *L'Étranger ou l'Union dans la différence*, 2d ed. (Paris: Desclée de Brouwer, 1991), chap. 3.

12 *L'Archibras*, no. 4 (no series), "Le surréalisme le 18 juin 68": 2.

13 In a lucid and vigorous report in which he emphasized "the right to produce culture or the right that is granted to a social group (possibly to every individual) of playing an active role in the community," Giulio Carlo Argan protested against "the idea of a monocentric culture with a periphery organized around a radiating core." Our technological culture, he added, "is only the most current and, perhaps, terminal phase of a cultural phenomenon that, since the eighteenth century, has been strictly tied to the European and American history of thought, politics, and economy"; it is not "universal" (Report for the "Meeting of Experts on Cultural Rights as Human Rights," UNESCO, Paris, July 8–13, 1968).

14 See especially the three latest works of Herbert Marcuse, *Soviet Marxism: A Critical Analysis* (London: Routledge and Kegan Paul, 1969), *Eros and Civilization: Philosophical Inquiry into Freud*, with a new preface by the author (Boston: Beacon Press, 1966), *One Dimensional Man: Studies in the Ideology of Advanced Industrial Societies* (Boston: Beacon Press, 1966).

15 Martin Heidegger, *Questions III* (Paris: Gallimard, 1955).

16 Herbert Marcuse, "Critique of Neo-Freudian Revisionism," in *Eros and Civilization*, 207–36.

17 Strongly marked by the failure of the revolution in Germany (1918), along with Georges Lukács and Karl Morsch, Marcuse was one of the thinkers of what has been called the "Dialectical School of European Marxism." Beginning in 1934, he taught at Columbia University, where his interests turned increasingly toward Freudian aesthetics and psychology.

18 In fact, one has to look elsewhere than in Marcuse for a serious presentation of socioeconomic structures. Thus, preferable to the Marcusian legend of the "consumer society" (however tempting it may be) is John Kenneth Galbraith's analysis of "technostructure" in *The New Industrial State* (Boston: Houghton Mifflin, 1967), 60–71. The study that Galbraith makes of relations between the "educational and scientific estate" (282–316) and the technostructure moreover underlines the conflicts and is inspired by theses contrary to those of Marcuse.

19 See Pierre Bourdieu and Jean-Claude Passeron, "L'examen d'une illusion," *Revue française de sociologie* 2, special issue on 1968 ("Sociologie de l'éducation"): 227–53.

20 Cf. René Kaës, *Les ouvriers français et la culture* (Paris; Dalloz, 1962); Paul-Marie de La Gorce, *La France pauvre* (Paris: Grasset, 1965); Michael Harrington, *L'autre Amérique* (Paris: Gallimard, 1967); and Jules Klanfer, *Le sous-développement humain* (Paris: Éditions Ouvrières, 1967), to cite only the most accessible titles. All of the conclusions tend to restore as a datum of *culture* this reality at once marginalized and fundamental that Oscar Lewis called "the culture or subculture of poverty" (*The Children of Sanchez* [New York: Random House, 1961], xxv) or the "culture de l'appauvrissement" (*Économie et humanisme*, no. 174 [May–June 1967]: 77–81).

21 André Glucksmann, *Stratégie et révolution en France: 1968* (Paris: Christian Bourgois, 1968), 80.

22 That is exactly what Michel Foucault recently recalled in the first part of his "Réponse à une question" (*Esprit*, May 1968, 850–74).

7

The Indian Long March

"Saturday afternoon, 14 July, 1973. The roads leading to Guambia began to be filled with Indians (*compañeros*). The first came from the neighbouring '*resguardos*',[1] ... Next came the Inganos and Kamsa,[2] who had travelled from Putumayo, and the representatives of the '*parcialidades*' of Narino,[3] along with the Aruacos of the Sierra Nevada of Santa Marta,[4] who had been travelling four days by foot, train and bus in order not to miss the Meeting.

"And later came those from the West, and after midnight the comrades from the East, from Tierradentro, who had come by way of the '*paramo*'.[5] There were already around two thousand of us. Since it was very cold and as our comrades from the hot climes hadn't even a *ruana* to put on, we made eleven fires to warm ourselves, then began warming ourselves, some chatting, others playing music and singing.

"From time to time we would drink a little coffee to stave off hunger. Sunday, 15 July, broke full of sunlight, and we were full of contentment. ..."[6]

"Some people walked all night to join the Indian *compañeros*", adds the editor of *La Lettre*. They are heading towards another morning. No longer devoured by poverty, as they were when I knew them in Misiones in Argentina ... – but determined to forge their own history. "Recent actions have changed our perspective: today more than reacting against imminent extinction, growth and development are our objectives."[7] The Meetings of Tribes and Assemblies of Chiefs are aimed at a reconquest. For both peasant and Indian a revolution is taking form in fact and in consciousness; it is already stirring up hitherto silent depths in the Latin American countries.

Memory or the Tortured Body

The time of oppression is still not over. On the contrary, by asserting their rights to the earth and organizing autonomous associations, the Indians are being met with a renewed wave of repressive measures. Recent events tend to prove this: the destruction of the E1 Cedro hamlet in the Indian region of Veraguas by the Panama National Guard (15 March 1976); the military interventions in the communes of Palenque Ocosingo and Chinon in Mexico ... (12–13 June 1976); the murders and imprisonment of Indians in Merure (Mato Grosso, Brazil) ... (15 July 1976); etc. A list of further misdeeds that echoed in the national or international press would be lengthy. Yet these bloody marks on the surface of news transmissions are far from signalling the ordinariness of the violence. And the imprisonments, the arsons, even the murders are probably less destructive than the economic alienation, cultural domination and social degradation – less dangerous than the entire process of an on-going, day-by-day ethnocide.

"You know," said Russell Means, "the Indian has a long memory. He doesn't forget his murdered heroes or his land occupied by the foreigner." In their villages, the Indians retain a keen awareness of their four and a half centuries of colonization. Dominated but not subjugated, they also remember what Westerners have "forgotten" – a continuous succession of uprisings and awakenings that have left almost no traces in the written historiographies of the occupiers. As much as and more than in the handed-down narratives, this history of resistance punctuated by cruel repression is marked upon the Indian body. This writing of an identity recognized through pain constitutes the equivalent of the indelible markings engraved on the bodies of the young in initiation tortures. In this form too "the body is a memory". It bears, it writes the law of the equality and non-submission that regulate not only the relation of the group with itself, but also its relations with the occupiers. Among the ethnic Indian groups (some 200) that inhabit "Latin" America, this tortured body and this other body, which is the altered earth, form the beginning from where once more the will to construct a political association is reborn. A unity fashioned by unhappiness and the resistance to unhappiness is the historic site, the collective memory of the social body, from whence originates a will that neither ratifies nor denies this writing of history and that deciphers the scars of the body itself – or the fallen "heroes" and "martyrs" who reflect them in narrative – as the index of a history to be made. "Today, in the hour of awakening, it is we who must be our own historians."[8]

The relationship of the "Race of the Sun" with the "scattered blood" that "obliges" and with which the lost earth awaits its "masters" seems to articulate fully the Indian political speech on the effectiveness of associative and rural strategies. In any event, ideology is most often absent from demands. In effect a common language would merely provide the groups with a substitutional body. It would finally replace ethnic groups by a unitary, comprehensive discourse. Here, on the contrary, the instituting alliance of each community with a body and with land upholds the real difference between specific situations. Action is thus aimed less at the construction of a common ideology than at the "organization" (this leitmotif word) of tactics and operations. In this connection, the political pertinence of a geographic distinction between distinct sites repeats – at the level of the association among ethnic groups – the distribution of sites of power and the rejection of centralization that is characteristic of the internal functioning of each of them. The Indian awakening thus takes on a democratic, autonomous form that can be recognized in the specific features of its political organization and in the objectives it concludes with its analyses.

A Political Awakening

What strikes us in the Indian manifestos is the distinction between, and yet the connection with, two essential givens: on the one hand a proper political form (which entails, for example, the refusal to participate in political parties – . . . on the other hand, an economic situation common to an entire rural Latin American proletariat (agricultural or underdeveloped journeyman workers, without contracts or guarantees, indebted victims of loans at exorbitant rates of interest; overtaxed small producers swallowed up by intermediaries who purchase their goods). The narrow articulation of the political and the economic avoids two quite frequent reductions: either the assimilation of the "proper" to a cultural "identity" frozen by the anthropologist; . . . or the effacement of an ethnic and political specificity by the generality of production relationships and class conflicts. To the alibi of a cultural identity . . . constructed by the science of anthropology or to the loss of self under the (effectively imperialist) control of socio-economic laws and conflicts imposed by the international market, the Indians prefer a third political path: that of changing by means of appropriate strategies a reality that gives them solidarity with other, non-Indian, peasant movements.

Thus, specificity no longer leads to a given, to a past, to a system of representations, to an object of knowledge (and/or exploitation), but is affirmed in a set of procedures – a way of doing – in the field structured by a global economic system that also sets up among those oppressed the bases of revolutionary alliances. "Cultural" specificity takes the form of a style of action that can be articulated on situations established by capitalist imperialism.

This political determination of cultural specificity is obviously the effect of a long historic experience, of a difference maintained through the anchoring of such ethnic groups on a homeland and their particular resistance to ideological seduction. Three aspects must be stressed.

First, the Spanish institution of the *encomienda* in the earliest colonial era, the privatization and capitalization of the land by its occupiers, the subsequent demographic foundering of the Indians, the artificial regrouping of the rest of the indigenous population into *reducciones* (those factory cities of the seventeenth century) or the institution of forced labour for groups brought together on large estates or in the mines – all these forms of colonization, and others as well, dissociate the labour force and the means of subsistence; they superimpose upon the destruction of former systems (which sometimes, as in Inca society, prefigured "feudal" organization) the framework of a palaeotechnical capitalism whose first proletarians were the Indians .... In this connection we can say that the critique of capitalism in recent Indian Declarations goes back to their earliest witnesses, to those whose experience extends over more than four centuries and who ... cannot dissociate the struggle for their political existence from a lucid analysis of that economic system.

Secondly, if the resistance of those spared has a political aspect, it is because despite the arrogation of the best land by the colonizers, despite the reduction and spatial distortion caused by the geographic expansion of those colonizers, as well as the pressure exerted on the Indian lands by smaller-scale colonial adventurers, ... and, finally, despite the movement ... that forced the Indians to abandon land too poor to nourish them and to find work elsewhere as agricultural or factory labourers, the surviving communities have never stopped making a periodic return to the village, to assert their rights to the land, and thus, through this collective alliance to a land, to maintain an anchorage in the particularity of a site .... This land was and remains a kind of palimpsest: the scription of the foreign *gringos*[9] does not eradicate the first text, which remains traced there, illegible to the passers-by who have manipulated these regions for four centuries, sacredly silent with "maternal forces", a tomb of fathers, and an indelible seal of a contract between members of the community....

Lastly, the style of Indian resistance is attached to the Indians' typical internal social organization. What has often been stressed ... is the lack of coercive power – in wartime – in their communities .... Instead of referring to an overt rejection of centralizing institutions, such a structure refers to a society that has no one particular representative (the chief) of the power that organizes it. In it, the law acts as a tacit co-ordination of received practices. It is the very functioning of the group – a non-isolated authority invested in practised norms. As linkage to a land minimizes the role of a system of representations and is articulated in gestural relationships between the body and the mother earth, the concert of social practices and functions composes an order that no single figure of power detach itself from the group or become visible in order to impose duties of submission or offer, to all, the opportunities for control or revision.... A plurality of communities and practices is still its structural form. At the level of the Association between communities it reproduces the type of organization proper to each of them. An ethnic difference is thereby affirmed in a different political model instead of being aligned upon ours to defend it.

A Revolution: Autonomous Federated Communities

In assembling the features that emerge from the Indian Manifestos, we have the following model: an associative tissue of socio-political micro-units, each characterized by an autonomous communality of goods (basically land) – in other words, by a distribution of complementary rights and duties over the same wealth and attributed to different parties over which no one possesses, with private title (as a physical or moral person), what we have called the right of property.... Thus as was stated in the Constitutive Act of the *Confederación de Indigenas de Venezuela* in 1973, the Indian communities "posit other models of society for developmental alternatives".

At a time when the notion and effectiveness of Western democracy are everywhere being undermined by the spread of economic and cultural technocracy and are slowly foundering with their inherent possibilities, ... at a time when the micro-experiences and research inherent in self-management tend to compensate for this centralizing evolution by recreating a diversity of local democracies, we have the Indian communities, oppressed and occulted by the Western "democracies", declaring themselves capable of offering self-management models supported by hundreds of years of history.... From the area those societies have most despised and that they fought and endeavoured to subjugate, there have emerged political alternatives and social models that may in themselves represent a corrective to the massive acceleration and reproduction of the totalitarian and levelling factors created by Western structures of power and technology....

This is precisely what Francisco Servin, *Pai-Tavytera*, stated at the Indian Parliament held in Paraguay in October 1974: "We were masters of the land but we have become veritable pariahs since the gringos came.... We have a hope that a day will come when they will realize that we are their roots and that together we must become a great tree, with all its branches and flowers."[10] Indeed, the dawn of this day has broken. The image of this tree, which once signified revolutions of liberty and popular solidarities, seems to be rising once again with the Indian awakening and with its correspondences in Western experiments and investigations. Perhaps an age of autonomy has been inaugurated by these odd coincidences between phenomena produced in rising and declining societies and by the different forms political change can take.

A maintenance and deepening of these differences will only add to the autonomous project that is taking shape. The political feature of Indian practices does not therefore set an example. It would serve only as a mystification, it would be merely an object produced by our discourse, were we to transform it into some utopian model, into a dream solution to all our difficulties or into some ideological substitute for the technical problems the autonomous project encounters in our societies. The Indian Declarations, however, are explicitly opposed to such ideological exploitation. They preach a labour of differentiation and egalitarian co-operation that can work both in favour of the relationship between communities and of their relationship with foreign societies. It is in that way that possible paths are defined and questions posed. A rapid summary of them serves to indicate the bases for demonstrating solidarity with the movement embodied in these Declarations.

First, the passage from a micro-politics (autonomous communities) to a macro-politics (federation), whereas in our societies such a passage corresponds to a hitherto uncrossed frontier created by the integrating structures of the State.

Secondly, the collective contracts with the land in their dual aspect – economic (rural co-operatives) and ecological (a harmony with nature) – whereas Western development, through the two-fold privilege it accords to industrialization and social conflicts, has acquired a "history" in which "nature" figures merely as the object of labour and the arena of socio-economic struggles that have no value other than the negative one of a peasant "resistance" to be overcome, of a biological limitation that must constantly be surmounted or of some traditionalist ballast to be cast overboard. . . .

Lastly, and equally essential to any autonomous plan, there is a cultural pluralism that assigns to schooling, which is brought under the control of the community and of "sages" (*amautas*), the task of teaching the social processes of a rural "co-operatism", the necessary agricultural know-how, the history of relations with the West, the mastery of the mother tongue as well as of the national language – in other words, the tools which enable one to use and to symbolize various practices, whereas the dominant culture and the "rural schools" established so far (a catastrophe) have hierarchized such practices and have debased or crushed the differences and thereby deprived democratic enterprise of all cultural content and technological wherewithal.

A space of exchange and of sharing is thereby set up: without fanfare. It is accompanied – and this ought not to astound us – by references to the Great Spirit, references that are modest because the everyday knowledge of the Invisible and the Eternal is mute. . . . Around such silences, the "cornerstones" of the community, the gestures, groups and federations of Indians form networks. On the frontiers of these Indian lands another sort of silence seems to reply to the inhabitants: the militant, unspectacular activities of the various religious or civil associations which, in Latin America, in the United States, in Germany, Sweden, Denmark and in many other distant countries, are devoting themselves to sharing information and to active solidarity. Since Barthélémy de las Casas, the rumblings of such solidarities have shaken the colonizing West. In this task, born of concern for others and destined to increase in concert with the Indian awakening, we readers are, in our turn, invited to join.

Notes

1 *Resguardos*: land reserved for the Indians by the Spanish Crown, then by the Colombian Republic.
2 *Kamsa*: groups, tribes.
3 *Narino*: state in the South, on the border of Ecuador.
4 *Santa Marta*: in the north of Colombia, between the coast and Venezuela.
5 The *Paramo*: a very cold zone, situated above 3000 metres.
6 Indian meeting of the Cauca, in Colombia, according to the account given by the regional Council of Cauca "as a contribution to our common struggle". The text has been published in *La Lettre*, no. 188 (April 1974), pp. 14–15.
7 Declaration of ANUC, and the indigenous regional Council of Cauca, Bogota, 31 August 1974.
8 Speech of Justino Quispe Balboa (Aymara, Bolivia) to the first Indian Parliament of South America, 13 October 1974, before the Paraguayan authorities and observers. J. Quispe Balboa was then twenty-one years old. Dial Document no. 196.
9 *Gringo*: the white man, the European or North American foreigner.
10 See Dial Document no. 196.

Part III

Other People: Ethnography and Social Practice

8

Introduction

Ian Buchanan

In order to assess accurately Certeau's contribution to cultural studies, his key works in the area need to be read as blueprints for something still to be constructed, not as maps of what already exists. His life was ended before this project could ever be completed. Therefore, it is inappropriate, I think, to ask whether it succeeded in its aims or not, but entirely proper to ask whether it could have succeeded. Any final determination of the success or failure of Certeau's work would be premature to say the least, because far too much of it was left undone.

The limited aim of *The Practice of Everyday Life* was simply to make a certain type of discussion possible, not to broach that discussion and carry it to its conclusions. It is therefore a tentative, searching work, not a polished, conclusive one. Yet this is not how most critics have approached it and, accordingly, it has tended to be perceived (unjustly, in my view) as a failed though admirable attempt to do something different within the constrained field of the human sciences. However, this is not an assessment we need accept. My position is that, despite the growing attention Certeau's work is currently receiving, we still do not know what his theory is capable of and we will never know unless we approach it from the perspective of his overall project. To that end, I will offer a schematic description of the overall project, which, in addition to the numerous cross-references it makes to its companion volume (written by Pierre Mayol and Luce Giard under Certeau's direction), speaks optimistically of a variety of never carried out analytic investigations.

So, let me start by sketching the primary aim of the project. Although he is often accused of writing in a slippery, fugitive style (not without justification, I might add), Certeau could not be more explicit in stating his aims. *The Practice of Everyday Life* is, he states, "part of a continuing investigation of the ways in which users – commonly assumed to be passive and guided by established rules – operate." Its aim "is not so much to discuss this elusive yet fundamental subject as to make such a discussion possible; that is, by means of inquiries and hypotheses, to indicate pathways for future." The measure of the success of the project will be whether or not the practices of everyday life remain in the background or not, whether, in other words, their specificity of operation is delineated and articulated, or not. The focus here, Certeau thoughtfully emphasizes, is on practices, not subjects; as such, his investigations imply neither a return to a liberal humanist concern for the individual nor a reiteration of the structuralist interest in the production of discourses. Neither an enunciating subject, nor a subject of enunciation, occupies the first position in Certeau's scheme: that honour is reserved for enunciation, or, to put it another way, the modality of practices, which, in reality, is the true subject of his inquiry. As Certeau himself puts it, "the question at hand concerns modes of operation or schemata of action, and not directly the subjects (or persons) who are their authors or vehicles." It is equally invalid, then, to say that Certeau privileges the ordinary man at the expense of the ordinary woman, as it is to say that he concentrates overmuch on the other (whether defined as woman, black, gay or Jew), since these are not his actual objects of inquiry, but merely effects of what he is really trying to specify, namely the operational logic of culture.

Although it is never announced as such, Certeau's method is plainly dialectical: the minutiae of everyday life are to be brought into view by way of their underpinning logic. It is the development of a notion of cultural logic that enables Certeau to realize his plan of moving more or less insignificant cultural practices such as cooking and walking into the foreground of critical attention. As it is this never fully specified logic that is supposed to account for the contrary view of culture that Certeau hopes to present by rendering logical, albeit still paradoxical, such apparently aberrant ideas as the power of the powerless, the activity of the passive, the productions of non-producers, escaping without leaving and so on, it is precisely that which should be the focus of our attention. Accepting the basic state of incompletion of Certeau's overall project is no impediment to this line of inquiry, since his blueprints are quite clear on how exactly this logic was to be derived. Indeed, in view of the fact that they describe the limits and aims of the project, they could be said to initiate it.

So, how did Certeau propose to derive a logic of culture? His first move is, as he called it, a negative one. He rules out any focus on the production of cultural difference by counter-culture groups, both because it is obvious and has been done before, and because such productions are in his view merely symptoms or indexes of deeper complexities. Like Deleuze's, Certeau's interest, as we shall see, is not in the production of difference, but in different productions, a fact which seems to have escaped many of even his most enthusiastic supporters, who, in cultural studies at least, deploy his ideas to valorize such trivial subversions as wearing jeans. This becomes obvious when we examine his three so-called positive determinations.

To begin with, Certeau proposes to combine two lines of inquiry that had hitherto been kept in a kind of quarantine from one another, namely the study of representations on the one hand, and the study of modes of behaviour on the other. What he had in mind, though, was not merely the combination of textual analysis and behavioural analysis, a convergence that today is practically a commonplace, but rather their synthesis. "For example, the analysis of the images broadcast by television (representation) and of the time spent watching television should be complemented by a study of what the cultural consumer 'makes' or 'does' during this time and with these images." The same applies to the use of space, Certeau goes on to suggest, as well as commodities purchased in supermarkets; even newspaper and magazine stories could be so regarded. Certeau defines this "making" as a poiesis whose chief characteristic is its lack of visibility. It is a hidden production because it takes places in fields already defined and occupied by large production-systems (television, urban development etc.), which according to a logic of scale tend to swamp the non-systemic with their outputs, and because there is no place where this other production could actually exhibit itself. There is no place to look for this production, then, except where by definition it cannot be seen. The difficulties do not end there, however. The task of articulating this other production is made even more frustrating by the fact that it does not manifest itself in products as such, "but rather through its ways of using the products imposed by a dominant economic order." Literally, then, this mode of production produces nothing but itself, but does not even have itself to show for its efforts, however great or small they may be. Such a production therefore cannot be said to be symbolic, but neither can it be said to be unreal or purely imaginary.

The second positive determination is inspired by Foucault's *Discipline and Punish*. Certeau is ambivalent about this book. On the one hand, he cannot but admire the deft way Foucault reorganizes an existing field of inquiry along new lines. As Certeau puts it, "instead of analysing the apparatus exercising power (i.e., the localisable, expansionist, repressive, and legal institutions), Foucault analyses the mechanisms (*dispositifs*) that have sapped the strength of these institutions and surreptitiously reorganised the functioning of power." In this way, Foucault has made possible a much richer, and much more fluid, understanding of the way power suffuses every aspect of social life, from the way we comport our bodies to the laws we observe. Perhaps most importantly, Foucault offers a productivist notion of power, in contrast to the then prevailing repressive conceptions of power (Marcuse, Reich, Brown). On the other hand, despite raising new and interesting questions about the way power operates, it "privileges the productive apparatus (which produces the 'discipline')" at the expense of the productions of the people it supposedly disciplines. Such productions are repressed by discipline, or better, redirected, which is the central job of education after all. Yet to repress is not to eradicate, something psychoanalysis at once explains and is premised on. Therefore, the truism that discipline has insinuated itself into every facet of daily life needs to be balanced against the fact that the everyday has not been reduced to a rigid set of regimes such as the notion of discipline implies. So, rather than extend its analyses into new fields but along the same lines, what Certeau proposes to do is explore the obverse side of Foucault's analyses, looking not for patterns of resistance, which Foucault postulates anyway, but subtle movements of escape and evasion. What Foucault's system lacks, in Certeau's assessment, which he then sets out to remedy himself, is an adequate account of the other: what emerges from this discussion is the need to develop new ways of articulating otherness.

The third positive determination is the assumption that the practices of everyday life must conceal a logic of their own, which may go back to primitive times. Such an idea is of course already enshrined in the aforementioned suggestion that cultural practices might be articulated by recourse to a notion of syntax. Here, though, it is not simply a matter of articulating an elusive set of phenomena by superimposing a grid, an approach already made standard by structuralism anyway; rather, it is saying that the practices themselves are conditioned by this grid, a still structuralist idea to be sure, but differing in one very important respect. Now, instead of saying that subjects obey an internalized logic they can neither know nor evade, Certeau is saying cultural logic is like a menu from which subjects choose already worked out actions according to their perceived needs. Insofar as those actions are adopted and personalized, they form a repertoire, which is as close to a habitus as Certeau is prepared to go. In order to grasp this logic, Certeau undertakes two types of investigations: he has a try at, on the one hand, description, initiating a kind of ficto-criticism, and, on the other, an examination of a range of possible hypotheses. Overall, the problem is how to articulate a set of productive practices that produce nothing and therefore seem silent without turning them into something they are not, a set of hollow symbols.

The project thus initiated, but never completed, Certeau called heterology.

9
Walking in the City

To *see* Manhattan from the 107th floor of the World Trade Center. Below the wind-stirred haze, the urban island, a sea upon the sea rises on the crested swell of Wall Street, falls into the trough of Greenwich Village, flows into the renewed crests of midtown and the calm of Central Park, before breaking into distant whitecaps up beyond Harlem. For a moment, the eye arrests the turbulence of this sea-swell of verticals; the vast mass freezes under our gaze. It is transformed into a texturology in which the extremes of defiance and poverty, the contrasts between races and styles, between yesterday's buildings already relegated to the past (New York, this anti-Rome, has never learned to age) and the new outcroppings that erect barriers to block space – all are conjoined. Paroxystic sites with monumental reliefs. The spectator can even read the fading urban universe. Inscribed upon it are the architectural figures of the *coincidatio oppositorum* sketched long ago in mystical miniatures and textures. On this concrete, steel and glass stage, bounded by the cold water of two oceans (the Atlantic and the American) the tallest letters in the world create this gigantesque rhetoric of excess in expenditure and production.[1]

To what erotics of knowledge can the ecstasy of reading such a cosmos be connected? Delighting in it as violently as I do, I speculate as to the origin of the pleasure of seeing such a world wrought by hubris "as a whole", the pleasure of looking down upon, of totalizing this vastest of human texts.

To be lifted to the summit of the World Trade Center is to be carried away by the city's hold. One's body is no longer criss-crossed by the streets that bind and re-bind it following some law of their own; it is not possessed – either as user or used – by the sounds of all its many contrasts or by the frantic New

York traffic. The person who ascends to that height leaves behind the mass that takes and incorporates into itself any sense of being either an author or spectator. Above these waters Icarus can ignore the tricks of Daedalus in his shifting and endless labyrinths. His altitude transforms him into a voyeur. It places him at a distance. It changes an enchanting world into a text. It allows him to read it; to become a solar Eye, a god's regard. The exaltation of a scopic or a gnostic drive. Just to be this seeing point creates the fiction of knowledge. Must one then redescend into the sombre space through which crowds of people move about, crowds that, visible from above, cannot see there below? The fall of Icarus. On the 107th floor, a poster poses like some sphinx, a riddle to the stroller who has been in an instant changed into a seer: "It's hard to be down when you're up."

The desire to see the city preceded the means of fulfilling the desire. Medieval and Renaissance painting showed the city seen in perspective by an eye that did not yet exist.[2] They both invented flying over the city and the type of representation that made it possible. The panorama transformed the spectator into a celestial eye. It created gods. Since technical processes created an "omnivisual power", things are different.[3] The fiction invented by the painters of the past slowly became fact. The same scopic drive haunts the architectural (and no longer pictorial) productions that give materiality to Utopia today. The 1350-foot tower, Manhattan's prow, continues the construction of a fiction that creates its readers, that transforms the city's complexity into readability and that freezes its opaque mobility into a crystal-clear text. Can the vast texturology beneath our gaze be anything but a representation? An optical artefact. The analogue to the facsimile which, through a kind of distancing, produces the space planner, the city planner or the map-maker. The city-panorama is a "theoretical" (i.e. visual) simulacrum: in short, a picture, of which the preconditions for feasibility are forgetfulness and a misunderstanding of processes. The seeing god created by this fiction, who, like Schreber's, "knows only corpses",[4] must remove himself from the obscure interlacings of everyday behaviour and make himself a stranger to it.

On the contrary, it is below – "down" – on the threshold where visibility ends that the city's common practitioners dwell. The raw material of this experiment are the walkers, *Wandersmänner*, whose bodies follow the cursives and strokes of an urban "text" they write without reading. These practitioners employ spaces that are not self-aware; their knowledge of them is as blind as that of one body for another, beloved, body. The paths that interconnect in this network, strange poems of which each body is an element down by and among many others, elude being read. Everything happens as though some blindness were the hallmark of the processes by which the inhabited city is organized.[5] The networks of these forward-moving, intercrossed writings form a multiple history, are without creator or spectator, made up of fragments of trajectories and alterations of spaces: with regard to representations, it remains daily, indefinitely, something other.

Eluding the imaginary totalizations of the eye, there is a strangeness in the commonplace that creates no surface, or whose surface is only an advanced limit, an edge cut out of the visible. In this totality, I should like to indicate the processes that are foreign to the "geometric" or "geographic" space of visual, panoptic or theoretical constructions. Such spatial practices refer to a specific form of *operations* (ways of doing); they reflect "another spatiality"[6] (an "anthropological", *poïétik* and mystical spatial experiment); they send us to an opaque, blind domain of the inhabited city, or to a *transhuman city*, one that insinuates itself into the clear text of the planned, readable city.

From Concept to Practices

The World Trade Center is the most monumental figure of a Western urbanism. The atopia-Utopia of optical science has long tried to surmount and articulate the contradictions created by the urban conglomeration. It is a question of working towards an increase in the human collection or accumulation. A perspective view or a prospective view, the dual projection of an opaque past and an unclear future on to an accommodating surface, it has (since the sixteenth century?) begun the transformation of the *urban reality* into the concept of *city*, and it has begun – long before the concept itself can become history – to make it part of an *urbanistic* ratio. The alliance of city and concept never makes them one; rather, it employs their progressive symbiosis: city planning is both to *give thought to the plurality* of the real and to *make effective* that notion of the plural – it is to know and to be able to articulate.

The "city" established by Utopian and urbanistic discourse[7] is defined by the possibility of a threefold operation: the creation of a *clean space* (rational organization should eliminate all physical, mental and political pollution); the substitution of a non-time or a synchronic system for the indiscernible, stubborn resistance of tradition (univocal strategies, made possible by the exhaustion of all data, should replace the tactics that cleverly play upon "opportunities", catch-occurrences, and the opacities of history); and finally the creation of a *universal and impersonal subject* (this is the city itself: as with its political model, the Hobbesian state, it is gradually possible to endow it with all the functions and predicates previously disseminated and allocated to many real subjects, groups, associations and individuals). Thus, the city enables us to conceive and construct a space on the basis of a finite number of stable and isolatable elements, each articulated to the other.

In this site organized by "speculative" and classifying operations,[8] management combines with elimination: on the one hand we have the differentiation and redistribution of the parts and function of the city through inversions, movements, accumulations, etc., and on the other hand we have the rejection of whatever is not treatable, and that thus constitutes the "garbage" of a functionalist administration (abnormality, deviance, sickness, death, etc.). Progress, of course, allows for the reintroduction of an increasing proportion of these wastes into the management network and the transformation of those very flaws (in health, security, etc.) into means for strengthening the system of order. In fact, however, it constantly produces effects that run counter to what it aims for: the profit system creates a *loss* which, with all the multifarious forms of poverty outside and waste inside, is constantly inverting production into "expenditure". Furthermore, rationalizing the city involves *mythifying* it through strategic modes of discourse. Lastly, by favouring progress (time), functionalist organization allows the condition of its feasibility – space itself – to be overlooked, and space then becomes the unanticipated factor in a scientific and political technology.[9] That is how the city concept functions, a site of transformations and appropriations, the object of interventions, but also a subject continually being enriched with new attributes: simultaneously the plant and the hero of modernity.

Whatever the past avatars of this concept, it must be noted that today, while in *discourse*, the city acts as a totalizing and almost mythic gauge of socio-economic and political strategies, *urban life* allows what has been excluded from it by the urbanistic plan to increase even further. The language of power is "urbanized", but the city is subjected to contradictory movements that offset each other and interact outside the purview of the panoptic power. The city becomes the dominant theme of political epic but it is no longer a theatre for programmed, controlled operations. Beneath the discourses ideologizing it, there is a proliferation of tricks and fusions of power that are devoid of legible identity, that lack any perceptible access and that are without rational clarity – impossible to manage.

The city-concept is deteriorating. Does that mean that the sickness of the mind that created it and its professionals is also the sickness of the urban population? Perhaps the cities are deteriorating together with the procedures that set them up. However, we must be wary of our analyses. Ministers of knowledge have always assumed that the changes that shake their ideologies and their positions are universe-threatening. They transform the evil of their theories into theories of evil. Transforming their aberrations into "catastrophes" or trying to lock the people into the "panic" of their discourse, must they still be right?

Rather than staying within a discourse that maintains its privileged position by inverting its content (catastrophe, not progress), there is another way:

analysing the microbial processes – both singular and plural – an urbanistic system should manage or eliminate and survive its decline; following the pullulation of those practices that, far from being controlled or eliminated by the panoptic administration, are abetted in their proliferating illegitimacy, developed and inserted into the networks of surveillance and combined according to strategies that, albeit unreadable, are stable to the extent that they constitute everyday rules and surreptitious creativities that serve only to conceal the frantic existing models and discourses of the observing organization. That path could be regarded as a continuation of – but also as the inverse of – Michel Foucault's analysis of power structures. Instead of focusing his analysis on localizable, dominant, repressive, legal centres, he turned it to bear on technical machinery and procedures, those "minor instrumentalities" that, through a mere organization of "details", can transform diverseness of humanity into a "disciplined" society, and manage, differentiate, classify and fit into a hierarchy every deviancy that can affect training, health, justice, the army or labour.[10] "The often tiny ploys of discipline", the "minor but flawless" machinery that has colonized and made uniform the institutions of the state, derive their effectiveness from a relationship between *procedures* and the *space* they redistribute to create an "operator". They set up an "analytic arrangement of space". From the standpoint of playing at (with) discipline, however, what spatial practices correspond to these disciplined space-creating apparatuses? In light of the current contradiction between the collective management mode and the individual mode of reappropriation, such a question is no less pressing – if we posit a society to be defined not only by its networks of technical surveillance, and if we further recognize that in fact spatial usage creates the determining conditions of social life. I should like to review some of the procedures – many-sided, resilient, cunning and stubborn – that evade discipline, without thereby being outside its sphere, and that can lead to a theory of daily practices, to a theory of experienced *space* and of the disturbing familiarity of the *city*.

Pedestrian Utterings

History begins at ground level, with footsteps. They are the number, but a number that does not form a series. They cannot be counted because each unit is qualitative in nature: a style of tactile apprehension and kinesic appropriation. They are replete with innumerable anomalies. The motions of walking are spatial creations. They link sites one to the other. Pedestrian motor functions thus create one of those "true systems whose existence actually makes the city", but which "have no physical receivability".[11] They cannot be localized: they spatialize. They are no more inscribed in a content than are the characters the Chinese sketch out on their hand with one finger.

Of course, the walking process can be marked out on urban maps in such a way as to translate its traces (*here* heavy, *there* very light) and its trajectories (*this* way, not *that*). However, these curves, ample or meagre, refer, like words, only to the lack of what has gone by. Traces of a journey lose what existed: *the act of going by* itself. The action of going, of wandering, or of "window shopping" – in other words, the activity of passers-by – is transposed into points that create a totalizing and reversible line on the map. It therefore allows for the apprehension of a mere relic set in the non-time of a projective surface. It is visible, but its effect is to make the operation that made it possible invisible. These fixations make up the procedures of forgetting. The hint is substituted for practice. It displays property (voracious) of the geographic system's ability to metamorphose actions into legibility, but it thereby causes one way of existing to be overlooked.

A comparison with the act of speaking enables us to go further[12] and not be restricted only to criticism of graphic representations as if we were aiming from the limits of legibility at some inaccessible Beyond. The act of walking is to the urban system what the act of speaking, the *Speech Act*, is to language or to spoken utterance.[13] On the most elementary level it has in effect a threefold "uttering" function: it is a process of *appropriation* of the topographic system by the pedestrian (just as the speaker appropriates and assumes language); it is a spatial *realization* of the site (just as the act of speaking is a sonic realization of language): lastly, it implies relationships among distinct positions, i.e. pragmatic "*contracts*" in the form of movements (just as verbal utterance is "allocution", "places *the others*" before the speaker, and sets up contracts between fellow speakers[14]). A first definition of walking thus seems to be a space of uttering.

We can extend this problem to the relationships between the act of writing and writing, if we like, and even transpose it to relationships of "touch" (the brush and its gestures) to the finished picture (forms, colours, etc.). First isolated in the field of verbal communication, uttering is only one of its applications, and its linguistic modality is only the first indication of a far more general distinction between the forms employed in a system and the ways in which the system may be employed, i.e. between two "different worlds", because the "same things" are there viewed according to opposed formalities.

Considered from this angle, the pedestrian's uttering displays three characteristics that immediately distinguish it from the spatial system: the present, the discontinuous and the "phatic". First, it is true that a spatial order sets up a body of possibilities (e.g. by a place) and interdictions (e.g. by a wall); the walker then *actualizes* some of them. He thereby makes them be as well as appear.

However, he also displaces them and invents others, since the crossings, wanderings and improvisations of walking favour, alter or abandon spatial elements. Thus Charlie Chaplin multiplied the possibilities of his japes: out of one thing he made other things, and he went beyond the limits that the purposes and functions of the object impose upon its user. In the same way, the walker transforms every spatial signifier into something else. And while, on the one hand, he makes only a few of the possibilities set out by the established order effective (he goes only here – not there), on the other hand, he increases the number of possibilities (e.g. by making up shortcuts or detours) and the number of interdictions (e.g. by avoiding routes regarded as licit or obligatory). In short, he selects: "The user of the city takes up fragments of utterance in order in secret to actualize them."[15] Thus he creates *discontinuity*, either by choosing among the signifiers of the spatial language or by altering them through the use he makes of them. He dooms certain sites to intertia or to decay, and from others he forms "rare" ("fortuitous") or illegal spatial "shapes". However, this is already inherent in a rhetoric of walking.

Within the framework of uttering, the walker, in relation to his position, creates a near and a far, a *here* and a *there*. In verbal communication, the adverbs *here* and *there* are actually the indicators of the locutory fact[16] – a coincidence that reinforces the parallelism between linguistic uttering and the pedestrian uttering – and we must add that another function of this process of location (*here/there*) necessarily entailed by walking and indicative of an actual appropriation of space by an "I" is to set up *another* relative to that "I", and thereby establish a conjunctive and disjunctive articulation of places. Above all, I highlight the "*phatic*" aspect – if by that we understand, as Malinowski and Jakobson have noted, the function of terms that establish, maintain or interrupt contact: terms like "hello", "well, well", etc.[17] Walking, which now pursues and now invites pursuit, creates a mobile organicity of the environment, a succession of phatic *topoi*. And although the phatic function – the effort to set up communication – can characterize the language of talking birds as it does "the first verbal function acquired by children", it is not surprising that, anterior to or parallel with informative declamation, it also skips along, crawls on all fours, dances and strolls, heavily or lightly, like a series of "hellos" in an echoing labyrinth.

We can analyse the modalities of the pedestrian's uttering hereby freed from the mapped route, i.e. the types of relationship it entertains with routes (or "utterances"), by assigning to them a value of truth ("alethic" modalities of the necessary, the impossible, the possible or the contingent), a value of knowledge ("epistemic" modalities of the certain, the excluded, the plausible or the arguable), or finally, a value regarding obligation ("deontic" modalities of the obligatory, the forbidden, the permissible or the optional).[18] Walking affirms, suspects, guesses, transgresses, respects, etc., the trajectories it "speaks". All modalities play a part in it, changing from step to step and redistributed in proportions, successions, intensities that vary with the moment, the route, the stroller. The indefinable diversity of these operations of utterance. They cannot be reduced to any graphic tracing.

Perambulatory Rhetorics

The paths taken by strollers consist of a series of turnings and returnings that can be likened to "turns of phrase" or "stylistic devices". A perambulatory rhetoric does exist. The art of "turning" a phrase has its counterpart in the art of "turning" course. As with everyday language,[19] this art entails and combines both *styles* and *usages*. Style specifies a "linguistic structure that can manifest on the symbolic level . . . one man's basic way of existing in the world":[20] it connotes a singular. Usage defines the social phenomenon by which a system of communication is actually manifested: it refers to a norm. Both are aimed at a "way of doing" (speaking, walking, etc.), but one as a singular treatment of the symbolic and the other as an element of a code. They intersect to form a style of usage, a way of being and a way of doing.[21]

In introducing the notion of an "inhabitant rhetoric" – a fertile path indicated by A. Médam[22] and systematized by S. Ostrovesky[23] and J.-F. Augoyard[24] – it was posited that the "tropes" catalogued in rhetoric furnished models and hypotheses for the analysis of the methods for appropriating sites. It seems to me that two postulates condition the validity of that application: spatial practices also correspond to *manipulations* of the fundamental elements of a constructed order; like rhetorical tropes, they are *divergent* from a kind of "literal" meaning defined by the urban system. Verbal figures and "perambulant" figures may be homologous (the latter already stylized in dance steps), for both are "treatments" or operations that affect isolable units,[25] and "ambiguous arrangements" that divert and move meaning towards the equivocal,[26] as when a moving image blurs and multiplies the photographed object. Both these modes make for analogy. I would add that the geometric space of city-planners and architects appears to have the validity of the "literal meaning" *constructed* by grammarians and linguists in order to establish a normal and normative level to which the deviations of the "figured" can be referred. In fact, this "literal" (without figures) is not to be found in ordinary usage, whether verbal or pedestrian: it is only the fiction produced by a usage that is also special – the metalinguistic usage of science that makes itself unique through that very distinction.[27]

The perambulatory gesture plays with spatial organizations, however panoptic: it is not foreign to them (it does not eschew them), nor does it conform to them (it does not take its identity from them). It creates of them shadow and ambiguity. It insinuates into them its multifarious references and citations (social models, cultural usage, personal coefficients). It is in itself the effect of the successive encounters and occasions that are constantly altering it into the advertisement for the other, the agent of whatever may surprise, cross or seduce its route. These different aspects establish a rhetoric; they even define it.

In analysing by means of the narratives of spatial practices this "modest art of everyday expression",[28] J.-F. Augoyard singled out two basic stylistic figures: synecdoche and asyndeton. I believe that this predominance, based on two complementary poles, establishes a formalism for such practices. Synecdoche is "employing the word in a sense that is part of another sense of the same word";[29] in essence, it is naming a part for the whole in which it is included: hence, "head" for "man" in the expression "I know not the fate of so dear a head"; and thus, in the narrative of a route the stone colonnade or the knoll stands for a park. Asyndeton is the elimination of linking words, conjunctions, adverbs, within a sentence or between sentences; it jumps over linkages and it omits whole parts (from this point of view, any promenade jumps or skips like a child playing hopscotch).

These two perambulatory figures are mutually reflective. One enlarges one element of space in order to make it play the role of a "more" (of a totality) and substitute itself for that (the motorbike or the furniture for sale in a shop window stands for an entire street or neighbourhood); the other, through elision, creates a "less" and makes gaps in the spatial continuum, retaining only selections or relics from it. Wholes are replaced by fragments (less in place of more); the other dissolves them by eliminating the conjunctive and consecutive (nothing in place of something). One concentrates: it amplifies detail and miniaturizes the whole. The other cuts: it dismantles continuity and weakens its verisimilitude. Thus handled and shaped by practices, space forms itself into enlarged anomalies and separate islets.[30] Through such swellings, diminutions and fragmentations – the tasks of rhetoric – a spatial sentencing is created, a sentence-making of an anthological (composed of juxtaposed quotations) and an elliptical (made up of gaps, slips and allusions) kind. The perambulatory figures substitute journeys with the structure of a myth for the technological system of a coherent, totalizing space, a "linked" and simultaneous space, at least if by "myth" we understand a discourse regarding the site/non-site (or origin) of concrete existence, a narrative cooked up out of elements drawn from shared sites, an allusive, fragmented tale whose gaps fall into line with the social practices it symbolizes.

Figures are the gestures of this stylistic metamorphosis of space; or rather, as Rilke put it, "gesture trees" in motion. They even affect the rigid and preplanned territories of the special educational institutions in which mentally ill children dance and act out their "spatial histories" at play.[31] These gesture trees are in motion everywhere. Whole forests of them stroll in the streets. They alter the scene, but image cannot fix them in one place. If despite everything we must have an illustration, it would be in transit images, in the yellow-green and electric-blue calligraphy that silently screams as it striates the city's underground – "embroideries" of letters and numbers, the perfect gestures of spray-painted acts of violence, handwritten Sivas, dancing graphics whose fleeting apparitions are accompanied by the roaring of subway trains: New York's graffiti. Indeed, while it is true that the forests of gesture can have meaning, their progress cannot be fixed by a picture, nor can the meaning of their movements be confined within a text. Their rhetorical transhumance carries away and off the analytical and coherent, literal, meanings of urbanism; it is "semantic wandering"[32] produced by the masses that make the city in some of its neighbourhoods disappear, that in others exaggerate it or infect it with a cancer; that twist it, break it up and divert it from its order, albeit immobile.

The Mythics of the Proper

The figures for these movements (synecdoches, ellipses, etc.) characterize both "symbolics of the unconscious" and "certain procedures typical of the subjectivity manifested in discourse".[33] The likeness created between "discourse"[34] and "dream"[35] by the use of the same "stylistic procedures" thus includes pedestrian activities. The "old catalogue of tropes" that, from Freud to Benveniste, furnished a suitable inventory for the rhetoric of the first two levels of expression is equally valid for the third. If parallelism exists it is not only because utterance dominates in all three regions, but also because its discursive progress (verbalized, dreamed or paced off) is established as a relationship between the *site* from which it issues (an origin) and the *non-site* it creates (a way of *passage*).

From this point of view, having linked linguistic formations with the perambulatory processes, they can be approached from the standpoint of oneiric figurations, or at least one can glimpse on that other bank what, in spatial practice, is indissociable from the site dreamed. *To walk is to lack a site.* It is the indeterminate process of being both absent and in search of the proper, of one's own. Undoubtedly the errancy that multiplies and assembles the city makes of it a vast social experience in site deprivation – an experience, true, that is weakened by innumerable and minuscule deportations (displacements, walks); that is fleshed out by the relationships and intersections of such exoduses, which create interweavings (the solidarity of the urban fabric) and are set within the framework of what must ultimately have been the *site* (the City). However, the identity created by this site is all the more *figured* since, despite the inequality in titles and profits, there is here only a swarming mass of passers-by, a network of dwellings taken over by traffic, a strolling through the semblances of the real, a universe of places haunted by a non-site or by dreamed sites.

An indication of the relationship between the practices of space and this lack is provided by the ways in which they play with and upon "proper" names. The relationships between the "sense" of a stroll and the sense of words set up two kinds of apparently contrary movement: one exterior (to walk is to go outdoors) and the other interior (mobility within the stability of the signifier). Walking, in effect, is subject to semantic tropisms; it is drawn to or repelled by things named in the *obscure* sense, while the city itself largely becomes a desert in which the bizarre, not to mention the terrifying, no longer takes on shadowy shapes but rather, as in Genet's plays, that of the *light* itself, which technocratic power creates everywhere and which places the dweller under surveillance (of what? who knows?): "The eye of the city is upon us, we cannot bear it without growing dizzy", as one inhabitant of Rouen said.[36] In those white spaces of some foreign logic, proper nouns plumb the reserves of hidden and familiar meanings. They "make sense", i.e. they impel movements, like the vocations and appeals that turn or divert the itinerary by making it resound with still uncertain meanings. They create non-sites within sites; they change them into passages.

A friend who lives in Sèvres is drawn when in Paris to the rue des Saints-Pères and the rue de Sèvres when he is on his way to visit his mother in another part of town; the names articulate a sentence that his feet construct without his being aware of it. Numbers (112th Street, or 9, rue Saint-Charles) also draw us towards them just as they can haunt our dreams. Another friend unconsciously represses streets that have the names of famous or forgotten persons; she prefers routes without signatures. This is another way such proper nouns move us. What are they spelling out? Once they were arranged in constellations that gave a semantic hierarchy and order to the face of the city, creators of chronologies and historical justifications; such names have little by little lost their graven surface validity, like worn coins, but their capability to signify has outlived them. Saints-Pères, Corentin Celton, Place Rouge – they offer themselves to the polysemes with which passers-by endow them; they become things apart from the places they were intended to define and turn into imaginary meeting-places in the journeys they map out, having become metaphors, for reasons foreign to their original validity, however known/unknown to the passers-by. A strange toponymy, detached from the sites, floating above the city like a misty geography of "suspended meaning" and from the heights directing physical displacements below: Place de l'Étoile, Concorde, Poissonnière. As Malaparte said, "The Place de la Concorde does not exist, it is a notion."[37]

It is more than a notion. We must multiply comparisons in order to talk of the magic powers of proper names, slipped to the stroller like jewels on to moving fingers, guiding them as they adorn them. They link gestures and steps, they open up meanings and directions; such words even act to empty and erode their primary function. They are liberated, occupiable spaces. Through semantic rarefaction, their rich vagueness earns them the *poetic* function of expressing an illogical geography: "With a lovely nave I shall fill this great empty space."[38] The relics of meaning, and sometimes their shells, the inverted leftovers of great ambitions, maybe for walking.[39] Nothings – or near-nothings – symbolize and direct our steps; names that have, precisely, ceased to be "proper".

Three distinct (but combined) functionings of the relationships between spatial practices and signifying practices are sketched in (and perhaps based on) these symbolizing nuclei: the *believable*, the *memorable* and the *primitive*. They indicate that which "authorizes" (or makes possible and believable) spatial appropriations, that which is repeated (or remembered) of a silent and convoluted memory, and that which is structured and still marked by an in-fantile (*in-fans*) origin. These three symbolic mechanisms arrange the *topoi* of the discourse on/of the city (legend, recollection and dream) in a way that is also beyond urbanistic systematicity. They can even be found in the functions of proper names: they make the place they clothe with a word habitable and believable (by calling their classifying power they put on authorization); they recall or evoke the phantoms (dead and supposedly gone) that still stir, lurking in gestures and walking bodies; and, as they name – i.e. as they impose a command issuing from the other (a history) – and as they alter functionalist identity by breaking off from it, they create in the site itself this erosion or non-site carved out by the law of the other.

Believabilia and Memorabilia: Habitability

By an all-too-obvious paradox, the discourse that creates belief is the discourse that takes away that which it enjoins, or which never gives what it promises. Far indeed from expressing a vacuum, from describing emptiness, it creates one. It makes room for a vacuum. Thus it makes openings; it "permits" play within a system of defined sites. It "authorizes" a playing-space (*Spielraum*) to be produced on a checkerboard that analyses and classifies identities. It makes habitable. As such I call it a "local authority". It is a flaw in the system that saturates sites with meaning and reduces them to the point of making them unbearable, "stifling". A symptomatic tendency of functionalist totalitarianism (even when it programmes games and festivals) is that it thus seeks to eliminate local authorities, for these comprise the system's univocity. It challenges what it quite rightly calls *superstitions*: superfluous semantic coverings that insinuate themselves "more" or "too much"[40] and that in a past or in a poetics alienate a part of the territory the partisans of technological motives and financiers have reserved for themselves.

In the end these proper names are already "local authorities" or "superstitions". Therefore, they are replaced by numbers. It is the same for the stones and legends that haunt the urban space like so many additional or superfluous inhabitants. They are the targets of a witch-hunt, if only because of the logic of the technostructure. Their extermination, however (like that of the trees, the woods and the dells where these legends live),[41] is turning the city into a "suffering symbol".[42] The habitable city is being wiped out. Thus, as a woman from Rouen says, here "there is no special place; except for my place, that's all. . . . There's nothing." Nothing "special", nothing unusual, nothing created by a memory or a tale, nothing made significant by someone else. The only thing that remains believable is the cave of one's own dwelling, for the present still permeable by legend, still touched with shadows. Aside from that, according to another city-dweller, there are only "places where you can no longer believe in anything".[43]

It is through the opportunity they afford of storing up pregnant silences and inarticulate stories – or rather through their ability to create cellars and attics everywhere – that local legends (*legenda*: that which must be read, but also that which can be read) create exits, ways of leaving and re-entering, and thus habitable spaces. The setting out and the journey complete and enlarge on departures, comings and goings that were once provided by a body of legend now lacking in sites. Physical movement has the itinerant function of yesterday's or today's "superstitions". And in the end what does travelling produce if not, through a sort of "going back", "an exploration of the deserts of my memory", a return to a close-by exoticism via far-off detours, the "invention" of relics and legends ("fleeting glimpses of the French countryside", "fragments of music and poetry"),[44] in short, a "total uprooting" (Heidegger)? This long peregrination leads directly to the body of legend that the close-by site now lacks; it is a fiction, one that also has, like the dream or the perambulatory rhetoric, the dual characteristic of being the result of movements and of condensations.[45] As a corollary, we can gauge the importance of such signifying practices as we do spatial practices.

From this viewpoint, their content is no less revealing, even more so their organizing principle. The narratives of sites are makeshift. They are made of fragments of world. Although literary form and actantial *schema* correspond to stable models whose structures and combinations have often been analysed over the past thirty years, their matter (all their "manifest" detail) is furnished by the leftovers of nominations, taxonomies, comic or heroic predicates, etc.: i.e. by fragments of scattered semantic sites. These heterogeneous – even opposite – elements fill out the homogeneous and given form of the narrative. Thus we have the actual relationship of the practices of space with the constructed order. On its surface, that is pierced and pitted by ellipses, asides and leakages of meaning, it is an order-sieve.

The verbal relics of which narrative is made up (fragments of forgotten stories and opaque gestures) are juxtaposed in a collage in which their relationships are not thought out and therefore form a symbolic whole.[46] They are articulated by lacunae. Thus, within the structured space of the text, they produce anti-texts, effects of dissimulation and fugue, opportunities for passage through to other landscapes, like cellars and copses: "Oh, massifs; oh, plurals!"[47] Through the processes of dissemination they open up, narratives contrast with *rumour*, which is always injunctive, the initiator and result of a levelling of space, the creator of mass motions that shore up an order by adding make-believe to make-do or -be. Narratives diversify; rumours totalize. Although there is always an oscillation from one to the other, it would appear that today there is more stratification: narratives are becoming more private and fading into out-of-the-way neighbourhoods, families or individuals, while rumour is rampant and, in the guise of the *City*, the key word of some private law takes the place of every proper name and obliterates or combats superstitions that are still guilty of resisting it.

The dispersal of narratives already means the dispersal of the *memorable*. In fact, memory is the anti-museum: it cannot be localized. Its remains can still be found in legend. Both objects and words are hollow. Some past lies sleeping there, as it does in the everyday gestures of walking, eating, sleeping – where ancient revolutions lie dormant. Memory is only a travelling Prince Charming who happens to awaken the Sleeping Beauty – stories without words. "*Here, there was* a bakery"; "*That* is where old Mrs Dupuis *lived*". We are struck by the fact that sites that have been lived in are filled with the presence of absences. What appears designates what is no more: "*Look*: here there *was* . . .", but can no longer be seen. Demonstratives utter the invisible identities of the visible: the very definition of the site is, in fact, to be this series of movements and effects between the shattered strata of which it is formed and to play upon those shifting levels.

"Memories are what keep us here. . . . It's personal – not interesting to anyone – but still, in the end that creates the spirit of the neighbourhood."[48] Every site is haunted by countless ghosts that lurk there in silence, to be "evoked" or not. One *inhabits* only haunted sites – the opposite of what is set forth in the *Panopticon*. However, like the royal Gothic statues of Notre-Dame that were walled up for 200 years in the basement of a building on the rue de la Chaussée-d'Antin,[49] such ghosts – broken, like the sculptures – neither speak nor see. A kind of knowing has fallen silent. Only whispers of what is *known* but is *silent* are exchanged "between us". Sites are fragmentary and convoluted histories, pasts stolen by others from readability, folded up ages that can be unfolded but that are there more as narratives in suspense, like a rebus: symbolizations encysted in the body's pain or pleasure. "I feel good here"[50] – an effect of space, set apart from language, where it suddenly bursts into light.

The Infancies of Sites

What is memorable is what we can dream about a site. In any palimpsestic site, subjectivity is already articulated on the absence that structures it like existence, and the fact of "being there", *Dasein*. We have seen, however, that that being acts only in spatial practices, i.e. in *ways of passing to something else*. We must ultimately recognize here the repetition in various metamorphoses of some decisive and basic experience: the child's differentiation of himself from his mother's body. Here the possibility of space and of a localization (an "I am not alone") of the subject has its origin. Without going into Freud's famous analysis of this prenatal and natal experience while watching the games of his one-and-a-half-year-old grandson, who was tossing a spool and contentedly crying "O-o-o-o!" (meaning *fort*, i.e. *there*, *gone* or *can't*) and pulling it back to him by its thread with a joyful *Da* (i.e. *here*, *returned*),[51] suffice it to note this (perilous and satisfying) abrupt emergence from indifferentiation with the mother's body for which the spool is the substitute: this departure of the mother (that she both disappears and is made to disappear by him) represents localization and exteriority against a background of absence. The jubilant physical feat enables him to "make" the material object "leave" and to make *himself* disappear (for he is identical to that object) – to be *there* (because) *without* the other, but in a *necessary relationship* with what has disappeared – that creates an "original spatial structure".

Undoubtedly, we can follow differentiation further back to the nomination that already cuts off from its mother the foetus identified as male (but what about the daughter, who is henceforth placed in another spatial relationship?). What is important in this initiatory game – as in the "gleeful behaviour" of the child who, before a mirror, recognizes *one* (the totalizable *he*), whereas it is only the *other* (there, an image with which he identifies himself)[52] – is this process of "spatial cognition" that inscribes the passage to the other as the law of the being and the law of the site. To employ space, therefore, is to repeat the joyous and silent experience of childhood: it is, in the site, *to be other* and *to pass to the other.*

Thus begins the progress Freud compares to strolling in the motherland.[53] This relationship of self to self controls the internal alterations of the site (inter-stratal play) or the promenade-like unfolding of the stories silted up on a site (movements and journeys). Childhood, which determines the practices of space, then augments its effects, proliferates and inundates private and public spaces and defaces their readable surfaces, and creates in the planned city a "metaphorical" city or a city in movement, like the one of Kandinsky's dreams: "A great city built in accordance with all the rules of architecture and suddenly shaken by an unpredictable and incalculable force."[54]

Notes

1 Consult "New York City" by Alain Médam, in *Les Temps modernes*, August–September 1976, pp. 15–33; and, by the same author, *New York Terminal* (Paris: Galilée, 1977).

2 Cf. H. Lavedan, *Les Représentations des villes dans l'art du Moyen-Age* (Paris: Van Oest, 1942); R. Wittkower, *Architecturals: Principles in the Age of Humanism* (London: Tiranti, 1962); L. Marin, *Utopiques: jeux d'espaces* (Paris: Minuit, 1973).

3 M. Foucault, "L'oeil du pouvoir", in J. Bentham, *Le Panoptique [Panopticon]* (1791) (Belfond, 1977) p. 16.

4 D. P. Schreber, *Mémoires d'un nécropathe*, trans. (Paris: Seuil, 1975) pp. 41, 60, etc.

5 In his *Regulae*, Descartes made the blind man the guarantor of the knowledge of things and places against the illusions and deceptions of sight.

6 M. Merleau-Ponty, *Phénoménologie de la perception* (Paris: Gallimard, 1976), pp. 332–3.

7 Cf P. Choay, "Figures d'un discours inconnu", in *Critique*, April 1978, pp. 293–317.

8 We cannot connect urbanistic techniques, which classify things spatially, with the tradition of the "art of memory" (cf. F. A. Yates, *L'Art de la mémoire* (Paris: Gallimard, 1975). The capacity to build a spatial organization of knowledge develops its procedures on the basis of that "art"; it determines Utopias; it was almost realized in Bentham's *Panopticon*. It is a stable form, despite the diversity of its content (past, future and present) and its plans (to conceive or to create) *vis-à-vis* successive modes of thought.

9 Foucault, "L'oeil du pouvoir", p. 13.

10 M. Foucault, *Surveiller et punir* (Paris: Gallimard, 1975).

11 C. Alexander, "La Cité semitreillis, mais non arbre", in *Architecture, Mouvement, Continuité* (1967).

12 Cf. R. Barthes' remarks in *Architecture d'aujourd'hui*, no. 153, December 1970–January 1971, pp. 11–13 ("We speak our city... simply by living in it, by travel-

ling through it, by looking at it"), and C. Soucy's comments in *L'Image du centre dans quatre romans contemporains* (Paris: CSU, 1971) pp. 6–15.

13 Cf. the many studies on the subject since J. Searle's "What is a Speech Act?", in Max Black (ed.), *Philosophy in America* (London: Allen & Unwin, 1965; Ithaca, NY: Cornell University Press, 1965) pp. 221–39.

14 É. Benveniste, *Problèmes de linguistique générale*, vol. 2 (Paris: Gallimard, 1974), pp. 79–88.

15 R. Barthes, quoted in C. Soucy, *L'Image du centre*, p. 10.

16 "*Here* and *now* demarcate the spatial and temporal instance, which is coextensive and contemporary with the present source of a discourse containing *I*" (É. Benveniste, *Problèmes de linguistique générale*, vol. I (Paris: Gallimard, 1966), p. 253.

17 R. Jakobson, *Essais de linguistique générale* (Paris: Seuil, 1970), p. 217.

18 On modalities, see H. Parret, *La Pragmatique des modalités* (Urbino, 1975), or A. R. White, *Modal Thinking* (Ithaca, NY: Cornell University Press, 1975).

19 See the analyses of P. Lemaire, *Les Signes sauvages: Philosophie du language ordinaire* (Paris: duplicated thesis, 1972), pp. 11–13.

20 A. J. Greimas, "Linguistique statistique et linguistique structurale", in *Le Français moderne*, October 1962, p. 245.

21 In a related field – rhetoric and the poetic in the sign language of mutes – see E. S. Klima and U. Bellugi, "Poetry and Song in a Language without Sound" (San Diego, California, 1975), and E. S. Klima, "The Linguistic Symbol With and Without Sound", in J. Kavanagh and J. E. Cummings (eds), *The Role of Speech in Language* (Cambridge, Mass: MIT Press, 1975).

22 A. Médam, *Conscience de la ville* (Paris: Anthropos, 1977).

23 UER de sociologie, Aix-en-Provence, France.

24 J.-F. Augoyard, *Le Pas. Approche de la vie quotidienne dans un habitat collectif à travers la pratique des cheminements* (Grenoble: duplicated thesis, 1976), pp. 163–255: "La rhétorique habitante".

25 In his analysis of culinary practices, P. Bourdieu considers not the ingredients but their treatments to be decisive ("Le sens pratique", in *Actes de la recherche*, February 1976, p. 77).

26 J. Sumpf, *Introduction à la stylistique du français* (Paris: Larousse, 1971), p. 87.

27 On the "theory of the literal" see J. Derrida, *Marges* (Paris: Minuit, 1972), pp. 247–324: "La mythologie blanche".

28 Augoyard, *Le pas*, p. 256.

29 T. Todorov, "Synecdoques", in *Communications*, no. 16, 1970, p. 30. Cf. also P. Fontanier, *Les figures du discours* (Paris: Flammarion, 1968), pp. 87–97, and J. Dubois et al., *Rhétorique générale* (1970), pp. 102–12.

30 On this space organized by practices into "islets", see P. Bourdieu, *Esquise d'une théorie de la pratique* (Geneva: Droz, 1972), pp. 215 ff., and his "Le sens pratique", pp. 51–2.

31 Cf. Anne Baldassari and Michel Joubert, *Pratiques relationnelles des enfants à l'espace et institution* (CRECELE, CORDES, 1976), and by the same authors, "Ce qui se trame", in *Paralleles*, no. 1, June 1976.

32 Derrida, *Marges*, p. 287, concerning metaphor.

33 Benveniste, *Problèmes de linguistique générale*, vol. 1, pp. 86–7.

34 For Benveniste, "discourse" "is language, as assumed by the speaking man and in a state of intersubjectivity" (ibid., p. 266).

35 Cf., for example, S. Freud, *La Science des rêves* (PUF, 1973) pp. 240–300, on condensation and transfer, which are "procedures of figuration" belonging to the "dreamwork".

36 P. Dard, F. Desbons et al., *La Ville: symbolique et souffrance* (Paris: CEP, 1975) p. 200.

37 See also, for example, the epigraph of *Place de l'Étoile* by Patrick Modiano (Paris: Gallimard, 1968).

38 Joachim du Bellay, *Regrets*, p. 189.

39 For example, *Sarcelles* – the name of a vast urban experiment – has taken on a symbolic value among the inhabitants of the city by becoming, for all of France, a benchmark of total failure. That extreme example ended up by lending its citizens an unexpected "prestige".

40 *Superstare*: to be above, like *more* or *too much*.

41 Cf. F. Lugassy, *Contribution à une psychosociologie de l'espace urbain: L'habitat et la forêt* (Paris: Publ. de Recherche urbaine, 1970).

42 Dard et al., *La ville*.

43 Quoted in ibid., pp. 174, 206.

44 C. Lévi-Strauss, *Tristes tropiques* (Paris: Plon, 1955), pp. 434–6.

45 One could say as much of snapshots brought back from a trip, substituted for (and changed into) legends of the site from which one left.

46 Terms whose relationships are not thought out but rather stated as necessary may be called *symbolic*. On this definition of symbolism as a cognitive mechanism characterized by a "deficit" of thought, see Dan Sperber, *Le Symbolisme en générale* (Paris: Hermann, 1974).

47 F. Ponge, *La Promenade dans nos serres* (Paris: Gallimard, 1967).

48 An inhabitant of Croix-Rousse, Lyon (interviewed by P. Mayol).

49 Cf. *Le Monde*, 4 May 1977.

50 See note 48 above.

51 See the two analyses in *The Interpretation of Dreams* and *Beyond the Pleasure Principle*, as well as Sami-Ali, *L'Espace imaginaire* (Paris: Gallimard, 1974), pp. 42–64.

52 J. Lacan, *Écrits* (Paris: Seuil, 1966), pp. 93–100.

53 S. Freud, *Inhibition, symptôme et angoisse* (PUF, 1968).

54 N. Kandinsky, *Du Spirituel dans l'art* (Paris: Denoël, 1969), p. 57.

10

Believing and Making People Believe

> I love the word "believe". In general, when one says, "I know", one does not know: one believes.
>
> Marcel Duchamp, *Duchamp du signe* (Paris: Flammarion, 1975, p. 185)

Leon Poliakov once said that Jews are Frenchmen who, rather than no longer going to church, no longer go to the synagogue. In the humorous tradition of the *Haggadah*, that joke relegates to the past beliefs that no longer organize practices. Today political convictions seem to be following the same path. One becomes a socialist *to have been* one, without going to demonstrations, without attending meetings, without paying dues – in short, without cost. More ceremonial than identification, "membership" is shown by what is called a *voice*, that leftover of a word: one vote a year. By living on a kind of "trust", the party carefully collates the relics of ancient convictions and through that fiction of legitimacy it succeeds in managing its affairs. It only needs, by means of opinion polls and statistics, to proliferate its citation of those phantom witnesses, thereby re-citing its litany.

A fairly simple technique upholds the acting out of this credibility. The polls need only concern not what directly links the "adherents" to the party, but that which does not attract them elsewhere – not the energy of convictions, but their inertia: "If it is not true that you believe something else, it is therefore true that you are still with us." The results of this operation rely upon remnants of the membership. They reckon on the very attrition of any conviction, for those remnants indicate both the *reflux* of what the respondents had believed in and the lack of a stronger credibility that might lead them away: the "voices" are not withdrawing; they are staying put; they are still there where they were, they give rise to the same total. The account becomes an accounting. This fiction could well serve as an appendix to Borges' *Esse est Percipi*.[1] It is the apologue of a shift that figures do not show, one that affects beliefs.

By way of an initial approximation, I take "belief" to mean not what is believed (a dogma, a programme, etc.), but the investiture of subjects in a proposition, the *act* of uttering it while holding it to be true[2] – in other words, a "modality" of the affirmation rather than its content.[3] Now, the capacity to believe seems to be receding everywhere in the political field. It underlay the functioning of "authority". Since Hobbes, political philosophy – especially in its English tradition – has deemed that connection to be fundamental.[4] Through that linkage, politics makes explicit its relationship of difference and continuity with religion. In both instances, however, the determination to inspire belief on which the institution lives is providing a respondent with a quest for love and/or identity.[5] It is therefore important to consider the forms taken by belief in our societies and the practices that form the origin of such displacements.

The Devaluation of Beliefs

For a long time it was supposed that the reserves of belief were indefinite. On the sea of credulity one needed only create islets of rationality to set out and ensure the fragile conquests of a critical method. The rest, seen as inexhaustible, was presumed transferable to other objects and other aims, as waterfalls are harnessed and used for hydroelectric power. One tried to "capture" this force and to move it from one place to another: from those so-called pagan societies in which it was at home it was directed towards the Christianity it was supposed to support; from the churches it was then moved on towards a monarchical politics; next, from a traditionalist religiosity towards the institutions of the Republic, of National Education or the types of socialism. Such "conversions" consisted in capturing the energy of belief by transporting it. What was not transferable – or had not yet been transferred – to the new realms of progress was regarded as "superstition"; what was usable by the ruling order was deemed "conviction". The resources were so rich that in exploiting them one forgot the need to analyse them. Campaigns and crusades entailed "investing" the energy of belief in good sites and good objects (of belief).

Gradually belief became polluted, like the air or the water. This motive energy – still resistant albeit manageable – began to run out. It was noticed, without knowing what it is. An odd paradox: all the polemics and reflections on ideological content and the institutional framework to be provided for it have not (except in English philosophy, from Hume to Wittgenstein, H. H. Price, Hintikka or Quine) been accompanied by any elucidation of the nature of the act of believing. Today it no longer suffices to manipulate, transfer and refine belief; its composition must be analysed, since we want to produce it artificially. Marketing (commercial or political) is still making only partial use of it.[6] Nowadays there are too many objects for belief and not enough credibility.

An inversion has taken place. The ancient powers managed their "authority" ably and thereby made up for their lack of technical or administrative machinery: this consisted of client systems, of allegiances, "legitimacies", and so forth. They tried none the less to make themselves more independent of the play of such fidelities through a rationalization, the control and organization of space. As an end result of that labour, the powers of our developed societies have fairly precise and compact procedures for the surveillance of every social network: such as the administrative and "panoptic" systems of police, school, health, security, etc.[7] However, they are slowly losing their credibility. They command more strength and have less authority.

Often the technicians do not concern themselves about this at all, busy as they are with extending and complicating the machinery for maintenance and surveillance. False confidence. The sophistication of discipline does not compensate for the disinvestment of subjects. In businesses the letting-go of workers is increasing more rapidly than the police control apparatus of which it is the target, the pretext and the effect. Waste of produce, misuse of time, "feather-bedding", job turnover and absenteeism among the staff, etc.: such things erode from within a system which, like the Toyota plants,[8] tends to become prison-like to prevent anything escaping. In administration, offices, and even in political or religious organizations, the cancer invading the machinery corresponds to the disappearance of convictions. It also causes it. Interest cannot replace belief.[9]

Belief is being exhausted. Or rather, it has sought refuge in the media and leisure activities. It has gone on vacation; yet it is none the less an object captured and dealt with by advertising, business and fashion. To regain those beliefs that are fading and becoming lost, business has set about manufacturing simulacra of credibility. Shell produces the Credo of "values" that "inspire" its management and that are to be adopted by its staff and its workers. The same holds true for a hundred other businesses, even if they are slow to take action and continue to rely on the fictitious capital of some outmoded "family" business or local "spirit".

The material with which to inject believability into the apparatus, where is it to be found? There are two traditional sources, one political, the other religious: in the first, the overdevelopment of administrative bodies and framework takes the place of mobility or reflux of convictions among militants. In the second, on the contrary, institutions in the process of decaying or of isolating themselves allow the beliefs that they had long fomented, maintained and controlled to become dissipated.

An Archaeology: the Transits of Belief

The relationships between these two "bases" are strange and longstanding.

1. Religiosity seems easier to exploit. Marketing firms are turning back enthusiastically to fragments of beliefs that were only yesterday violently being combatted as superstitions. Advertising is becoming evangelical. Many administrators on the economic and social levels, who are disturbed by the slow sinking of the Churches in which respose the remains of the "values", are trying to re-enlist their services by christening them "up to date". Before these beliefs can go down with the ships that carry them they are precipitously being unloaded by businesses and administrations. The people who use these relics no longer believe in them. Nevertheless, they employ them and imbue them with kinds of "integrist" and ideological and financial associations in order to recaulk these old leaky tubs and turn the churches into museums of beliefs without believers, thus preserved for exploitation by liberal capitalism.

Such a salvage operation works on the basis of two tactical hypotheses – both probably false. The first postulates that belief remains attached to its objects and that by preserving the latter you retain the former. In fact (as demonstrated by both history and semiotics), the investment of belief passes from myth to myth, from ideology to ideology, or from utterance to utterance.[10] Thus, belief withdraws from a myth and leaves it more or less intact, but disarmed and changed into a document.[11] In the course of these transits, the conviction that is still attached to the terrain it is gradually abandoning cannot win out against the currents that are moving elsewhere. There is no equivalence between the objects that still cleave to it and those that mobilize it elsewhere.

The other tactic no longer assumes that belief remains tied to its prime objects, but rather that, on the contrary, it can be separated from them artificially; that its flight towards the narratives of the media, towards leisure "paradises", towards inner or communal retreats, etc., can be halted or diverted; that one might thus bring it back to the fold, to the disciplinary order it has left. However, conviction does not so easily resprout in the fields it has abandoned. It cannot be so easily brought back to administrations or businesses that have become "unbelievable". The liturgies that attempt to "enliven" and "revalue" the workplace do not transform its functioning; they do not therefore produce believers. The public is not that credulous. It is amused by such festivals and simulacra. It does not "go along".

2. *Political* organizations are slowly replacing Churches as the sites of the practices of belief, but because of this they appear to have been haunted by the return of a very ancient (pre-Christian) and very "pagan" alliance between power and the religious life. It is as though when the religions ceased to be an autonomous power ("spiritual power" as it was called), politics once again became religious. Christianity had cut through the interlacing of the visible objects of belief (political authorities) and its invisible objects (gods, spirits, etc.). But it retained that distinction only by establishing a clerical, dogmatic and sacramental power in the place left vacant by the temporary deterioration of the political at the end of the age of antiquity. In the eleventh and twelfth centuries, ecclesiastical power, under the banner of "The Peace of God", imposed its "order" on clashing civil powers.[12] Succeeding centuries were marked by the deterioration of that order to the benefit of princes. In the seventeenth century the Churches received their models and their rights from the monarchies, even if they still evidenced a "religiosity" that legitimized power and that it little by little turned to its credit. With the crumbling of this ecclesiastical power three centuries ago, beliefs flowed back towards the political, but without carrying with them the divine or celestial values the Churches had set aside, controlled and taken in hand.

This complicated round trip, which passed from politics to Christian religion, and from that religion to a new politics,[13] resulted in an individualization of beliefs (common frames of reference breaking down into social "opinions" or private "convictions") and of their fields of action in an increasingly diversified network of possible objects. The notion of democracy was consonant with the will to control this multiplication of convictions that had replaced the faith upon which an order had been based. It is striking that in breaking down the old system – i.e. the religious credibility of politics – Christianity finally compromised the feasibility of that religion it had detached from politics, it contributed to the devaluation of what it had appropriated in order to render it autonomous, and it thereby made possible the reflux of beliefs towards political authorities hitherto deprived of (or freed from) those spiritual authorities that had once been as much a principle of relativization as of legitimization. The return of a "pagan" repression had thus been affected by this fall from the "spritual". The erosion of Christianity left an indelible mark on modern times: the "incarnation" or historicization that Rousseau, in the eighteenth century, was already calling a "civil religion".[14] In contrast to the pagan State, which "drew no distinction between its gods and its laws",

Rousseau posited a citizen's "religion", "whose articles it was up to the sovereign to establish". "If anyone, after having publicly accepted those dogmas, behaves as if he does not believe in them, he is to be put to death." Different from this civil religion of the *citizen* was a spiritual religion of *man*: the individual, asocial and universal religion of *la Profession de foi du vicaire savoyard*. That prophetic view – far less incoherent than has been suggested – already articulates the development of a body of "civil" and political dogma on the radicalization of an individual conscience *freed* from all dogma and deprived of power. Sociological analysis has since proved that prediction to be correct.[15]

Hence belief is reinvested solely in the political system, to the extent that the "spiritual powers" – which had guaranteed civil powers in antiquity and which entered into competition with those of the Christian West – fall out of circulation and are disseminated or miniaturized.

The Institution of the Real

The media change the profound silence of things into its opposite. Once constituted in secret, the real now jabbers away. We are surrounded by news, information, statistics and opinion polls. Never has history talked so much or shown so much. Never, indeed, have the gods' ministers *made them speak* so continuously, in such detail and so injunctively as the producers of revelations and rules do today *in the name* of topicality. Our orthodoxy is made up of narrations of "what's going on". Statistical debates are our theological wars. The combatants no longer bear ideas as offensive or defensive arms. They move forward camouflaged as facts, data and events. They set themselves up as messengers of a "reality". Their uniform is the colour of the economic and social earth. When they advance, the ground itself seems to advance. But in fact they manufacture it, they simulate it, they cover themselves with it, they believe in it – they thus create the stage of their law.

Malville, Kalkai, Croissant, the POLISARIO Front, the nuclear question, Khomeini, Reagan, etc.: these fragments of history organize themselves into doctrinal articles. "Be silent!" says the speaker or the political officeholder. "There are the facts. Here are the data, the circumstances, etc. Therefore, you must . . . " The real, as told to us, interminably dictates what must be believed and what must be done. And what can one reply to such facts? We can only bow down and obey what they – those oracles – "signify", as with the oracle at Delphi.[16] Thus the manufacture of simulacra provides the means of producing believers and, therefore, adherents. This institution of the real is the most visible form of our contemporary dogma. It is also, therefore, the most disputed among parties.

It no longer has its own site, its own headquarters or its own ultimate authority. Information, a private code, innervates and saturates the social body. From morning till evening, unceasingly, streets and buildings are haunted by narratives. They articulate our existences by teaching us what they should be. They "cover the event", i.e. they *make* our legends (*legenda* = that which must be read and said). Seized from the moment of awakening by the radio (the voice is the law), the listener walks all day through a forest of narrativities, journalistic, advertising and televised, which, at night, slip a few final messages under the door of sleep. More than the God recounted to us by the theologians of the past, these tales have a function of providence and predestination: they organize our work, our celebrations – even our dreams – in advance. Social life multiplies the gestures and modes of behaviour *imprinted* by the narrative models; it continually reproduces and stores up the "copies" of narratives. Our society has become a *narrated* society in a threefold sense: it is defined by *narratives* (the fables of our advertising and information), by *quotations* of them, and by their interminable *recitation*.

Such narratives have the strange and twofold power of changing sight into belief and of manufacturing reality out of simulacra: a dual inversion. On the one hand, modernity – once born of an observant will struggling against credulity and basing itself on a contract between the seen and the real – has now transformed that relationship and gives to be seen precisely what must be *believed*. The scope, the status and the objects of vision are defined by fiction. The media, advertising or political representation all function in this way.

Of course, fiction also existed in the past, but within circumscribed aesthetic and theatrical sites: fiction indicated itself as such (thanks to perspective, for example, the art of illusion); with its own ground-rules and production conditions, it provided its own metalanguage.[17] It spoke solely in the name of language. It narrativized symbolics, leaving the truth of things suspended and almost secret. Today, fiction claims to presentify the real, to speak in the name of facts, and thus to cause the simulacrum it produces to be taken as a system of reference. Those to whom these legends are addressed (and who pay for them) are therefore no longer obliged to believe what they cannot see (the traditional position), but rather to believe what they do see (the contemporary position).

This inversion of the terrain on which beliefs develop is the result of a mutation in the paradigms of knowledge: the visibility of the real is substituted for the earlier postulate, its invisibility. The socio-cultural scene of modernity refers back to a "myth". It defines the social referent by its visibility (and thus by its scientific or political representivity); on the basis of this new postulate (the belief that the real is visible), it articulates the possibility of what we know, what we observe, our proofs and our practices. In this new arena – the infinitely extendable field of optical investigations and of a scopic drive –

there still remains the strange collusion between *belief* and the question of the real. But now it is played out within the element of the *seen*, the *observed* or the *shown*. In short, the contemporary simulacrum[18] is the last localization of the belief in sight. It is the identification of the *seen* with what is to be *believed* – once we have abandoned the hypothesis that holds that the waters of an invisible ocean (the Real) haunt the shores of the visible and create the effects, the decipherable signs or the misleading reflections of its presence. The simulacrum is what the relationship of the visible to the real becomes when the postulate of an invisible immensity of the Being (or beings) hidden behind appearances crumbles.

Society Recited

In the face of narratives of images – which nowadays are no more than "fictions", visible and readable productions – the spectator-observer *knows perfectly well* that they are but simulacra, the results of manipulations ("I know perfectly well it's a joke"), *but even so*, he assumes for those simulations the status of reality:[19] a belief survives the denial created by all that we know about their manufacture. As a television viewer has said, "Had it been untrue, you would have been able to tell." He postulated *other* social sites that could guarantee what he knew to be fictitious, and that is what allowed him to believe it "anyway": as though belief could no longer be couched in direct convictions, but only through the detour of what others are supposed to believe. Belief is no longer based on an invisible otherness concealed behind signs, but on what other groups, other fields or other disciplines are supposed to be. The "real" is what, in each place, the reference to another causes to be believed. And the same holds for the scientific disciplines. For example, the relationship between computing and history functions on the basis of an astonishing *quid pro quo*: from computers historians seek the accrediation of a "scientific" power that can lend a technical, real weight to their discourse; from history, the computer scientists seek validation through the "reality" created by "concrete" manifestations of knowledge. Each expects from the other a guarantee that gives weight to their simulacrum.[20]

The same holds true politically. Each party derives its credibility from what it believes and causes to be believed about its referent (the revolutionary "miracles" performed in the East?) or its adversary (the faults and woes of the wicked on the other side). Each political discourse creates effects of reality out of what it assumes and causes to be assumed about the economic analysis on which it is based (an analysis that is itself validated by this reference to the political). Within each party, the professional discourses of the "responsible" leadership *stand up* thanks to the credulity those leaders assume on the part of the rank and file militants or the voters and, on the other hand, the "I am well aware that it's a joke" of many voters is countered by what they postulate, out of conviction or out of knowledge, about the cadres of the political apparatus. Belief thus functions on the basis of the value of the real that is assumed "anyway" in the other, even when one knows perfectly well – all too well – the extent to which "it's all bullshit" on one's own side.

Quotation, then, is the ultimate weapon for making one believe. Because it plays upon what the other is assumed to believe, it is the means by which "reality" is instituted. To quote the other on one's own behalf is thus to make believable the simulacra produced in a particular place. Opinion "polls" have become the most elementary and the most passive procedure for doing this. Perpetual self-quotation – the proliferation of polls – is the fiction through which the country is brought to believe in what it *is*. Each citizen assumes for all the others what he takes to be their belief – without believing in it himself. By replacing doctrines that have become unbelievable, quotation allows the technocratic apparatuses to make themselves feasible for each person *in the name of the others*. To quote is to give reality to the simulacrum a power produces by causing a belief that others believe in it, but without furnishing any believable object. However, it is also to designate the "anarchists" or "deviants" (to quote them to the public), to hand over to the aggressivity of the public those who, affirming through their deeds that they do not believe in it, destroy the fictitious "reality" that no one can support "anyway" except as the conviction of the others.

To the extent that this "opinion-making" instrument can be manipulated by those who wield it, one is quite justified in wondering about the ability it offers to change "belief" into "distrust", into "suspicion" – even into denunciation, and about whether citizens can control politically that which provides the circular and pointless trustworthiness to political life itself.

Notes

1 See Jorge Luis Borges, *Chroniques de Bustos Domeq*, and the chapter "Esse est percipi" (to be is to be seen).

2 Cf. the remarks in W. V. Quine and J. S. Ullian, *The Web of Belief* (New York: Random House, 1970), pp. 4–6.

3 Cf. on this subject: Jaakko Hintikka, *Knowledge and Belief: An Introduction to the Logic of the Two Notions* (Ithaca, NY: Cornell University Press, 1969); Rodney Needham, *Belief, Language and Experience* (Oxford: Basil Blackwell, 1972); Ernest Gellner, *Legitimation of Belief* (Cambridge: Cambridge University Press, 1974); John M. Vickers, *Belief and Probability* (Dordrecht: Reidel, 1976); *Langages*, no. 43 on "modalities", September 1976.

4 Cf., for example, R. S. Peters and Peter Winch, "Authority", in Anthony Quinton (ed.), *Political Philosophy* (Oxford: Oxford University Press, 1973), pp. 83–111.

5 Pierre Legendre, *L'Amour du censeur* (Paris: Seuil, 1974) p. 28.

6 Cf., for example, Dale Carnegie, *Public Speaking and Influencing Men in Business* and, especially, Martin Fishbein and Icek Ajzen, *Belief, Attitude, Intention and Behavior* (Reading, Mass: Addison-Wesley, 1975).

7 Cf. Michel Foucault, *Surveiller et punir* (Paris: Gallimard, 1975) etc.

8 Kamata Satoshi, *Toyota: l'usine de désespoir* (Paris, Ouvrières edn, 1976): a system which is still "palaeotechnical", in which the goal is to *control* every activity; not make them cohere by means of values designed to create believers. See Miklos Haraszti, *Salaire aux pièces* (Paris: Seuil, 1976).

9 Pierre Gremion further states that in local administration, and especially in the urban sub-system, the mechanisms of legitimation "no longer exist". See P. Gremion, *Le Pouvoir périphérique: Bureaucrates et notables dans le système politique francais* (Paris: Seuil, 1976), pp. 416ff.

10 Cf. M. de Certeau, *La Culture au pluriel* (Paris: 10/18, 1974), pp. 11–34: "Les révolutions du croyable". From the standpoint of logic, it is precisely to these shifts of belief from utterance to utterance that Quine and Ullian devoted their first analyses (Quine and Ullian, *Web of Belief*, pp. 8–9).

11 To the analysis of the journeys which lead the myth from tribe to tribe, and "wear it out" little by little into legendary tradition, fantastic elaboration or political ideology (see Lévi-Strauss, *Anthropologie structurale, deux* (Paris: Plon, 1973), pp. 301–15, "Comment meurent les mythes"), we must thus add that of these slow disinvestments through which belief moves away from a myth.

12 See Georges Duby, *Guerriers et paysans* (Paris: Gallimard, 1976), pp. 184ff.

13 See M. de Certeau, *L'Écriture de l'histoire*, 2. edn (Paris: Gallimard, 1978), pp. 152–212: "La formalité des pratiques. Du système religieux à l'éthique des lumières (XVIIe–XVIIIe siècle)."

14 J.-J. Rousseau, *Le Contrat social*, IV, ch. 8.

15 Cf. Robert N. Bellah, *Beyond Belief: Essays on Religion in a Post-Traditional World* (New York, 1970) pp. 168–89, concerning "civil religion" in the United States.

16 *To signify* in the sense of the Heraclitian fragment: "The oracle which is Delphi does not speak; it does not dissimulate: it *signifies*" (fragment 93, in Diels).

17 See Erwin Panovsky, *La Perspective comme forme symbolique* (Paris: Minuit, 1975); E. H. Gombrich, *L'Art et l'illusion* (Paris: Gallimard, 1971), pp. 255–360; R. Klein, *La Forme et l'intelligible* (Paris: Gallimard, 1970).

18 On simulacra see Jean Beaudrillard, *L'Échange symbolique et la mort* (Paris: Gallimard, 1976), pp. 75–128, "L'ordre des simulacres"; and, by the same author, "La précession des simulacres", in *Traverses*, no. 10 (1978), pp. 3–37.

19 See O. Mannoni, *Clefs pour l'imaginaire ou l'Autre Scène* (Paris: Seuil, 1969), pp. 9–33: "Je sais bien mais quand même" (on belief).

20 M. de Certeau, "Science et fiction: l'histoire, de l'informatique à l'anthropologie", in *Nouvelles littéraires*, January 1977.

11

Ethno-Graphy

Speech, or the Space of the Other: Jean de Léry

Jean de Léry's Writing Lesson (1578)

Although his text is based on a long medieval tradition of utopias and expectations in which was already mapped the locus that the "noble savage" would soon inhabit, Jean de Léry provides us with a "modern" point of departure. In fact, he assures us of a transition.

Published in 1578, his *Histoire d'un voyage faict en la terre du Brésil*... is the story of a journey into the Bay of Rio in the years 1556–1558. This voyage is part of a number of successive "retreats." A partisan of the Reformation, Léry flees France in favor of Geneva; he leaves Geneva, and with a few companions he sails off for Brazil in order to take part in the foundation of a Calvinist sanctuary. From the island in the Bay of Rio, where the admiral Nicolas Durant de Villegagnon received the Protestant mission after a treaty with Calvin, he withdraws again, disgusted by the admiral's theological fluctuations. He wanders for three months among the Tupinambous along the coast, from the end of October 1557 until the beginning of January 1558, before following the same road in the opposite direction, from Brazil to Geneva, and from Geneva to France, where he settles down as a pastor. His is a reverse pilgrimage: far from rejoining the referential body of an orthodoxy (the sacred city, the tomb, the basilica), his itinerary goes from the center to the borders, in searching for a space where he can find a ground. Upon that ground he envisions building the language of a new – a reformed – conviction. At the end of his journey, after all the comings and goings, the Savage is invented.[1]

In 1556 Jean de Léry is twenty-four years old. Published twenty years later, his *Histoire* casts the movement of departure that had gone from over here (in France), to over there (among the Tupis), into circular form. It transforms the voyage into a cycle. From over there it brings back a literary object, the Savage, that allows him to turn back to his point of departure. The story effects his return to himself through the mediation of the other. Yet something still remains over there, which the words of the text cannot convey; namely, the speech of the Tupis. It is that part of the other that cannot be retrieved – it is an evanescent act that writing cannot convey.

Thus, in the jeweled setting of the tale, native speech takes on the figure of a missing precious stone. It is the moment of ravishment, a stolen instant, a purloined memory beyond the text: "Such a joy it was [writes Léry about his impressions during a Tupi assembly hearing the beautifully measured rhythms of such a multitude – and especially the cadence and refrain of the ballad, all of them together raising their voices to each couplet, saying: *heu, heuaüre, heüra, heüraüre, heüra, heüra, oueh* – that I remained completely ravished. But moreover, every time the memory comes back to me, my heart throbs, and it seems as if their music still rings in my ears."[2] An absence of meaning opens a rift in time. Here the chant measures *heu, heuaüre* or, further, *Hé, hua, hua*, just as a voice utters *re re*, or *tralala*. Nothing can be either transmitted, conveyed, or preserved. But immediately afterward, Léry appeals to his interpreter for a translation of several things that he was unable to comprehend. With this passing to meaning occurs the task that transforms the ballad into a product that can be put to good use. From these voices the deft translator extracts the story of an initial deluge "which is," Léry notes, "what most resembles Scripture among them":[3] a return is accomplished, to the West and to writing, to which the gift of this confirmation is taken from the distant Tupi shores, a return to the Christian and French text through the exegete's and the voyager's combined efforts. Productive time is sewn back into the fabric, history is generated anew, after the break precipitated by the throbbing heart that was going back over there, toward that instant when, "totally ravished," fascinated by the other's voice, the observer forgot himself.

The connection between speech and writing is staged on one other occasion in the *Histoire*. This connection discreetly focuses the entire narrative, but Léry clarifies his position in a key episode, in the central chapter in which he deals with religion,[4] that is, with the relation that the Christianity of Scripture holds with the oral traditions of the indigenous world. At the dawn of modern times, this episode inaugurates the series of analogous scenes that so many travelogues will project over the next four centuries... In the form assumed here, the scene already puts all kinds of sacred and profane writings together in order to appropriate them to the West, the subject of history, and to allocate to them the function of being an expansionist *labor* of knowledge.

As for writing, whether sacred or profane, not only are the Indians unaware of what it is, but moreover, they are deprived of characters with which they might otherwise be able to signify things: when I was in their country in the beginning and learning their language, I used to write a few sentences. Then, in reading to them afterward, in their eyes it all seemed like some kind of sorcery. One would say to the other: Is it not a marvel that he could not utter a word in our language yesterday, but by virtue of this paper that he keeps and that makes him speak the way he does, we can understand him today?

Which is the same opinion held among the natives of the Spanish Island who were the first there.[5] For he who wrote its *History* thus states:[6] The Indians, knowing that the Spanish conquerors, without either seeing or speaking to one another, except by sending letters from place to place, could be understood in this fashion, believed either that the European had the gift of prophecy or that the missives spoke. In such a way, he said, the savages, fearing being discovered and surprised in guilt, were held to their duties so well through these means that they no longer dared either to lie or steal from the Spaniards.

For this reason I say that whoever wishes to amplify this matter here has a handsome topic, both to praise and exalt the art of writing and, too, to show how much the nations that inhabit these three parts of the world – Europe, Asia, and Africa – can praise God beyond the savages of this fourth part called America: for unlike those who are unable to communicate anything except through verbal means,[7] to the contrary we have this advantage, that without budging an inch, by means of writing and the letters we send, we can declare our secrets to whomever we please, even if they are removed to the other end of the world. Thus beyond the sciences that we learn through books, of which the natives are seemingly entirely deprived, this invention of writing at our fingertips, which they are also totally lacking, must be even more advanced to the rank of the unique gifts that men of our lands have received from God.[8]

Scriptural Reproduction

Between "them" and "us" there exists the difference of possessing "either sacred or profane" writing, which immediately raises the question of a relation of *power*.... Sorcery, say the Tupinambous, is the power of the strongest. But they are deprived of it. The Westerners have the advantage. They accredit it as being one of the unique gifts that men from their country received from God. Their cultural power is countersigned by the absolute itself; it is not only a fact, but also a right, the effect of an election, a divine heritage.

Still more characteristic is the nature of the rift. It does not result essentially from a selection between (primitive) error and (Christian) truth. Here the decisive element is the possession or privation of an *instrument* that can at the same time "keep things in all their purity" (as Léry will remark further on)[9] and stretch all the way "to the other end of the world." In combining the power to keep the past (while the primitive "fable" forgets and loses its origin)[10] with that of indefinitely conquering distance (while the primitive "voice" is limited to the vanishing circle of its auditors), writing *produces history*. On the one hand, it accumulates, it keeps an inventory of the secrets from the West, it loses nothing, it preserves them in an intact state. Writing is an archive. On the other hand, it declares, it goes to the end of the world, toward those destined to receive it according to the objectives that it desires – and "without budging an inch," without having the center of its action being moved, without any change in it through its progress. With writing the Westerner has a sword in his hand which will extend its gesture but never modify its subject. In this respect, it repeats and diffuses its prototypes.

The power that writing's expansionism leaves intact is colonial in principle. It is extended without being changed. It is tautological, immunized against both any alterity that might transform it and whatever dares to resist it. It can be taken as the play of a double *reproduction* which, as history and as orthodoxy, preserves the past and which, as mission, conquers space by multiplying the same signs. Léry's is the period when critical research on the return to origins – exhuming written "sources" – is built over the innovation of the new empire that, with printing, is permitted by an indefinite reproduction of the same products.

To writing, which invades space and capitalizes on time, is opposed speech, which neither travels very far nor preserves much of anything. In its first aspect speech never leaves the place of its production. In other words, *the signifier cannot be detached from the individual or collective body*. It cannot be exported. Here speech is the body which signifies. Statements are separated neither from the social act of enunciation, nor from a presence that is given, dispensed, and lost in the act of naming. Writing is found only where the signifier can be isolated from presence, while the Tupinambous see a bizarre form of speech, the action of a force, in characters drawn on paper; in their eyes, writing is a form of sorcery; for the Indians of the Spanish Island, missives speak.

In order that writing can function from afar, it has to maintain its relation to the place of production, even from a distance. For Léry, who still bears witness to reformed biblical theology, writing implies a faithful transmission of the origin, a being-there of the Beginning which lasts, intact, throughout avatars of generations and mortal societies. Writing is itself a body of truth, hence it can be isolated from the Church or community. This true object brings from the past to the present the statements that an originary and founding enunciation has produced "without budging." Léry's is a world which is no longer natural but which has become literary, in which the power of a distant (absent) author is reiterated. The religious cosmos – a creature signifying the creator – already appears to be replaced by the text, but in a miniaturization that fashions for man's profit a faithful and mobile instrument in an endless space. Speech is now located in an entirely different position. It does not preserve. That is its second feature. In respect to a Tupi oral tradition concerning the deluge that would have drowned "everyone in the world, except for their grandfathers who took refuge in the highest trees of their country," Léry notes that "being deprived of all kinds of writing, they retain things in their purity only with difficulty; like poets, they added this fable about their grandfathers who took refuge in the treetops."[11] Thanks to his scriptural standard, Léry knows how to determine what orality adds to things, and he knows exactly how things had been. He becomes a historian. Speech, to the contrary, has much to do with custom, which "turns truth into falsehood." And more fundamentally, the Tupi's account is a fable (from *fari*, to speak). So *fable is a drifting away* – adjunction, deviation, diversion, heresy, and poetry of the present, in relation to the "purity" of primitive law.

Through all this Jean de Léry appears to be a good Calvinist. He prefers the letter to a church body; the text to the voice of a presence; origins related by writing to the elocutionary experience of a fugitive communication. But he is already displacing the theology that inspires him. He is laicizing it. To be sure, in his view nature is still a sign to which he responds, while traveling under blooming trees, by singing the 104th Psalm: such a form of "speech" turns his heart to the whispers of the forest and the voices of the Tupis.[12] It is in syncopation with his ravishment at the sound of the communal ballad. The religious elements of the *Histoire* go in the direction of the almost ecstatic and prophetic speech of the primitives, but these elements are dissociated from the *labor* connoted by writing. A structure already appears to be in place. From festive, poetic, ephemeral speech are delineated the tasks of conserving, of verifying, and of conquering. A will to power is invested in its form. It discreetly transforms the Christian categories which provide it with a language. Ecclesial election is turned into a Western privilege; originary revelation into a scientific concern for upholding the truth of things; evangelization into an enterprise of expansion and return to one's self. Writing designates an *operation organized about a center*: departures and dispatches still depend on the impersonal will which is developed there and to which they return. The multiplicity of procedures in which "declarations" of this will are written elaborates the space of an organization around the *same*, which extends without undergoing any modification. These are scriptural organizations, commercial, scientific, and colonial. The "paths of writing" combine a plurality of itineraries with the singularity of the place of production.

A Hermeneutics of the Other

Signified through a concept of writing, the work of redirecting the plurality of ways toward the single productive center is precisely what Jean de Léry's story attains. As his preface already indicates, the tale is fabricated from "memoirs . . . written in Brazilian ink and in America itself," a raw material doubly drawn from the tropics, since the very characters that bring the primitive object into the textual web are made from a red ink extracted from the *pau-brasil*, a wood that is one of the principal imports to sixteenth-century Europe.

Yet only through the effect of its organization does the *Histoire* "yield profit." To be sure, the literary *operation* that brings back to the producer the results of signs that were sent far away has a condition of possibility in a *structural* difference between an area "over here" and another "over there." The narrative plays on the relation between the structure which establishes the separation and the operation which overcomes it, creating effects of meaning in this fashion. The break is what is taken for granted everywhere by the text, itself a labor of suturing.

The Break. At the manifest level, in the distribution of masses, the separation (between "over here" and "over there") first appears as an occanic division: it is the Atlantic, a rift between the Old and the New World. In telling of tempests, sea monsters, acts of piracy, "marvels," or the ups and downs of transoceanic navigation, the chapters at the beginning and at the end (chapters 1–5 and 21–22) develop this structural rupture along the historical line of a chronicle of a crossing: each episode modulates uncanniness according to a particular element of the cosmological range (air, water, fish, bird, man, etc.), adding its proper effect to the series, in which difference is simultaneously the generative principle and the object to be made credible. The chapters that present Tupi society (7–19), bordered by the preceding, exhibit the same principle but now systematically, according to a scheme of dissimilarity that must affect every genre and every degree of being in order to situate the "over there" within the cosmos: "This American land where, as I shall be deducing, everything that is seen, whether in the customs of its inhabitants, the shapes of its animals, or in general in what the earth produces, is *dissimilar* in respect to what we have in Europe, Asia, and Africa, might well in our eyes be called a *new* world."[13]

In this landscape the figure of dissimilarity is either a deviation from what can be seen "over here" or, more often, the combination of Western forms that seem to have been cut off, and whose fragments seem to be associated in unexpected ways. Thus, among the four-footed animals (of which there exists "not one . . . that in any or every aspect in any fashion can resemble our own"), the *tapiroussou* is "half-cow and half-donkey," "being both of the one and of the other."[14] The primitives incorporate the splitting that divides the universe. Their picture of the world follows a traditional cosmological order whose scaffolding is exposed, but it is a picture covered with countless broken mirrors in which the same fracture is reflected (half this, half that).

The Work of Returning. This structural difference, particularized in the accidents that happen along the way or in the portraits in the gallery of primitives, only forms the area where an operation of return is effected, in a mode drawn according to the literary zones that it crosses. The narrative as a whole belabors the division that is located everywhere in order to show that the *other returns to the same*. In this fashion it inserts itself within the general problem of *crusade* that still rules over the discovery of the world in the sixteenth century: "conquest and conversion."[15] But this narrative displaces that problem through an effect of distortion that is introduced structurally by the breakage of space into two worlds. . . .

A part of the world which appeared to be entirely other is brought back to the same by a displacement that throws uncanniness out of skew in order to turn it into an exteriority behind which an interiority, the unique definition of man, can be recognized.

This operation will be repeated hundreds of times throughout ethnological works. In Léry's case we see it evinced in the staging of the primitive world, through a division between *Nature*, whose uncanniness is exteriority, and *civil* society, in which a truth of man is always legible. The break between over here and over there is transformed into a rift between nature and culture. Finally, nature is what is other, while man stays the same. By the way, we can observe that this metamorphosis, a product of the displacement generated by the text, makes of nature the area where *esthetic* or *religious* experience and admiration are expressed and where Léry's prayer is spoken, while the social space is the place where an *ethics* is developed through a constant parallel between festivity and work. In this already modern combination, social production, what reproduces sameness and marks an identity, posits nature, esthetics, and religiosity outside of itself.

We can follow in some detail the arc traced by the story. . . . In a first movement, it goes toward alterity: first the travel in the direction of the land over there (chapters 1–5), and then the overview of marvels and natural wonders (chapters 7–13). This movement has its final punctuation with the ecstatic song glorifying God (the end of chapter 13). The poem, Psalm 104, marks a vanishing point opening onto alterity, what is out of this world and unspeakable. At this point, with the analysis of Tupi society (chapters 14–19), a second movement begins: it goes from the most uncanny (war, chapter 14; anthropophagia, chapter 15) in order to progressively unveil a social model (laws and police, chapter 18; therapeutics, health, the cult of the dead, chapter 19). Then passing through the oceanic break, the narrative can bring this civilized primitive as far back as Geneva by way of return (chapters 21–22).

This work is indeed a *hermeneutics of the other*. Onto the shores of the New World it transports the Christian exegetical apparatus which, born of a necessary relation with Jewish alterity, has been applied in turn to the biblical tradition, to Greco-Latin antiquity, and to many more foreign totalities. On one more occasion it draws effects of meaning from its relation with the other. Ethnology will become a form of exegesis that has not ceased providing the modern West with what it needs in order to articulate its identity through a relation with the past or the future, with foreigners or with nature.

The functioning of this new hermeneutics of the other is already sketched in Léry's text in the shape of two problematic issues that transform its theological usage. These are the linguistic operation of translation, and the position of a subject in relation to an expanse of objects. In both cases the (oceanic) break that characterizes the difference is not suppressed; on the contrary, the text presupposes and thwarts this break in order to be grounded as a discourse of knowledge.

The bar between the Old and the New World is the line on which an *activity of translation* can be seen replacing a theological language. This discreet transformation is indicated by two chapters of which both – since one is devoted to departure and the other to return – constitute a navigational lock, a transit, between the travelogue and the picture of the Tupi world. The first, chapter 6, tells of theological debates at Fort Coligny in the Rio Bay and of the "inconstancy and variation" of Villegagnon "in matters of religion," the cause for the disembarkation of the Huguenot mission among the Tupis on the coast, "who were incomparably more humane with us."[16] The other, chapter 20, which Léry designates as the "colloquy of the savage's language,"[17] is a dictionary – or rather a French–Tupi Berlitz guide.

According to the first account, the Island of Coligny mediates between the Old and the New World and is a place where divisiveness and the confusion of languages reign supreme. It is a Babel in the twilight of the universe. Yet confusion is no longer avowed here. It is hidden in a language of hypocrisy (that of Villegagnon), where what is said is not what is thought, much less what is done. At the end of the globe, at the threshold of the unknown Tupi world, deception proliferates beneath the veil of a literal reproduction of Calvinist theology: such are the public prayers of the "zealot" Villegagnon, whose "inner side and heart it was discomfiting to get to know."[18] Is this not tantamount to saying that at this point language no longer holds an anchor in reality, and that at the farthest borders of the West it floats detached from its truth and from any firm grounding, caught up into the indefinite turnings of a lure?

Chapter 20 comes at the end of the description of the Tupi lands. After the linguistic confusion surrounding the Island of Coligny, this vast picture of the primitive world is an epiphany of things, the *discourse of an effectivity*. Clearly the contents were first given as antinomic, but they were divided and elaborated in such a way as to become, in their human sector, a world which does justice to the truth of Geneva. Thus, a reality is already there, and it saturates Léry's statements. What separates the Western world from that world is no longer an array of things, but their appearance – essentially, a foreign language. From stated difference there only remains a *language to be translated*. Whence the chapter which provides the code for linguistic transformation. It allows unity to be restored by folding upon one another all the heterogenous peelings that cover an identity of substance.

The dictionary becomes a theological instrument. Just as religious language is perverted by a usage which is "discomfiting to get to know" and which refers to unfathomable intentions or "heart,"[19] now, situated on the very line that the rift of the universe demarcated, translation *lets* primitive reality pass into Western discourse. All that is needed is to have one language "converted" into another. As Calvin already suggested,[20] the operation of translation frees one from reducing language to a first tongue from which all others would be derived; it replaces the being-there of a beginning with a transformation which unravels on the surface of languages, which makes a single meaning pass from tongue to tongue, and which will soon provide linguistics, the science of these transformations, with a decisive role in all recapitulative strategies.

In the place where the *Histoire* locates it, foreign language already acquires the double function of being the way by which a substance (the effectivity of primitive life) happens to uphold the discourse of a European knowledge, and of being a fable, a speech which is unaware of what it expresses before decipherment can provide it with meaning and practical usage. The being which authenticates the discourse is no longer directly received from God; it is made to come from the foreign place itself, where it is the gold mine hidden under an exotic exteriority, the truth to be discerned beneath primitive babble.

For Léry this economy of translation entails, moreover, a general problematic. For example, it orders the analysis of living beings and therein becomes specific. In effect, plants and animals are classified according to the modulations of a constant distinction between what is seen (appearance) and what is eaten (edible substance). Exteriority captivates the eye, it astonishes or horrifies, but this theater is often a lie and a fiction in respect to edibility, which measures the utility, or the essence, of fruits and animals. The double diagnostic of taste corrects seductions or repulsions of the eye: is it healthy or not to eat, raw or cooked? The same holds for exotic fable, the enchanting but often deceptive voice: the interpreter discriminates in terms of utility when, first creating a distance between what it says and what it does not say, he translates what it does not say in forms of truth that are good to hear back in France. An intellectual edibility is the essence that has to be distinguished from ravishments of the ear.

From the baroque spectacle of flora and fauna to their edibility; from primitive festivals to their utopian and moral exemplariness; and finally from exotic language to its intelligibility, the same dynamic unfolds. It is that of *utility* – or, rather, that of *production*, at least insofar as this voyage which increases the initial investment is, analogically, a productive labor, "a labor that produces capital."[21] From the moment of departure from Geneva a language sets out to find a world; at stake is a mission. Deprived of effectivity – without grounding – at the furthermost borders of the West (on the Island of Coligny, chapter 6), it finally appears as a language of pure conviction or subjectivity, a language that is incapable of defending its objective statements against deceptive use, leaving its speakers no recourse but to flee. This language is opposed, on the other side of things, to the world of total alterity, or of primitive nature. Here effectivity is at first uncanniness. But within the breadth of this alterity, analysis introduces a rift between exteriority (esthetics, etc.) and interiority (meaning that can be assimilated). It causes a slow reversion, beginning with the greatest exteriority (the general spectacle of nature, then the forests, etc.), and progresses toward the regions of greater interiority (sickness and death). It thus prepares primitive effectivity to become, by means of translation (chapter 20), *the world that is spoken by an initial language*. The point of departure was an over here (a "we") relativized by an elsewhere (a "they"), and a language deprived of "substance." This point of departure becomes a place for *truth*, since here the *discourse which comprehends the world* is in use. Such is the production for which the primitive is useful: it makes language move from the affirmation of a conviction into a position of knowledge. Yet if, from its point of departure, the language to be restored were theological, what is reinstated upon return is (in principle) either scientific or philosophical.

This position of knowledge is upheld by using the line between *over here and over there* in a way that also results from the transformation that is being performed. This line is used to distinguish between the ethnological subject and object. In Léry's text it is drawn through the difference between two literary forms, that which narrates tales of travel (chapters 1–6 and 21–22), and that which describes a natural and human landscape (chapters 7–19). . . .

On the first is written the chronicle of facts and deeds by the group or by Léry. These events are narrated in terms of *tense*: a *history* is composed with a chronology – very detailed – of actions undertaken or lived by a *subject*. On the second plane *objects* are set out in a space ruled not by localizations or geographical routes – these indications are very rare and always vague – but by a taxonomy of living beings, a systematic inventory of philosophical questions, etc.; in sum, the catalogue raisonné of a knowledge. The historical parts of the text value time "as an accomplice of our will"[22] and the articulation of *Western acting*. In relation to this subject who acts, *the other is extension*, where understanding delimits objects.

For Léry, the book is a "History" in which "seen things" are still attached to the observer's activities. He combines two discourses that will soon be separated from one another. One discourse is attached to science; as opposed to "natural history" (left to the philosopher) and to "divine history" (left to the theologian), it assumes its task, according to Jean Bodin, to be one of "explaining the actions of contemporary man living in society" and analyzing "the productions of the human will" insofar as it is *semper sui dissimilis*.[23] In the sixteenth century, at least for theologians, history takes for granted the autonomy of a political and juridical *subject* of actions (the prince, the nation, the "civil order") on the one hand, and on the other, of *fields* where dissimilitudes between various expressions of man's will (law, language, institutions, etc.) can be measured. In Léry's case the subject is momentarily an "exiled prince," a man lost between sky and earth, between a God who is disappearing and an earth that is yet to be discovered; the subject's itinerancy connects a language left vacant to the work needed to provide another effectivity for this language. Later there will be "ethnology," when the picture of the primitive world will have acquired a homogeneity independent of the displacements of actual journeys; in other words, when the space of "objective" representation will be distinguished from the observing judgment, and when it will have become futile to present the subject in the text of a constructive operation.

Eroticized Speech

If, in this *Histoire*, meaning moves in the direction of what writing produces (it constructs the meaning of the Tupi "experiment" – just as an experiment in physics is constructed), the savage is reciprocally associated with the seduction of speech. What travel literature really fabricates is the primitive as *a body of pleasure*. Facing the work of the West, that is, Western man's actions that manufacture time and reason, there exists in Léry's work a place for leisure and bliss, the Tupi world, indeed a feast for the eyes and ears. Such eroticizing of the other's body – of the primitive nudity and the primitive voice – goes hand in hand with the formation of an ethics of production. At the same time that it creates a profit, the voyage creates a lost paradise relative to a body-object, to an erotic body. This figure of the other has no doubt played a role in the modern Western *epistemè*, more crucial than that of the critical ideas circulated through Europe by travel literature.

As we have observed, the profit "brought back" through writing appears to delimit a "remainder" which, although it is unwritten, will also define the primitive. The trace of this remainder is pleasure: Léry's "ravishments," the Tupi festivals – sylvan psalms for the one, dances and country ballads for the others. *Excess* is the quality they share. But they are ephemeral and irrecoupable, unexploitable moments that will neither be regained nor redeemed. Something of Léry himself does not return from over there. These moments rend holes in the fabric of the traveler's time, just as the Tupis' festive organization was beyond all economy of history. Spending and loss designate *a present*; they form a series of "snippets," nearly a lapsus in Western discourse. These rips seem to come in the night to undo the utilitarian construct of the tale. It is the "un-heard" that purloins the text or, more precisely, is stolen from the thief; it is exactly what is *heard* but not understood, hence ravished from the body of productive work: speech without writing, the song of pure enunciation, the act of speaking without knowing – a pleasure in saying or in hearing.

At issue here are not the extraordinary deeds or experiences of which hagiographic or mystical discourses make use, each in their own way, to establish the status of a language of "truth." In the *Histoire*, marvels – the visible marks of alterity – are used not to posit other truths or an other discourse, but, on the contrary, to found a language upon its operative capacity for bringing this foreign exteriority back to "sameness." The "remainder" or "leftover" is more likely a fallout, an aftereffect of this operation, a waste that it produces through succeeding in doing what it does, but which comes as a by-product. This waste product of constructive thinking – its fallout and its repressed – will finally become the other.

That the figure of the other, eliminated from objective knowledge, returns in another form along the margins of this knowledge is what the eroticized voice makes manifest. But this displacement has to be situated in the totality which prepares for it, for it is relative to the general representation of the tale, which turns the primitive society into a festive body and an object of pleasure. A series of stable oppositions globally upholds the distinction between the primitive and the civilized man throughout the entire text. Thus:

PRIMITIVE	VS.	CIVILIZED
nudity	vs.	clothing
(festival) ornament	vs.	finery (stylishness)
hobby, leisure, festival	vs.	work (occupation)
unanimity, proximity, cohesion	vs.	division, distance
pleasure	vs.	ethics

Tupis are feathered (from birds to man, the primitive world modulates the combinations of plumed ornaments and pristine nudity). "Frolicking, drinking, and *liquoring* [*caouiner*] is almost their everyday occupation."[24] For Léry, who is an artisan, what are they really doing – or what are they producing? They spend their time celebrating, in pure expression that neither preserves anything nor accrues profit, in a present, eternal time *off*, a pure excess. In the Tupi mirror, the image of the worker appears thus inverted. But the operation which leaves nothing more to difference than an exteriority effectively transforms it into a festive theater. It produces *an estheticization of the primitive*.

A character from a spectacle, the primitive man represents an economy other than work. He reintroduces the other economy into the general picture. By way of hypothesis we can state that in an esthetic and erotic fashion, he is the return of what the economy of production had to repress in order to be founded as such. In the text he is situated in effect at the juncture of a prohibition and a pleasure. For example, the primitive festival is what surprises Léry (he is "ravished"), but equally it is what he surprises, penetrating the Tupi world by effraction. Here we witness a double transgression, in respect both to his law and to theirs. In the village where they are gathered, he feels "some fears" in hearing them sing in the distance: "All the same, after all these indistinct noises and howls turned to silence, the men paused for a moment (the women and children remained very coy all this time), and from then on we heard them singing and making their voices sound on such a marvelous note that, once I regained my confidence in hearing these softer and more gracious sounds, it hardly need be asked if I wanted to see them more intimately."[25]

After a moment of suspense, because of danger, he moves forward in spite of his translator (the interpreter who "had never dared to be seen among the natives during such a festival"): "Thus approaching the place where I heard this singing, as the natives' houses are either very long or are built in a round fashion and (as we might say of the pergolas in our gardens over here) are covered with grasses all the way from the ground to the roof: in order better to see *at my pleasure*, with my hands I fashioned *a little aperture* through the covering."[26] He finally penetrates this area of pleasure protected by a wall, as are the gardens of his native land.

There, pointing my finger at two Frenchmen who were looking at me – themselves having been emboldened by my example and having approached with neither obstacle nor difficulty – all three of us went into the house. Hence seeing that the primitives were not at all startled (as the interpreter had expected), but rather, on the contrary, held their rank and order in an admirable fashion, and continued to sing their songs, we withdrew quite gently to a corner where we contemplated them *at our delight*.[27]

The tale tells of the pleasure afforded by seeing through the "little aperture," as if it were a keyhole, before the men taking refuge in a corner where they can be fully delighted in the joy of this "sabbath" and these "Bacchanals."[28] Moreover, Léry says the pleasure of hearing the frightening and seductive noises from close proximity makes the temerity of approaching them quite irresistible. Such scenes of ethnological eroticism will repeat themselves in every travelogue. . . .

The "noises" that resound from the primitive men's festival, like the "inarticulate sounds" that indicate that of "men-women," have no intelligible content. These are "vocations" loosened from the orbits of meaning. An oblivion of precaution, losses of understanding, ravishments – that kind of language draws its power no longer from what it says, but from what it does or from what it is. Thus it cannot be either true or false. It is beyond or before this distinction. The "over there" comes back in this form. Like a cry, the act of enunciation inverts the statement and the whole organization of form, object, or referent. It is senseless. It partakes of orgasm.

Responding to this calling, the gesture of coming nearer reduces but never eliminates distance. It creates a situation of "inter-dict." The voice moves, in effect, in a space between the body and language, but only in a moment of passage from one to the other and as if *in* their weakest difference. Here there is neither the contact of body against body in the violence of love (or festivity), nor the contact of word against word (or text against text) in the semantic order proper to a linguistic linearity. The body, which is a thickening and an obfuscation of phonemes, is not yet the death of language. The articulation of signifiers is stirred up and effaced; there remains nonetheless the vocal modulation, almost lost but not absorbed in the tremors of the body; a strange interval where the voice emits a speech lacking "truths," and where proximity is a presence without possession. The moment evades the legalities and the disciplines of meaning as it evades the violence of bodies. It is the cerebral and illegal pleasure of being right there, where language, as it swoons, announces the coming of a coveted, feared violence which is held at a distance by the space through which one hears. This erotic "excess" plays upon the preservation of the very system that makes the body the observer's other. It takes for granted the legality that it transgresses. That "desire may be the underside of the law" is what the audible voice utters over and over again.[29]

Seen and/or Heard: The Eye and the Ear

The suppression of the native's effective uncanniness corresponds to the replacement of his exterior reality by a voice. This is a familiar displacement. The other returns in the form of "noises and howls," or "softer and more gracious sounds." These ghostly voices are blended into the spectacle to which the observing and scriptural operation has reduced the Tupi. The space in which the other is circumscribed composes an opera. But if the figures and voices, all remnants transformed from medieval festival, are associated coextensively with pleasure and together form a theater of the esthetic behind which the founding wills (preserved by writing) of operations and judgments on things themselves are upheld, the picture is made double by an opposition between the heard and the seen. In the fashion of those images in books that appear to move when looked at through a pair of spectacles whose lenses are tinted differently, one green, the other red, the native shifts within a single frame according to the way he is perceived, with the eye or with the ear.

We must add a third term to the two others in order to complete the series corresponding to the different ways in which the native can be perceived: *the mouth, the eye, the ear.* The Indian's "edibility" pertains to the *oral* instance, a matter of defining his "substance" and, from the standpoint of the Westerner, confronting his anthropophagia – an obsessive topic whose study has always been central and which establishes the status of future ethnology. Inscribed in the text, as we have seen, this relation of power is moreover what makes the text possible. Here the tale has at its command the object that has been prepared for it through this preliminary action. From now on the compositions of the eye and traversals of voice go along different tracks. For the audiovisual is split into two parts.

The eye is in the service of a "discovery of the world." It is the front line of an encyclopedic curiosity that during the sixteenth century "frenetically heaps up" materials in order to posit the "foundations of modern science." The rare, the bizarre, the unique – objects already collected through medieval interest – are apprehended in the fervor of an englobing ambition: "that nothing will remain foreign to man and that everything will be at his service."[30] There exists a "dizzying curiosity" that the development of all "curious" or occult sciences will be orchestrating. The frenzy of knowing and the pleasure of looking reach into the darkest regions and unfold the interiority of bodies as surfaces laid out before our eyes.

This conquering and orgiastic curiosity, so taken with unveiling hidden things, has its symbol in travel literature: the dressed, armed, knighted discoverer face-to-face with the nude Indian woman. A New World arises from the other side of the ocean with the appearance of the Tupi females, naked as Venus born in the midst of the sea in Botticelli's painting. To Léry's stupor, these Indian women wish "to remain nude forever": "With their two hands they douse water over their heads . . . wash themselves and plunge their whole bodies in every fountain and glassy river like reeds of sugar cane, and on one such day, even more than twelve times."[31]

Apparitions of this kind on the banks of glassy rivers have their nocturnal doubles on the Island of Coligny where the French make the Indian women, "prisoners of war," work like slaves: "As soon as night had fallen, from their bodies they secretly stripped the shirts and other tatters that had been given to them. For their pleasure, before going to bed they went about to stroll in the nude all about our island."[32]

The nakedness of these night women wild with pleasure is a very ambivalent vision. Their savagery fascinates and threatens, erupting from an unknown world where the women are, according to Léry, the only persons who work tirelessly and actively, and who, voracious souls that they are, are yet the first to practice anthropophagia. Thus the action of the woman who had been awarded, as a "husband" to look after, a prisoner doomed to be eaten:

> As soon as the prisoner would have been beaten to death, if he had a wife (as I have noted are awarded to a few of them), she placed herself beside his body as if she were mourning him a little. I note "a little," for truly following what is said to be the way of the crocodile – that is, once having killed a man, the animal weeps beside the body before devouring him – immediately after having expressed such sorrow and shed a few false tears over her dead husband, if possible she will be the first to partake of him. That being done, the other women, and most of the old ones (among whom many covet eating human flesh more than the young women, and constantly solicit all who have prisoners in order to have them dispatched in that way), appear with hot water that they have taken from the fire, rub and scald the dead body in such a way that once they have removed the first layer of skin, they blanch the body just as, over here, cooks prepare a suckling pig that will be roasted on a spit.[33] . . .

This native reenacts the Western phantasm of witches dancing and crying in the night, wild with pleasure and glutting themselves on children. The "sabbath" that Léry evokes is in continuity with what the Carnival of antiquity has since become, now progressively excluded from cities with the development of bourgeois towns, exiled into the countryside, the forests, and the night. This festive, prohibited, threatening world appears again exiled to the other side of the universe, at the outer limit of the conquerors' enterprise. And like the exorcist, his colleague from over here, the explorer-missionary assigns himself the task of expelling witches from the foreign land. But he does not succeed so well in localizing them on the stage of ethnological exorcism. The other returns: with the image of nudity, "an exorbitant presence";[34] with the phantasm of the *vagina dentata*, which looms in the representation of feminine voracity; or with the dancing eruption of forbidden pleasure. More basically, the native world, like the diabolical cosmos, becomes Woman. It is declined in the feminine gender.

But another image reminiscent of witches is superimposed over this one. In relation to "us," the Tupi are "stronger, sturdier and fuller, fitter, and immune to disease: and there is hardly ever a cripple, a one-eyed, deformed, or baleful soul among them. Furthermore, how many of them live to the age of one hundred or one hundred and twenty years . . . there are few in their old age who have either grey or white hair."

Akin to gods, "they all truly drink from the Fountain of Youth." "The little concern and worry they have for things of this world" harmonizes with a paradise in which "the woods, grasses, and fields are ever greening."[35] In the midst of this endless spring, one of the "doubly strange and truly marvelous things that I observed among these Brazilian women," notes Léry, was their nudity. It is not only innocent, "without any sign of shame or disgrace,"[36] but primal, prior to human history. In many images from the Renaissance, nudity has the value of a divine attribute. It is in effect the sign of theophanies, unveilings of divine Love that a series of paintings contrasts with the festivals depicting earthly Love, which is clothed and decorated. . . .

These women in whom the diabolical and the divine alternate, who oscillate between the over-there and the over-here of the human sphere ("This animal takes so much delight in this nudity," writes Léry),[37] are nevertheless an *object* placed in the space in which the looking itself becomes conspicuous. An image, and no longer an origin – even if the apparition keeps the uncanniness of what it is replacing. As in painting of the Renaissance, the unclothed Venus replaces the Mother of men, the mystery of Mary or Eve, and as in Venus the naked truth is what the *eye is allowed to see*, in the same way the Indian women indicate the secret that a knowledge transgresses and disenchants. Like the Indian woman's naked body, the body of the world becomes a surface offered to the inquisitions of curiosity. During Léry's time the same will hold true for the bodies of the city and of the diseased, which are transformed into *legible* spaces. Through the "little apertures" of successive "experiments" the traditional veil that covers the opacity of things is torn and lets the "world be recognized in ocular ways."[38]

Of the transgression that accompanies the birth of a science, Léry provides a summary with two elements: "a good foot, a good eye."[39] On another occasion he writes, "See and visit."[40] ... From this labor, the women naked, seen, and known designate the finished product metonymically. They indicate a new, scriptural relation with the world; they are the effect of a knowledge which "tramples" and travels over the earth visually in order to fabricate its representation. For Heidegger, "The fundamental event of the modern age is the conquest of the world as a picture."[41] But the apparition of women in the *Histoire* still retains the traces of risk and incertitude that in the sixteenth century go hand in hand with the inversion of the mother-earth into the earth-object. Through the women the tale therefore tells both of the beginning and of the temerity of a scientific *point of view.*

Whereas the object beheld can be written – made homogeneous with the linearities of stated meaning and constructed space – the *voice* can create an *aparté*, opening a breach in the text and restoring a contact of body to body. "Voice off." What comes from the mouth or goes into the ear can produce ravishment. Noises win over messages, and singing over speech. A break of direction and time follows the coming of a "song rally" among both the Indians and the "great forest": "Hearing the chant of an infinity of birds nightingaling through the woods where the sun was shining; seeing myself, I say, as a soul invited to praise God among all these things; moreover with a cheerful heart, I took to singing Psalm 104 out loud: Hark, hark my soul, I must tell you, etc."[42]

There is an analogical structure – resembling many others – in the vocation the "gracious" sounds brought to him through the Tupi festival, and the calling that came from the "birds nightingaling," inviting him to sing. The Indian shaman's vocation often comes of hearing a bird in the forest and gaining the will and the ability to sing. Almost immediately affected with a meaning (whether religious or not), the voice creates the rift of a lapse of memory and an ecstasy. Unlike in shamanism, Léry's calling has no social function; to the contrary, it crosses language, it makes of the senseless soul the void through which an irresistible poem comes to life. "I must tell you": it is still a received formula, but it marks already the locus where the rupture of an excess will expand in the urgency of a "saying," of an act of speech which will be neither docile to a spoken truth nor subject to a statement. The formula no longer goes in the direction of a will conserved in its purity through the writing whose powers Jean de Léry had praised. In a sensorial and symbolic sheath of the winds, of whispers, and of noises foreign to normal sounds is hidden a *birth through the ear.* It designates a violation (or a "ravishment") which cuts across social reason; it is acquiescence to *the other's voice*, "his master's voice" and the voice of the father, the voice of conscience; the voice where there is indication – originally represented in myth as the incestuous demand for sacrifice – of the "obscene and ferocious figure of the super-ego."[43]

This figure designates the insurmountable alterity from which the subject's desire is modeled. I evoke it here only to emphasize a crucial point. What is heard is not what is expected. What appears "doesn't resemble anything." Hence it cannot be truthful. "Meaning is truthful"; and inversely, "Truthfulness is nothing more than meaning"; finally, "Truthfulness has but one constant characteristic: it *means*, it has the sense of a *meaning*."[44] In this fashion what was heard *cannot be put into words*, unless indirectly, through a metaphorical disruption, breaking the linearity of discourse. It insinuates a rift, a jump, a confusion of genres. It is a *metabasis eis allo genos*, a "passage to another genre" as Aristotle puts it.

Generally speaking, voice itself would have a metaphorical – a delineraizing and altering – function to the degree that it cuts across the metonymical schema of sight. If, as "derision of the signifier," metaphor "is placed at the exact point where meaning is produced in non-meaning,"[45] it would be in effect the movement by which one signifier is replaced by its other: "one word for another," but also the very ruse that subverts the word. Through these metaphorical eruptions of fable and these lapses of meaning, voice, exiled to the distant shores of discourse, would flow back, and with it would come the murmurs and "noises" from which scriptural reproduction is distinguished. Thus an exteriority, with neither beginning nor truth, would return to visit discourse.

In respect to a single text, would it be too much to recognize already in the gap between what is seen and heard the distinction between two functionings of the savage world in relation to the language that deals with it? Either as an *object* of a discourse that constructs schemes and pictures, or as a *distortion*, a rapture, but also a calling of this discourse? These two functions are combined, for the vocal exteriority is also the stimulus and the precondition of its scriptural opposite. It is necessary – insofar as necessity, as Jacques Lacan says, is precisely "what never ceases to be written."[46] The savage becomes a senseless speech ravishing Western discourse, but one which, because of that very fact, generates a productive science of meaning and objects that endlessly writes. *The locus of the other* that this speech represents is hence doubly fabulous: first by virtue of a metaphorical rupture (*fari*, the act of speech not having a subject that can be named), and then by virtue of an object that can be understood (a fiction that can be translated into the terms of knowledge). A saying *arrests* what is said – it is the erasure of writing – and forces it to extend its production; it generates writing.

At the very least, Léry's story sketches the science of this fable, which essentially will become ethnology – or the manner of its intervention in history.

Notes

1 The Léry dossier is important. I will be quoting from Paul Gaffarel's edition of the *Histoire d'un Voyage* – the only exact and complete one – except for some details, checked based on the Geneva edition of 1580 (Paris, B. N.: 8° Oy 136 B), in two volumes (Paris: A. Lemerre, 1880). I will refer to this text hereafter with G. followed by the volume and page numbers. . . .

2 G. 2:71–72.

3 G. 2:72.

4 "Ce qu'on peut appeler religion entre les Sauvages Amériquains . . . " [What Can Be Called Religion Among the American Native Indian Savage . . .], G. 2:59–84.

5 "L'Isle espagnole": Hispaniola, which is to say Haiti.

6 F. Lopez de Gomara, *Historia de las Indias, con la conquista del Mexico y de la nueva España*, book I, ch. 34, p. 41.

7 This was an error, but of importance here is the coalescence between "primitive" and "oral" or "verbal."

8 G. 2:60–61.

9 G. 2:73.

10 Ibid.

11 G. 2:72–73.

12 G. 2:27 and G. 2:80. In both cases it is a question of psalm 104.

13 G. 1:34–35; my emphasis.

14 G. 1:157.

15 Alphone Dupront, "Espace et humanisme," *Bibliothèque d'Humanisme et Renaissance* (1946), 8:19.

16 G. 1:112.

17 G. 1:12. . . . This text, whose author probably is not Léry, is part of the *Histoire* from the first edition. It is one of the oldest documents concerning the Tupi language.

18 G. 1:91–96.

19 The effort of numerous French "spirituals" in the seventeenth century will consist specifically in going back from objective religious language that has since become ambivalent and deceptive to "intentions," to "motifs," to one's "heart," and to the "mystical" conditions of a good "style of speech."

20 See *Commentaires de M. Jean Calvin sur les cinq livres de Moyse* (Geneva, 1564), on Genesis (pp. 20–21), and Claude-Gilbert Dubois, *Mythe et langage au siezième siècle* (Bordeaux: Ducros, 1970), pp. 54–56.

21 Here we can refer to Marx's analyses in *Introduction to a Critique of Political Economy* and in his *Principles of a Critique of Political Economy*, in *The German Ideology* (New York: International Publishers, 1978).

22 Louis Dumont, *La Civilisation indienne et nous* (Paris: Armand Colin, 1964), p. 33.

23 Jean Bodin, *Methodus ad facilem historiarum cognitionem* (1566), cap. primum, in *Oeuvres philosophiques*, Mesnard, ed. (Paris: PUF, 1951), pp. 114–15.

24 G. 1:130. *Caouiner* means to celebrate by drinking *caouin*, a potion made from corn called *Avati*.
25 G. 2:69.
26 G. 2:69–70; my emphasis.
27 G. 2:70.
28 G. 2:71 and 73.
29 Jacques Lacan, "Kant avec Sade," in *Ecrits* (Paris: Seuil, 1966), p. 787. [My translation – Tr.]
30 Alphonse Dupront, "Espace et humanisme," *Bibliothèque d'Humanisme et Renaissance* (1946), 8:26–33, on "curiosity."
31 G. 1:136.
32 G. 1:137.
33 G. 2:47–48.
34 Emmanuel Levinas, *Totalité et infini* (The Hague: Nijhoff, 1971), p. 234, on "exhibitionistic nudity of an exorbitant presence," "lacking signification."
35 G. 1:123.
36 G. 1:136 and 123.
37 G. 1:136.
38 Marc Lescarbot, *L'Histoire de la Nouvelle France* (Paris, 1609), p. 542.
39 G. 1:138. [The French proverb is *bon pied, bon oeil*. – Tr.]
40 "For the entire year I lived in this country, I was so *curious* about *contemplating* the big and small that, being of the opinion that I always *see them before my eyes*, I would forever have the *idea and image* in my mind." But "to partake in the pleasures, you must *see and visit* them in their country" (G. 1:138; my emphasis). [The French locution is *voir et visiter*. – Tr.]
41 Martin Heidegger, "The Age of the World Picture," in *The Question Concerning Technology and Other Essays* (New York: Harper and Row, 1977), p. 134.
42 G. 2:80.
43 Jacques Lacan, *Ecrits* (Paris: Seuil, 1966), pp. 360, 619, 684.
44 Julia Kristeva, *Sèméiotikè: Recherches pour une sémanalyse* (Paris: Seuil, 1969), pp. 211–12. [My translation – Tr.]
45 Lacan, *Ecrits*, pp. 557 and 508.
46 Jacques Lacan, *Le Séminaire*, book 20, *Encore* (Paris: Seuil, 1975), p. 99.

Part IV

Other Languages: Speech and Writing

12 Introduction

Jeremy Ahearne

Speech and writing, reading and listening constitute a dominant organizing problematic across the plurality of Certeau's intellectual ventures. From *The Capture of Speech* (originally published in 1968) to *The Writing of History* (1975), from *Une politique de la langue* (1975) to *The Mystic Fable* (1982 – note the Latin *fari*, to speak) and *The Everyday Nature of Communication* (1983), these issues supply the reader of Certeau's oeuvre with a transversal thread to follow.[1] The three texts in this part provide an introduction to the central questions informing Certeau's approach to these issues.

Certeau's reflection on the relations between writing, reading, and orality shapes decisively the central theses of *The Practice of Everyday Life*. The book traces on the one hand how powerful strategies organized through writing prescribe or program the conditions of social life; and on the other hand how "ordinary" folk may subject such imposing prescriptions to oblique forms of reading, or how a murmur of common voices may at least put in question the implementation of such programs. "The Scriptural Economy," taken from *The Practice of Everyday Life*, maps out some of the key terms in this analysis. It also supplies a convenient historical frame through which to read the other two texts in this part. It is worth signaling here one key aspect of this frame, since it functions as a pivotal feature of Certeau's work. This concerns the gradual historical transition, over the early modern and modern period, from a traditional society informed by the centrality of Scripture to a society literally constituted and regulated by "modern" practices of writing. For Certeau, this represents a transition from one broad order or "economy" of writing to another.

"The World of the Vowel" gives a suggestive perspective on the conquering spread of these modern practices of writing. It is taken from the as yet untranslated book *Une politique de la langue. La Révolution française et les patois* (*A Politics of Language: the French Revolution and Patois*).[2] The book is based on an analysis of a particularly intriguing corpus of material. In Prairial, Year II of the French Revolution (May–June 1794), the Abbot Grégoire, an influential republican cleric and deputy, addressed a report to the National Convention entitled "On the necessity and means of annihilating patois and of universalizing the use of the French language." The title testifies eloquently enough to an enduring will to universalize a model of language prescribed in the capital and to remove the "variations" and manifold "resistance" to progress represented by the various oral patois of the regions. Certainly, there were good reasons why philanthropists in Paris might have wanted to do this. Certeau, however, is drawn to the material generated by Grégoire's preparation for this report. In August 1790, Grégoire sent out a questionnaire to various provincial contacts, concerning the vitality of different patois throughout France, as well as the possible means and effects of their elimination. It is in the responses of these correspondents that Certeau detects a revealing struggle. These local notables are torn, with varying degrees of intensity, between the lure of belonging to a Parisian enterprise (associated with writing, progress, Enlightenment, a certain social distinction) and the pull of their native patois (associated with orality, nature, passion). On one level, they are vehicles through which models of writing will colonize and remap social space. At another less manifest level, they come to play out an inner struggle between the increased discipline and distance imposed on the psyche by writing, and the "ease" and "intimacy" which orality will henceforth come to represent.

The final text in this part brings together concisely a number of elements that would receive more extensive treatment in *The Mystic Fable*. Again, we can read it as a detailed case study of the turbulence introduced by the transition from one broad order of writing and speech to another. Holy Scripture, by the sixteenth and seventeenth centuries, was ceasing to "speak" to believers as it had once done. The world itself was coming to seem opaque, unreadable: it too could no longer be perceived as the ongoing "utterance" of a divine speaker. In response to this progressive "disenchantment," a proliferation of instrumental writings were setting out to construct, as it were, islands of political and rational order among the "ruins" of an older order. There was, then, an abundance of language – but nothing, for the early modern mystics studied by Certeau, that might satisfy a nostalgia for words that could, in their terms, speak to the soul, that could touch and call forth the subject in his or her affective recesses. Hence their recourse to tactics of "utterance": how might they find or invent places where a certain "voice" within might speak? And how might this voice, felt not to be one's own, though more essential to oneself than one's own, be made to resonate effectively for others? Their writings were produced in the service of this "speech." Their writings are, of course, all that we now have, and Certeau is careful to stress the insuperable distance and "modesty" of ambition which such a "scriptural" relation imposes on his interpretation. They do nonetheless represent a peculiar kind of limit-case: they are writings at the frontier of orality, imagined as utterances rather than as repositories of knowledge.[3] Thus they lend themselves supremely well to Certeau's magisterial reading in terms of "voicing" (who is speaking to whom? how?) and modes of "utterance."

It will be helpful to give a preliminary gloss on certain key terms which figure in Certeau's analyses.

One should demarcate Certeau's use of the term "economy" somewhat from that industrial, financial, and political object studied by contemporary "economists." I shall propose three related levels of meaning which will enable us to explore more fully what Certeau understands by an "economy of writing." For each of these levels, one should bear in mind the wider sense of the term "economy," defined by the *Oxford English Dictionary* as "the organization, internal constitution, apportionment of functions, of any complex unity." First, at a general sociopolitical level, Certeau considers changing techniques of writing to be of fundamental importance in determining the ways in which a society orders, manages, and distributes its material and intellectual resources. These techniques comprise, for example, operations of recording, transcription, registering, stocking, and standardization, as well as the accumulation and dissemination of information. The resulting "economies" of writing work to organize and divide social space. The second level of meaning I wish to propose is a function of the first, but concerns more directly the individual subject. As Walter Ong and others have shown, the interiorization of different techniques of writing (chirography, typography, etc.) creates different intellectual "economies" in the human mind: they determine the way we "process" – generally unconsciously – the data of the world and turn them into knowledge, as well as the way we accumulate these data and imagine our own psychic resources.[4] Certeau's unfolding model of "economies of writing" likewise brings light to bear at this level. Third, in order to follow through the implications of Certeau's thought in this regard, one should bear in mind the psychoanalytic resonance of the term "economy" at an affective rather than strictly intellectual level. The individual subject must manage a certain amount of psychic "energy" and instinctual demands for "work"; the interiorization of a given "economy of writing" will have a bearing on the paths taken by this energy as it is invested, disinvested, and reinvested.[5]

The model of an "economy of writing" occupies a strategic place in Certeau's thought, though it is fair to say that its ramifications had not yet been fully explicated by the time of his death. However, if we bear in mind the three related levels of meaning I have suggested – sociopolitical, intellectual, psychoanalytic – then we will at least develop a sense of what is at issue. Last but not least, one should note that the "scriptural" of "scriptural economy" has a heavy connotation. It can refer in a neutral manner simply to "writing." But it can also signify specifically Christian Scripture – the regular frequentation and subsequent interiorization of which was of decisive importance in the formation of Certeau's own intellectual economy.

Certeau himself stresses that speech and writing should not be conceived in terms of a simple opposition between two distinct systems or processes. He assumes, as Derrida argues, that they are "relative" terms in a strong sense: their meaning for us is inconceivable outside the relation that generates it. Moreover, as processes of signification, they are caught up through and through in changing historical configurations – neither writing nor speech corresponds for us to what they were either for early modern mystics or for Grégoire's correspondents.

Nevertheless, this is not to say that certain formal constants do not emerge across the historical range of Certeau's objects of study. A sustained focus on marks of orality, one might say, foregrounds fundamental aspects of language which an investment in the apparent autonomy and self-sufficiency of texts has tended throughout the modern era to occult. One can see his recourse to a linguistics of "utterance" and a theory of "speech acts," as well as to much older categories of "rhetoric," as a means of sharpening this focus.[6] They direct attention not to the language deceptively "contained" in books, but to language as it is "incorporated" by human subjects who must "appropriate" it afresh each time they would speak (or write); less to language as a means of storing information than to language as a means for somebody to do something to somebody else, through a "performance" shaped by a particular form of interlocutory relation, tied to a particular place and time; not just to a language which clarifies ideas, but also to a language which calls forth emotion and passion. The implied line of demarcation here is not that between the intrinsic properties of "writing" and "orality." It corresponds instead to the frontier separating the conquests of those practices of writing constitutive of modernity, and what they progressively turned into their other.

For some time now, we ourselves have been caught in the turbulence of yet another transition from one broad economy of writing to another, based on the unprecedented achievements of new intellectual technology for processing, recoding, and transforming both writing and speech. Certeau's analyses provide us with reflective tools which can help us to measure these achievements against what an unqualified investment in the corresponding technology may condemn us, in our turn, to miss.

Notes

1 *Une politique de la langue. La Révolution française et les patois* has not yet been translated, though an extract appears in this part of the reader. It was co-authored with Dominique Julia and Jacques Revel, though Certeau himself wrote seven of the nine chapters. *The Everyday Nature of Communication* is available in the collection *The Capture of Speech and Other Political Writings*, pp. 89–139.

2 See note 1 above.

3 Compare Walter Ong's observations on the general transition from a manuscript to a print culture, in W. Ong, *Orality and Literacy: the Technologizing of the Word* (1982; London and New York: Routledge, 1988), pp. 125–6.

4 The level of meaning I have in mind here corresponds to what Ong calls a "noetic economy" (see *Orality and Literacy*, pp. 42, 98, 100, 152, etc.). See also Jack Goody, *The Domestication of the Savage Mind* (Cambridge: Cambridge University Press, 1977).

5 See, for example, J. Laplanche and J. B. Pontalis, *The Language of Psychoanalysis*, trans. D. Nicholson-Smith (1967; London: Karnac Books, 1988), pp. 127–30. The German word *Besetzung*, which becomes in English the technical term *cathexis*, becomes in French *investissement* (ibid., p. 62).

6 For "utterance" (*énonciation*), see, for example, the section "Man and Language" in Emile Benveniste, *Problems in General Linguistics*, trans. M. Meek (1966; Miami: University of Miami Press, 1971), pp. 193–246; for "speech acts," see J. L. Austin, *How to Do Things with Words* (Oxford: Clarendon Press, 1962).

13

The Scriptural Economy

"Only words that stride onward, passing from mouth to mouth, legends and songs, keep a people alive"

N. F. S. Grundtvig[1]

The dedication to Grundtvig, the Danish poet and prophet whose pathways all lead toward "the living word" (*det levende ord*), the Grail of orality, authorizes today, as the Muses did in earlier ages, a quest for lost and ghostly voices in our "scriptural" societies. I am trying to hear these fragile ways in which the body makes itself heard in the language, the multiple voices set aside by the triumphal *conquista* of the economy that has, since the beginning of the "modern age" (i.e., since the seventeenth or eighteenth century), given itself the name of writing. My subject is orality, but an orality that has been changed by three or four centuries of Western fashioning. We no longer believe, as Grundtvig (or Michelet) did, that, behind the doors of our cities, in the nearby distance of the countryside, there are vast poetic and "pagan" pastures where one can still hear songs, myths, and the spreading murmur of the *folkelighed*[2] (a Danish word that cannot be translated: it means "what belongs to the people"). These voices can no longer be heard except within the interior of the scriptural systems where they recur. They move about, like dancers, passing lightly through the field of the other.

The installation of the scriptural apparatus of modern "discipline," a process that is inseparable from the "reproduction" made possible by the development of printing, was accompanied by a double isolation from the "people" (in opposition to the "bourgeoisie") and from the "voice" (in opposition to the written). Hence the conviction that far, too far away from economic and administrative powers, "the People speaks." This speech is alternately seductive and dangerous, unique, lost (despite violent and brief outbreaks), constituted as the "Voice of the people" by its very repression, the object of nostalgic longing, observation and regulation, and above all of the immense campaign that has rearticulated it on writing by means of education. Today it is "recorded" in every imaginable way, normalized, audible everywhere, but only when it has been "cut" (as one "cuts a record"), and thus mediated by radio, television, or the phonograph record, and "cleaned up" by the techniques of diffusion. Where it does manage to infiltrate itself, the sound of the body often becomes an imitation of this part of itself that is produced and reproduced by the media – i.e., the copy of its own artifact.

It is thus useless to set off in quest of this voice that has been simultaneously colonized and mythified by recent Western history. There is, moreover, no such "pure" voice, because it is always determined by a system (whether social, familial, or other) and codified by a way of receiving it. Even if the voices of each group composed a sonic landscape – a site of sounds – that was easily recognizable, a dialect – an accent – can be discerned by the mark it leaves on a language, like a delicate perfume; even if a particular voice can be distinguished among countless others by the way it caresses or irritates the body that hears it, like a musical instrument played by an invisible hand, there is no unique unity among the sounds of presence that the enunciatory act gives a language in speaking it. Thus we must give up the fiction that collects all these sounds under the sign of a "Voice," of a "Culture" of its own – or of the great Other's. Rather, orality insinuates itself, like one of the threads of which it is composed, into the network – an endless tapestry – of a scriptural economy.

It is through an analysis of this economy, of its historical implantation, of its rules and the instruments of its success – a vast program for which I shall substitute a mere sketch – that one can best begin to locate the points at which voices slip into the great book of our law. I shall try simply to outline the historical configuration that has been created in our society by the disjunction between writing and orality, in order to indicate some of its effects and to point out a few current displacements that take the form of tasks to be accomplished.

I want to make clear at the outset that in referring to writing and orality I am not postulating two opposed terms whose contradiction could be transcended by a third, or whose hierarchization could be inverted. I am not interested in returning to one of the "metaphysical oppositions" (writing vs. orality, language vs. speech-acts, etc.) concerning which Jacques Derrida has very correctly said that "they have as their ultimate reference . . . the presence of a value or of a *meaning* (*sens*) that is supposed to be anterior to difference."[3] In the thought that asserts them, these antinomies postulate the principle of a unique origin (a founding archeology) or a final reconciliation (a teleological concept), and thus a discourse that is maintained by this referential unity. On the contrary, although this is not the place to explain my reasons in detail, I shall assume that plurality is originary; that difference is constitutive of its terms; and that language must continually conceal the structuring work of division beneath a symbolic order.

In the perspective of cultural anthropology, we must moreover not forget that:

(1) These "unities" (e.g., writing and orality) are the result of reciprocal distinctions within successive and interconnected historical configurations. For this reason, they cannot be isolated from these historical determinations or raised to the status of general categories.

(2) Since these distinctions present themselves as the relation between the delimination of a field (e.g., language) or a system (e.g., writing) and what it constitutes as its outside or its remainder (speech or orality), the two terms are not equivalent or comparable, either with respect to their coherence (the definition of one presupposes that the other remains undefined) or with respect to their operativity (the one that is productive, predominant, and articulated puts the other in a position of inertia, subjection, and opaque resistance). It is thus impossible to assume that they would function in homologous ways if only the signs were reversed. They are incommensurable; the difference between them is qualitative.

Writing: a "Modern" Mythical Practice

Scriptural practice has acquired a mythical value over the past four centuries by gradually reorganizing all the domains into which the Occidental ambition to compose its history, and thus to compose history itself, has been extended. I mean by "myth" a fragmented discourse which is articulated on the heterogeneous practices of a society and which also articulates them symbolically. In modern Western culture, it is no longer a discourse that plays this role, but rather a transport, in other words a practice: writing. The origin is no longer what is narrated, but rather the multiform and murmuring activity of producing a text and producing society as a text. "Progress" is scriptural in type. In very diverse ways, orality is defined by (or as) that from which a "legitimate" practice – whether in science, politics, or the classroom, etc. – must differentiate itself. The "oral" is that which does not contribute to progress; reciprocally, the "scriptural" is that which separates itself from the magical world of voices and tradition. A frontier (and a front) of Western culture is established by that separation. Thus one can read above the portals of modernity such inscriptions as "Here, to work is to write," or "Here only what is written is understood." Such is the internal law of that which has constituted itself as "Western."

What is writing, then? I designate as "writing" the concrete activity that consists in constructing, on its own, blank space (*un espace propre*) – the page – a text that has power over the exteriority from which it has first been isolated. At this elementary level, three elements are decisive.

First, the *blank page*: a space of its own delimits a place of production for the subject. It is a place where the ambiguities of the world have been exorcised. It assumes the withdrawal and the distance of a subject in relation to an area of activities. It is made available for a partial but regulatable operation. A separation divides the traditional cosmos, in which the subject remained possessed by the voices of the world. An autonomous surface is put before the eye of the subject who thus accords himself the field for an operation of his own. This is the Cartesian move of making a distinction that initiates, along with a *place* of writing, the mastery (and isolation) of a subject confronted by an *object*. In front of his blank page, every child is already put in the position of the industrialist, the urban planner, or the Cartesian philosopher – the position of having to manage a space that is his own and distinct from all others and in which he can exercise his own will.

Then *a text* is constructed in this place. Linguistic fragments or materials are treated (factory-processed, one might say) in this space according to methods that can be made explicit and in such a way as to produce an order. A series of articulated operations (gestural or mental) – that is what writing *literally* is – traces on the page the trajectories that sketch out words, sentences, and finally a system. In other terms, on the blank page, an itinerant, progressive, and regulated practice – a "walk" – composes the artefact of another "world" that is not received but rather made. The model of a productive reason is written on the nowhere of the paper. In many different forms, this text constructed on a proper space is the fundamental and generalized utopia of the modern West.

Thirdly, this construction is not merely a game. To be sure, in every society, play is a stage on which the formality of practices is represented, but the condition of its possibility is that it be detached from actual social practices. On the contrary, the "meaning" ("*sens*") of scriptural play, the production of a system, a space of formalization, refers to the reality from which it has been distinguished *in order to change it*. Its goal is social efficacity. It manipulates its exteriority. The writing laboratory has a "strategic" function: either an item of information received from tradition or from the outside is collected, classified, inserted into a system and thereby transformed, or the rules and models developed in this place (which is not governed by them) allow one to act on the environment and to transform it. The island of the page is a transitional place in which an industrial inversion is made: what comes in is something "received," what comes out is a "product." The things that go in are the indexes of a certain "passivity" of the subject with respect to a tradition; those that come out, the marks of his power of fabricating objects. The scriptural enterprise transforms or retains within itself what it receives from its outside and creates internally the instruments for an appropriation of the external space. It stocks up what it sifts out and gives itself the means to expand. Combining the power of *accumulating* the past and that of making the alterity of the universe *conform* to its models, it is capitalist and conquering. The scientific laboratory and industry (the latter correctly defined by Marx as the "book" of "science")[4] are governed by the same schema. And so is the modern city: it is a circumscribed space in which the will to collect and store up an external population and the will to make the countryside conform to urban models are realized.

Revolution itself, that "modern" idea, represents the scriptural project at the level of an entire society seeking to *constitute itself* as a blank page with respect to the past, to write itself by itself (that is, to produce itself as its own system) and to produce *a new history* (*refaire l'histoire*) on the model of what it fabricates (and this will be "progress"). It is necessary only for this ambition to multiply scriptural operations in economic, administrative, or political areas in order for the project to be realized. Today, by an inversion that indicates that a threshold in this development has been crossed, the scriptural system moves forward on its own; it is becoming self-moving and technocratic; it transforms the subjects that controlled it into operators of the writing machine that orders and uses them. A cybernetic society.

It is thus not without reason that for the past three centuries learning to write has been the very definition of entering into a capitalist and conquering society. Such is its fundamental initiatory *practice*. It was only when the disturbing effects of this prodigious growth of writing were noticed that we came to have doubts about modern children's education by means of a scriptural practice. . . .

In analyzing *writing*, this modern mythical practice, I do not in any way deny that we all owe it a great deal, especially those of us who are more or less intellectuals, and therefore the children, professionals, and beneficiaries of writing in a society which draws its strength from it. I would even point out two further aspects of writing that will make the dynamic of this strength clearer. They are connected with my subject because they concern the relation between writing and the loss of an identifying Spoken Word, on the one hand, and on the other, a new treatment of language by the speaking subject.

One could hardly overestimate the importance of the fundamental relationship between Western culture and what was for centuries considered writing par excellence, the Bible. If we simplify history (I am constructing an artifact, knowing that a model is judged not by the proofs advanced in support of it, but by the results it produces in interpretation), one can say that before the "modern" period, that is, until the sixteenth or seventeenth century, this writing (Holy Scripture) speaks. The sacred text is a voice, it teaches (the original sense of *documentum*), it is the advent of a "meaning" (*un "vouloir-dire"*) on the part of a God who expects the reader (in reality, the listener) to have a "desire to hear and understand" (*un "vouloir-entendre"*) on which access to truth depends. For reasons analyzed elsewhere, the modern age is formed by discovering little by little that this Spoken Word is no longer heard, that it has been altered by textual corruptions and the avatars of history. One can no longer hear it. "Truth" no longer depends on the attention of a receiver who assimilates himself to the great identifying message. It is the result of work – historical, critical, economic work. It depends on a "will to do" (*un vouloir-faire*). The voice that today we consider altered or extinguished is above all that great cosmological Spoken Word that we notice no longer reaches us: it does not cross the centuries separating us from it. There is a disappearance of the places established by a spoken word, a loss of the identities that people believed they received from a spoken word. A work of mourning. Henceforth, identity depends on the production, on the endless moving on (or detachment and cutting loose) that this loss makes necessary. Being is measured by doing.

Writing is progressively being overturned by this development. Another writing is imposed little by little in scientific, erudite or political forms: it is no longer something that speaks, but something made. Still linked to what is disappearing, indebted to what is moving away into the distance like a past but remains an origin, this new writing must be a practice, the endless production of anidentity that is supported only by an activity (*un faire*), a moving on (*une marche*) that always depends on something else to provide an available space for its advance, to the degree that the voice proper to Christian culture becomes its other and that the presence given in the signifier (the very definition of voice) is transformed into a past. The capitalist scriptural conquest is articulated on that loss and on the gigantic effort of "modern" societies to redefine themselves without that voice. The revolutionary task is only a major result of this effort. It is inseparable from the message that up to that point had always signified their end for other civilizations (none of them survived the death of its gods): "Our gods no longer speak to us – God is dead."

Along with writing, the relationship to language was also transformed. The two are always interdependent, but the relationship to language must also be stressed in order to be able to grasp the form in which the spoken word comes back with a new importance today. Another historical outline may be used to suggest it. The turning point that inaugurates the modern age is marked first, in the seventeenth century, by a devaluation of the statement (*l'énoncé*) and a concentration on the act enunciating it (*l'énonciation*). When the speaker's identity was certain ("God speaks in the world"), attention was directed toward the deciphering of his statements, the "mysteries" of the world. But when this certitude is disturbed along with the political and religious institutions that guaranteed it, the questioning is directed toward the possibility of finding substitutes for the unique speaker: who is going to speak? and to whom? The disappearance of the First Speaker creates the problem of communication, that is, of a language that has to be *made* and not just *heard and understood*. In the vast sea of a progressively disseminated language, a world without closure or anchorage (it becomes doubtful, eventually improbable, that a Unique subject will appropriate it and make it speak), every particular discourse attests to the absence of the position which the organization of a cosmos formerly assigned to the individual, and thus to the necessity of carving out a position by one's own way of treating a particular area of language. In other words, it is because he loses his position that the individual comes into being as a *subject*. The place a cosmological language formerly assigned to him and which was understood as a "vocation" and a placement in the order of the world, becomes a "nothing," a sort of void, which drives the subject to make himself the master of a space and to set himself up as a producer of writing.

Because of this isolation of the subject, language objectifies itself, becoming a field to be plowed rather than to be deciphered, a disorderly nature that has to be cultivated. The dominant ideology is transformed into a technique that has for its essential program to *make* language and no longer to *read* it. Language itself has to be fabricated, "written." For Condillac, constructing a science and constructing a language amount to the same task, just as for the revolutionaries of 1790 establishing the revolution required the creation and imposition of a national French language.[5] This implies a distancing of the living body (both traditional and individual) and thus also of everything which remains, among the people, linked to the earth, to the place, to orality or to non-verbal tasks. The mastery of language guarantees and isolates a new power, a "bourgeois" power, that of making history and fabricating languages. This power, which is essentially scriptural, challenges not only the privilege of "birth," that is, of the aristocracy, but also defines the code governing socioeconomic promotion and dominates, regulates, or selects according to its norms all those who do not possess this mastery of language. Writing becomes a principle of the social hierarchization that formerly privileged the middle class and now privileges the technocrat. It functions as the law of an educational system organized by the dominant class, which can make language (whether rhetorical or mathematical) its instrument of production. Here again Robinson Crusoe sheds light on the situation: the subject of writing is the master, and his man Friday is the worker, who has a tool other than language.

Inscriptions of the Law on the Body

This historical mutation does not transform the whole organization that structures a society through writing. It initiates another use, a new way of using that organization, a different functioning. It is therefore necessary to connect its establishment with the virtually immemorial effort to place the (social and/or individual) body under the law of writing. This effort preceded the historical form that writing has taken in modern times. It will outlive this particular form. It is interwoven into this form and determines it like a continuing archeology whose name and status we are unable to determine. What is at stake is the relation between the law and the body – a body is itself defined, delimited, and articulated by what writes it.

There is no law that is not inscribed on bodies. Every law has a hold on the body. The very idea of an individual that can be isolated from the group was established along with the necessity, in penal justice, of having a body that could be marked by punishment, and in matrimonial law, of having a body that could be marked with a price in transactions among collectivities. From birth to mourning after death, law "takes hold of" bodies in order to make them its text. Through all sorts of initiations (in rituals, at school, etc.), it transforms them into tables of the law, into living tableaux of rules and customs, into actors in the drama organized by a social order. And for Kant and Hegel, there is even no law unless there is capital punishment, that is, unless in extreme cases the body signifies by its destruction the absolute power of the letter and of the norm – a questionable assertion. However that may be, it remains that the law constantly writes itself on bodies. It engraves itself on parchments made from the skin of its subjects. It articulates them in a juridical corpus. It makes its book out of them. These writings carry out two complementary operations: through them, living beings are "packed into a text" (in the sense that products are canned or packed), transformed into signifiers of rules (a sort of "intextuation") and, on the other hand, the reason or *Logos* of a society "becomes flesh" (an incarnation).

A whole tradition tells the story: the skin of the servant is the parchment on which the master's hand writes. . . . Every power, including the power of law, is written first of all on the backs of its subjects. Knowledge does the same. Thus Western ethnological science is written on the space that the body of the other provides for it. One might thus assume that parchments and papers are put in place of our skins and that when, in good times, they have been substituted for it, they form a sort of protective coating around it. Books are only metaphors of the body. But in times of crisis, paper is no longer enough for the law, and it writes itself again on the bodies themselves. The printed text refers to what is printed on our body, brands it with a red-hot iron with the mark of the Name and of the

Law, and ultimately affects it with pain and/or pleasure so as to turn it into a symbol of the Other, something *said*, *called*, *named*. The printed setting represents the social and amorous experience of being the writing of something one cannot identify: "My body will be no more than the graph that you write on it, a signifier that no one but you can decipher. But who are you, Law who transforms the body into your sign?" The act of suffering oneself to be written by the group's law is oddly accompanied by a pleasure, that of being recognized (but one does not know by whom), of becoming an identifiable and legible word in a social language, of being changed into a fragment within an anonymous text, of being inscribed in a symbolic order that has neither owner nor author. Every printed text repeats this ambivalent experience of the body written by the law of the other. In some cases it is only a distant and worn metaphor of this experience that no longer works on incarnate writing: in others, it is a living memory of this experience aroused when reading touches the body at the points where the scars of the unknown text have long been imprinted.[6]

In order for the law to be written on bodies, an apparatus is required that can mediate the relation between the former and the latter. From the instruments of scarification, tatooing, and primitive initiation to those of penal justice, tools work on the body. Formerly the tool was a flint knife or a needle. Today the instruments range from the policeman's billyclub to handcuffs and the box reserved for the accused in the courtroom. These tools compose a series of objects whose purpose is to inscribe the force of the law on its subject, to tattoo him in order to make him demonstrate the rule, to produce a "copy" that makes the norm legible. This series forms an in-between; it borders on the law (it is the law that provides it with weapons) and it aims at the body (in order to mark it). An offensive frontier, it organizes social space: it separates the text and the body, but it also links them, by permitting the acts that will make the textual "fiction" of the model reproduced and realized by the body.

This panoply of instruments for writing can be isolated. It is put in reserve in storage places or in museums. It can be collected, before or after use. It remains there, ready for use or left over after use. This hardware can be used on bodies that are still far away, unknown, and can be re-employed in the service of laws other than those whose "application" they have made possible. These objects made for squeezing, holding up, cutting, opening, or confining bodies are displayed in fantastic showcases: shining iron and steel, dense wood, solid and abstract figures arranged like lines of print, instruments, curved or straight, constraining or bruising, that outline the movements of a suspended justice and already mold the parts of the body that are to be branded but are still absent. Between the laws that change and the living beings that pass by, the exhibits of these stable tools punctuate space, form networks and branching patterns, referring on one side to the symbolic corpus and on the other to carnal beings.

No matter how disseminated it may be (like the tiny bones of a skeleton), this panoply outlines in dotted line the relations between rules and bodies that are equally mobile. In detached pieces, it is the writing machine (*la machine à écrire*) of the Law – the mechanical system of a social articulation.

From One Body to Another

This machinery transforms individual bodies into a body politic. It makes these bodies produce the text of a law. Another machinery runs parallel to the first, but it is medical or surgical in type, and not juridical. It is in the service of an individual and not a collective "therapeutics." The body it treats is distinguished from the group. After having long been only a "member" – arm, leg, or head – of the social unit or a place in which cosmic forces or "spirits" intersected, it has slowly emerged as a whole, with its *own* illnesses, equilibriums, deviations and abnormalities. A long historical development stretching from the fifteenth to the eighteenth century was required before the individual body could be "isolated" in the way one "isolates" an element in chemistry or microphysics; before it could become the basic unit of a society, after a time of transition in which it appeared as a miniaturization of the political or celestial order – a "microcosm."[7] A change in sociocultural axioms occurs when the unit referred to gradually ceases to be the body politic in order to become the individual body, and when the reign of a *juridical* politics begins to be replaced by the reign of a *medical* politics, that of the representation, administration, and well-being of individuals.

Individualistic and medical classification delimits a "bodily" space of its own in which a combinative system of elements and the laws governing their exchanges can be analyzed. From the seventeenth to the eighteenth century, the idea of a physics of bodies in movement within this very body haunts medicine,[8] until this scientific model is replaced in the nineteenth century by one based on thermodynamics and chemistry. The dream of a mechanics of distinct elements correlated by propulsive forces, pressures, changes in equilibrium and maneuvers of every kind. The opera of the body: a complex machinery of pumps, pipes, filters, and levers, through which liquids circulate and organs respond to each other.[9] The identification of the pieces and their operations makes it possible to substitute artificial parts for those that wear out or have some defect, and even to construct automatons. The body can be repaired. It can be educated. It can even be fabricated. The panoply of orthopedic instruments and means of treatment expands in proportion to what one can henceforth take apart and repair, cut off, replace, take out, add, correct, or straighten. The network of these tools becomes more complex and extensive. It still remains in place today, in spite of the transition to a chemical medicine and to cybernetic models. Countless delicate steel instruments are adjusted to the innumerable possibilities that the mechanization of the body offers them.

But has their proliferation modified their functioning? In changing jobs, moving from the "application" of the law to that of surgical and orthopedic medicine, the apparatus of tools retains the function of marking or shaping bodies in the name of a law. If the *textual corpus* (scientific, ideological, and mythological) has been transformed, if bodies have become more autonomous with respect to the cosmos and take on the appearance of mechanical constructions, the task of relating the textual corpus to these bodies remains, no doubt emphasized by the multiplication of the possible means of treatment, but still defined by the writing of a text on bodies, by the incarnation of knowledge. The stability of the instrumentation. A strange functional inertia of these tools that are nevertheless active in cutting, gripping, shaping the flesh constantly offered up to a creation that makes it into bodies in a society.

A necessity (a destiny?) seems to be indicated by these steel and nickel objects: the necessity that introduces the law into the flesh by means of iron and that, in a culture, neither authorizes nor recognizes as bodies flesh that has not been written out by the tool. Even when, at the beginning of the 19th century, medical ideology is slowly inverted, as a therapeutics of extraction (the disorder is caused by an excess, something extra or superfluous – which has to be taken out of the body through bleeding, purging, etc.) is for the most part replaced by a therapeutics of addition (the disorder is a lack, a deficit, which has to be compensated for or replaced by drugs, supports, etc.), the apparatus of *instrumentality* continues to play its role of writing social knowledge's new text on the body in place of the old one. . . .

Mechanisms of Incarnation

From the seventeenth-century movement that attracted Puritan reformers as well as jurists to the medical theorists of the doctors who were known precisely as *Physicians*, a great ambition arose: to produce a new history on the basis of a text.[10] The myth of the Reformation is that the Scriptures provide, in the midst of a corrupt society and a decadent Church, a model one can use to reform both society and the Church. A return to the origins, not only those of the Christian West, but also that of the universe itself, to find a genesis giving a body to the *Logos* and incarnating it so that it can once again but in a different way "become flesh." The variants of this myth are found everywhere, in this time of Renascences, along with the utopian, philosophical, scientific, political or religious conviction that Reason must be able to establish or restore a world, and that it is no longer a matter of deciphering the secrets of an order or a hidden Author, but of *producing* an order so that it can be *written* on the body of an uncivilized or depraved society. Writing acquires the right to reclaim, subdue or educate history.[11] It becomes a power in the hands of a "bourgeoisie" that substitutes the instrumentality of the letter for the privilege of birth, a privilege linked to the hypothesis that the world as it is, is right. Writing becomes science and politics, with the assurance, soon transformed into an axiom of Enlightenment or revolution, that theory must transform nature by inscribing itself on it. It becomes violence, cutting its way through the irrationality of superstitious peoples or regions still under the spell of sorcery.

Printing represents this articulation of the text on the body through writing. The order thought (the text conceived) produces itself as a body (books) which repeats it, forming paving stones and paths, networks of rationality through the incoherence of the universe. The process later becomes more widespread and diverse. At this point it is only the metaphor of the more successfully rationalized techniques that later transform living beings themselves into the printed texts of an order. But the fundamental idea is already present in this logos that becomes books and in these books which the Age of Enlightenment thought would produce a new history. It could also have as its symbol the "constitutions" that proliferate in the eighteenth and nineteenth centuries: they give the text the status of being "applicable" to public or private bodies, of defining them and thus finding its effectiveness.

This grand mythical and reforming passion functions on the basis of three terms that characterize it: first, a model or "fiction," i.e., a *text*; second, the instruments of its application or writing, i.e., *tools*; third, the material which is both the support and the incarnation of the model, i.e., a nature, essentially a *flesh*, which writing changes into a *body*. Using tools to make a body conform to its definition in a social discourse: that is the movement. It sets out from a normative idea whose vehicles are a code of economic exchanges or the variants of this code presented by stories from the common legendary lore and by the new products of scientific knowledge. At the beginning, there is a fiction determined by a "symbolic" system that acts as a law, and thus a representation (a theater) or a fable (a "saying") of the body. That is to say, a body is postulated as the signifier (the term) in a *contract*. This discursive image is supposed to inform an *unknown* "reality" formerly designated as "flesh." The transition from the fiction to the unknown that will give it a body is made by means of instruments that multiply and diversify the unpredictable resistances of the body to be (con)formed. An indefinite fragmentation of the apparatus is necessary in order to adjust and apply each of these sayings and/or types of knowledge about the body, which work as unifying models, to the opaque carnal reality that gradually reveals its complex organization as it resists successive efforts to modify and control it. Between the tool and the flesh, there is thus an interaction that shows itself on the one hand by a change in the fiction (a correction of knowledge) and, on the other, by the cry, which shrieks an inarticulable pain and constitutes the unthought part of bodily difference.

As the products of a craft, and later of an industry, these tools multiply around the images which they serve and which are the empty centers, the pure signifiers of social communication, "non-entities"; the tools represent in concrete form the tortuous knowledge, sharp sinuosities, perforating ruses, and incisive detours that penetration into the labyrinthine body requires and produces. In that way, they become the metallic vocabulary of the knowledge that they bring back from these expeditions. They are the figures of an experimental knowledge won through the pain of the bodies that change themselves into engravings and maps of these conquests. The flesh that has been cut out or added to, putrefied or put back together tells the story of the high deeds of all these tools, these incorruptible heroes. Over the span of a life or a fashion, they illustrate the actions of a tool. They are its human, ambulatory, and transitory stories. . . .

The Machinery of Representation

Two main operations characterize their activities. The first seeks primarily to *remove* something excessive, diseased, or unesthetic from the body, or else to *add* to the body what it lacks. Instruments are thus distinguished by the action they perform: cutting, tearing out, extracting, removing, etc., or else inserting, installing, attaching, covering up, assembling, sewing together, articulating, etc. – without mentioning those substituted for missing or deteriorated organs, such as heart valves and regulators, prosthetic joints, pins implanted in the femur, artificial irises, substitute ear bones, etc.

From the inside or the outside, they correct an excess or a lack, but in relationship to what? As in the case of removing the hair from one's legs or putting mascara on one's eyelashes, having one's hair cut or having hair reimplanted, this activity of extracting or adding on is carried out by reference to *a code*. It keeps bodies within the limits set by a norm. In this respect, clothes themselves can be regarded as instruments through which a social law maintains its hold on bodies and its members, regulates them and exercises them through changes in fashion as well as through military maneuvers. . . . The foods that are selected by traditions and sold in the markets of a society also shape bodies at the same time that they nourish them; they impose on bodies a form and a muscle tone that function like an identity card. Glasses, cigarettes, shoes, etc., reshape the physical "portrait" in their own ways. Is there a limit to the machinery by which a society represents itself in living beings and makes them its representations? Where does the disciplinary apparatus[12] end that displaces and corrects, adds or removes things from these bodies, malleable under the instrumentation of so many laws? To tell the truth, they become bodies only by conforming to these codes. Where and when is there ever anything bodily that is not written, remade, cultured, identified by the different tools which are part of a social symbolic code? Perhaps at the extreme limit of these tireless inscriptions, or perforating them with lapses, there remains only the cry: it escapes, it escapes them....

This first operation of removing or adding is thus only the corollary of another, more general operation, which consists in *making the body tell the code*. As we have seen, this work "realizes" a social language, gives it its effectiveness. This is an immense task of "machining" bodies to make them spell out an order.[13] Economic individualism is no less effective than totalitarianism in carrying out this articulation of the law by means of bodies. It just proceeds by different methods. Instead of crushing groups in order to mark them with the unique brand of a power, it atomizes them first and multiplies the constraining networks of exchange that shape individual units in conformity with the rules (or "fashions") of socioeconomic and cultural contracts. In both cases, one may wonder why it works. What desire or what need leads us to make our bodies the emblems of an identifying law? The hypotheses that answer this question show in another way the power of the links that tools forge between our infantile "natures" and the forms of social discourse.

The *credibility* of a discourse is what first makes believers act in accord with it. It produces practitioners. To make people believe is to make them act. But by a curious circularity, the ability to make people act – to write and to machine bodies – is precisely what makes people believe. Because the law is already applied with and on bodies, "incarnated" in physical practices, it can accredit itself and make people believe that it speaks in the name of the "real." It makes itself believable by saying: "This text has been dictated for you by Reality itself." People believe what they assume to be real, but this "reality" is assigned to a discourse by a belief that gives it a body inscribed by the law. The law requires an accumulation of corporeal capital in advance in order to make itself believed and practiced. It is thus inscribed because of what has already been inscribed: the witnesses, martyrs, or examples that make it credible to others. It imposes itself in this way on the subject of the law: "The ancients practiced it," or "Others have believed it and done it," or "You yourself already bear my signature on your body."

In other words, *normative* discourse "operates" only if it has already become a *story*, a text articulated on something real and speaking in its name, i.e., a law made into a story and historicized (*une loi historiée et historicisée*), recounted by bodies. Its being made into a story is the presupposition of its producing further stories and thereby making itself believed. And the tool ensures precisely the passage from discourse to the story through the interventions that incarnate the law by making bodies conform to it and thus make it appear to be recited by reality itself. From initiation ceremonies to tortures, every social orthodoxy makes use of instruments to give itself the form of a story and to produce the credibility attached to a discourse articulated by bodies.

Another dynamics completes the first and interlaces with it, the dynamics that leads living beings to become signs, to find in a discourse the means of transforming themselves into a unit of meaning, into an identity. To finally pass from this opaque and dispersed flesh, from this exorbitant and troubled life, to the limpidness of a *word*, to become a fragment of language, a single name, that can be read and quoted by others: this passion moves the ascetic armed with instruments for mortifying his flesh, or the philosopher who does the same to language, "recklessly," as Hegel put it. But it does not matter who the person is that is moved by this passion, eager to finally have or be a name, to be called, to be transformed into a *saying* (*dit*), even at the price of his life. The intextuation of the body corresponds to the incarnation of the law; it supports it, it even seems to establish it, and in any case it serves it. For the law plays on it: "Give me your body and I will give you meaning, I will make you a name and a word in my discourse." The two problematics maintain each other, and perhaps the law would have no power if it were not able to support itself on the obscure desire to exchange one's flesh for a glorious body, to be written, even if it means dying, and to be transformed into a recognized word. Here again, the only force opposing this passion to be a sign is the cry, a deviation or an ecstasy, a revolt or flight of that which, within the body, escapes the law of the named.

Perhaps all experience that is not a cry of pleasure or pain is recuperated by the institution. All experience that is not displaced or undone by this ecstasy is captured by "the love of the censor,"[14] collected and utilized by the discourse of the law. It is channeled and instrumented. It is written by the social system. Thus we must seek in the area of these cries what is not "remade" by the order of scriptural instrumentality.

"Celibate Machines"

To the establishment of a new scriptural practice, marked on the sky of the eighteenth century by the laborious insularity of Robinson Crusoe, we can now compare its generalization as represented by the fantastic machines whose images emerge around 1910–1914 in the works of Alfred Jarry (*Le Surmâle*,

1902; *Le Docteur Faustroll*, 1911), Raymond Roussel (*Impressions d'Afrique*, 1910; *Locus Solùs*, 1914), Marcel Duchamp (*Le Grand Verre: La mariée mise à nu par ses célibataires, même*, 1911–1925), Franz Kafka (*Die Strafkolonie*, 1914), etc.[15] These are the myths of an incarceration within the operations of a writing that constantly makes a machine of itself and never encounters anything but itself. There are no ways out except through fictions, painted windows, mirror-panes. No rips or rents other than written ones. These are comedies about people stripped naked and tortured, "automatic" stories about defoliations of meaning, theatrical ravagings of disintegrating faces. These productions are fantastic not in the indefiniteness of the reality that they make appear at the frontiers of language, *but in the relationship between the mechanisms that produce simulacra and the absence of anything else.* These novelistic or iconic fictions tell us that there is no entry or exit for writing, but only the endless play of its fabrications. If every event is an entry or an exit, then the myth tells the nowhere (*non-lieu*) of the event or of an event that does not take place (*qui n'a pas lieu*). The machine producing language is wiped clean of history, isolated from the obscenities of reality, absolute and without relation to the "celibate" other.

This is a "theoretical fiction," to borrow an expression from Freud, who sketched out in 1900 a sort of celibate machine that manufactured dreams – going forward during the day, and backward at night.[16] Such a fiction is written in a language without homeland and without body, with the whole repertory of a fatal exile or an impossible exodus. The solitary machine makes the Eros of the dead function, but this ritual of mourning (there is no other) is a comedy played within the tomb of the departed (*l'absent(e)*). There are no dead in the field of graphic and linguistic operations. The "torture" of the separation or putting to death of the body remains literary. Wounding, torturing, killing, it develops within the confines of the page. Celibacy is scriptural. Characters transformed into cylinders, drums, ruins, and springs put together and painted on the "glass" where their perspective representation mixes with the objects located behind (the glass is a window) and in front (the glass is a mirror) represent not only, in the painting-glass-mirror constituted by Duchamp's *La Mariée mise à nu* hanging in the library of Miss Dreier's country house,[17] the dissemination of the subject of painting, but the lure of communication that the transparency of the pane of glass promises. A laughable tragedy of language: being mixed together by an optical effect, these elements are neither coherent nor conjoined. Spectators that happen to look at them associate but do not articulate them. Stripped naked (*mise à nu*) by a mechanically organized deterioration, the bride (*la mariée*) is never married to a reality of a meaning.

To be sure, only an erotic drive, a desire for the absent other, is capable of putting the productive apparatus in motion, but it aims at something that will never be *there* and that makes the voyeur's gaze obsessive when he is gripped by his double reflected on the mirror, moving in the middle of the things offered/refused in the windowpane-mirror. In the reflected image, the spectator sees himself dispersed among what cannot be grasped (the painted images of things). The graph painted on Marcel Duchamp's glass figures the trompe-l'oeil image of a stripping-naked by and for voyeur-spectators who will always remain celibate. The vision indicates and frustrates the absent communication. Other celibate machines function in the same way, identifying sex with its mechanical image and sexuality with an optical illusion. Thus, in Alfred Jarry's *Les Jours et les nuits*, an inscription hangs over the glass wall that encircles the island of the nereid, a woman surrounded by glass in the midst of a military décor; the inscription speaks of "the man who passionately embraces his Double through the glass": "The glass takes on life at one point and becomes a sexual organ, and being and image make love through the wall."[18] On this "island of lubricious glass," machines produce a giant windowpane which shapes itself into whatever sexual organ is required at whatever point it happens to be touched. In the same way, in *Les Dix mille milles*, a pane of glass separates the woman shut up in a railway car from the males on bicycles who race against the train.

These tragi-comedies, fragments of myths, recognize the impossibility of communication, of which language is both the promise and the phantasm. A poetics, once again, has preceded theory. Since then, reflection has moved in that direction. In Lacan's work, the category of "*lalangue*" connects speaking with the impossibility of conjoining ("there is no sexual relationship"); it connects the very possibility of language to the impossibility of the communication it is supposed to produce. A linguist adds: "Just as the philosopher's language is the place of the impossibility of mutual knowledge, *lalangue* is the place of the impossibility of the sexual relationship."[19] Among desiring subjects, there remains only the possibility of loving the language that substitutes itself for their communication. And that is indeed a model of language furnished by the machine, which is made of differentiated and combined parts (like every enunciation) and develops, through the interplay of its mechanisms, the logic of a celibate narcissism.

"It is a matter of *exhausting* the meaning of words, of playing with them until one has done violence to their most secret attributes, and pronounced at last the total divorce between the term and the expressive content that we usually give it."[20] Henceforth, the important thing is neither *what is said* (a content), nor the *saying* itself (an act), but rather the *transformation*, and the invention of still unsuspected mechanisms that will allow us to multiply the transformations.[21]

The time is thus over in which the "real" appeared to come into the text to be manufactured and exported. The time is over when writing seemed to make love with the violence of things and place them in a rational order. Verism was merely apparent, the theater of verisimilitude. After Zola, came Jarry, Roussel, Duchamp, *et al.*, that is, the "theoretical fictions" of the impossible other and of a writing given over to its own mechanisms or to its solitary erections. The text mimes its own death and makes it ridiculous. No one any longer respects this writing, this exquisite cadaver. It is no more than the illusory sacrament of the real, a space of laughter at the expense of yesterday's axioms. In it is deployed the ironic and meticulous work of mourning.

The key parts of the writing triumphant in Defoe's work are compromised: the blank page is only a pane of glass to which representation is attracted by what it excluded; the written text, closed on itself, loses the referent that authorized it; expansionist utility is inverted into the "sterile gratuitousness" of a celibate Don Juan or of a "widower" having no generation other than a symbolizing one, a man without woman and without nature, without an other. Writing has become an "inscription island," a *locus solus*, a "penal colony" – a laborious dream, occupied by this "impossible" to which or about which it thinks it "speaks."

It is through this stripping naked of the modern myth of writing that the celibate machine becomes, in a derisive mode, blasphemy. It attacks the Occidental ambition to articulate the reality of things on a text and to reform it. It takes away the *appearance* of being (i.e., of content, of meaning) that was the sacred secret of the Bible, transformed by four centuries of bourgeois writing into the power of the letter and the numeral. Perhaps this anti-myth is still ahead of our history, even if it is repeatedly confirmed by the erosion of scientific certainties, the massive "boredom" of people at school, or the progressive metaphorization of administrative discourses. Or perhaps it has simply been placed "alongside" a galloping technocratization, like a suggestive paradox, a little white pebble.

Notes

1 Translated from Grundtvig, *Budstikke i Høinorden* (1864), 31 X 527; text quoted by Erica Simon, *Réveil national et culture populaire en Scandinavie. La genèse de la Højskole nordique, 1844–1878* (Copenhagen, 1960), 59.

2 Simon, *Réveil national et culture populaire*, 54–59.

3 J. Derrida, *Positions* (Paris: Minuit, 1972), 41; *Positions*, trans. A. Bass (Chicago: University of Chicago Press, 1981).

4 Karl Marx, "1844 Manuscripts," in Marx and Engels, *Werke* (Berlin: Dietz, 1961), I, 542–544.

5 See M. de Certeau et al., *Une Politique de la langue* (Paris: Gallimard, 1975).

6 See Lucette Finas, *La Crue* (Paris: Gallimard, 1972), preface, on the reading that is an inscription of the text on the body.

7 On this history, A. Macfarlane, *The Origins of English Individualism* (Oxford: Blackwell, 1978); and earlier, C. B. Macpherson, *The Political Theory of Possessive Individualism. Hobbes to Locke* (Oxford: Oxford University Press, 1964).

8 See especially Charles Webster, *The Great Instauration. Science, Medicine and Reform, 1626–1660* (New York: Holmes & Meier, 1975), 246–323.

9 Jean-Pierre Peter, "Le Corps du délit," *Nouvelle revue de psychanalyse*, No. 3 (1971), 71–108: the three successive figures of the body distinguished by Peter could be related to the three paradigms from physics of which they are variants and applications, namely, the physics of impacts (seventeenth century), the physics of action at a distance (eighteenth century) and thermodynamics (nineteenth century).

10 Webster, *The Great Instauration*, especially his "Conclusions," 484–520.

11 On this new power of writing over history, see M. de Certeau, *L'Ecriture de l'histoire*, 2nd ed. (Paris: Gallimard, 1978).

12 A reference to Michel Foucault, *Surveiller et punir* (Paris: Gallimard, 1975), *Discipline and Punish*, trans. A. Sheridan (New York: Pantheon, 1977), whose analyses open a vast field to be explored and inventoried, extending even beyond the panoptical mechanisms.

13 It was one of Durkheim's ideas that the social code inscribes itself on an individual nature and so mutilates it. The first form of writing would thus be *mutilation*, which gives it an emblematic value. See Emile Durkheim, *Les Formes elémentaires de la vie religieuse* (Paris: PUF, 1968); *The Elementary Forms of the Religious Life*, trans. J. W. Swain (New York: Free Press, 1972).

14 See Pierre Legendre, *L'Amour du censeur* (Paris: Seuil, 1974).

15 Michel Carrouges, *Les Machines célibataires* (Arcanes, 1954) and the revised and augmented edition (1975); and *Junggesellen Maschinen/Les Machines célibataires*, ed. Jean Clair and Harold Szeemann (Venice: Alfieri, 1975).

16 See *The Interpretation of Dreams* (*Die Traumdeutung*), Chapter VII, on the "psychischen Apparat." The expression "theoretische Fiktion" refers particularly to "the fiction of a primitive psychical apparatus."

17 See Katherine S. Dreier and Matta Echaurren, "Duchamp's Glass 'La Mariée mise à nu par ses célibataires, même'. An Analytical Reflection" (1944), in *Selected Publications, III: Monographs and Brochure* (New York: Arno Press, 1972).

18 Alfred Jarry, *Les Jours et les nuits* (1897).

19 Jean-Claude Milner, *L'Amour de la langue* (Paris: Seuil, 1978), 98–112.

20 Michel Sanouillet, in Marcel Duchamp, *Duchamp du signe, Ecrits*, ed. M. Sanouillet (Paris: Flammarion, 1975), 16.

21 See Jean-François Lyotard, *Les Transformateurs Duchamp* (Paris: Galilée, 1977), 33–40.

14
The World of the Vowel

Pronunciation

It is when it addresses pronunciation (question 14) that the questionnaire touches upon the sensitive area.[1] Patois *varies*. It escapes from the regular and fixed forms of the national language [*la "langue"*].[2] It is the mobile voice through which the stable features of writing vanish, as "pronunciation is always changing and spelling always remains the same." Jean-Jacques Rousseau had noted this, adding that, through the insinuation of the voice, "language [*la langue*] changes by degrees in spirit and in character."[3] Admittedly, he meant to defend "the living voice,"[4] its natural *intimacy* and *intimation*, prior to all discourse;[5] he wanted to promote an orally based form of teaching. Yet he nevertheless noted the fact which the correspondents of Grégoire take as their point of departure: "Prosody and accent get progressively lost and disfigured as one gets further from the capital."[6] This is how patois appears in the gregorian corpus: it is the vocal subversion of scriptural norms, but also the warmth of origins, the richness of affections – "one conveys one's feelings when one speaks, and one's ideas when one writes."[7] An ambivalent aura envelops patois, which is thought of as feminine, like the voice and the vowel. It is both the witch and the siren.

Pronunciation also introduces with respect to local dialects the "agreeable" or the "disagreeable," the "soft" and the "hard." It opens within linguistic analysis a poem of "charm," serving as a counterpoint to the hostility aroused by its ungraspable mobility. Around a patois described as "very pleasing to the ear" (Andriès), there develops a problematic of auditory pleasure (see Gers 2,

G. 113–14), which is, however, inseparable from a fear of losing the order edified at a high price by the Enlightenment. In truth, the ear of the correspondents, sensitive to the "accents" of idioms, is not simply striving like the Abbot Grégoire to pinpoint the "sound of the voice";[8] their perception of this voice is tactile, they feel its "softness" or "harshness." The ear is the delicate skin which sound caresses or irritates: an erogeneous zone exacerbated, one might say, by the prohibitions banishing coarseness, vulgarity, and finally passion from the national language and accepted moral codes. A practice of asceticism constructs the code of Parisian and revolutionary culture which is imposed on local activists. But, repelled by the (written) law, the eroticism which has been exiled from writing seems to return in this ear touched by the voices emerging from valleys and woods. "The first languages were sung and impassioned" (Rousseau). Metamorphosed in our corpus into acoustic forms and disguised as pronunciation, the sorceresses of times past still come to haunt the linguistic landscape of the eighteenth century.

"The pronunciation is intoxicating," says Lequinio (Britanny, G. 287). Through it, a world of feelings awakens in the text. According to the categories of Jean-Jacques, it comes under "expression," which he opposed to the "precision" of ideas. But here the acoustic universe of what is "agreeable" and "disagreeable," identified with patois, is established *beside* that of the "thoughts articulated" by "language" [*la "langue"*]. The distinction formerly divided language; it henceforth divides space. In the representation given here, a region of vocalization is isolated. The act of utterance [*l'énonciation*] is extraposed in relation to what is said [*les énoncés*], and forms a separate site, connoted by the proliferation of feelings. Patois, a realm of voices, is the locus of affectivity. "Soft, agreeable, sonorous, expressive, abundant, solemn and proper for the expression of the great movements of the soul": a hundred passages in our corpus repeat this description by Aubry (Bouillon 2, G. 292), which gathers together in the same place the impoverishment of meaning (semantic redundancy), the multiplication of feeling (impressions), and the mobility of pleasures or desires ("movements"). For others, patois is "hissing" or "guttural," "harsh" and "disagreeable": for them, the same register of perception is in play, but in the mode of displeasure.

This patois, then, is heard and not read, pronounced rather than articulated; it is acoustic matter caught up in an aesthetics. This introductory picture can be completed by an element which is in itself the object of a question: "Do words end more commonly with vowels or consonants?"[9] This strange preoccupation attributes a particular importance to word-endings. It receives a twofold response: on the one hand, in three-quarters of cases, the word-ending is characterized by a *vowel*;[10] on the other hand, it is for the most part *not mute*, and one can find *a*, *o*, and *i* at the end of words which in French finish in a mute *e*. The first feature is attributed to an "easier" pronunciation (G. 233); the second distinguishes "dialect" from the "national language" (G. 14), perhaps because "the mute *e* is said to be a refinement introduced by peoples grown soft" (Saint-Claude, G. 201). These two marks (signifiers directly linked to a lived reality) are the sign of words still opened by (and to) the voice, but a voice close to the primal *a* and the originary cry, and which the consonantal "refinement" of culture has not reduced to the function of a "mute."

The Vowel, or Difference

However, this is not the essential issue in the responses. Instead, they tell the story of a struggle. For pronunciation introduces variation into the national language; that is to say, the "frightening spectre of the multitude of tongues [*langues*]," as Court de Gébelin said. This unceasing phonetic movement threatens the urban order of writing; it proliferates around this order like a virgin forest; it insinuates its way into the forum through the word as it is actually spoken, with the "imperceptible variations" which alter, "disfigure," and "undo" a language unaware of what is happening to it. The defense of the national language had inspired the advice which the most lucid observers – Jean-Jacques Rousseau[11] and many others, such as Jérémie-Jacques Oberlin – addressed to grammarians, urging them to give up the obsession which fixed their attention on writing and to endeavor to "determine the nuances and the principles of the nuances which make language vary from one village to the next."[12] It was vain advice. "The more the art of writing is perfected, the more that of speaking is neglected."[13] This disparity of treatment pushes orality in the direction of an alterity becoming gradually uncanny. By retreating back on to the written word (spelling, etymology, syntax), the analysis of language sets up the region which it abandons as a space of disorder. In times past, the woods would fill with witches' sabbaths for the population then gathering in the municipalities and towns. In the same way, an enchantment of voices accompanies here the rational "disenchantment" for which the written word is both the object and the means. The introduction of vocalization into a linguistic imagination seems to be the converse of what the written word is becoming for science.

For patois splits, divided in its entirety between what can be written down and what remains vocal: where the former applies, it is the same; where the latter applies, it is the other. "The writing of this patois is the same as for French, while the accentuation varies" (Mont-de-Marsan, G. 150). The "basic core," signifying "the same," is opposed to what "varies."[14] "The essential difference . . . comes from the pronunciation" (Carcassonne, G. 14). In this scheme, difference is reduced to a mere surface effect in relation to the stable identity designated by the "basic core." It is also put down to the vowel. It is through the vowel that mobility insinuates its way into the permanence of consonants. The "variations" are the doing of this heretic. "The substitution of one vowel for another" and "the omission or addition of a vowel" (Mâconnais, G. 221; Lyons, B.N. 29; etc.): such are the processes which explain "difference," illustrated by numerous examples. Added to these (see, for example, Mâconnais, G. 221) is "the transposition of the letters which compose the word," but no examples are given, as though a received generality were being noted which remains nevertheless inert in the analysis. What is striking here is that the same explanation is deemed valid at one moment for the changes in the same patois between one village and another,[15] and at the next moment for the difference between patois and the national language.[16] Even if, in the case of Flemish or Breton, the responses defend the autonomy of patois, they themselves are also based on these two convictions: *patois represents variation*, and *its nature is designated by the vowel.*

For the vowel marks in language *the singularity of the soil and the body.* It indicates there the site of utterance – and first and foremost of "home." "One recognizes, by the manner of their pronunciation ... people who live in the same place" (Bresse, B.N. 51; cf. Limoges, G. 166; etc.). The mountain and the valley, the bocage and the forest have their own accents. Ultimately, each "parish" has its own. The air, the climate, the altitude, the distance from other villages and towns are subject to an acoustic recording, which can be vivacious or drawling, high or low-pitched, hard or soft.[17] In this universe of vowels, there is a ubiquitous murmur of particularities. A vocal realm of local idiom [*idiotisme*] is opposed to the consonantal realm of "ideas," which is that of the universal, of the national language, and of the Enlightenment. But what can be heard in patois are also the sounds of the body. Its "organs" offer themselves up to perception: the mouth ("with a full mouth"[18]), the lips, the throat speak in these voices from which the expression of thought is no longer expected. They are signs of a singularity which is eroticized as it moves away into the distance. The plurality of this native region and of bodily experience becomes opaque. Conversely, rooted in the earth, the body is the noise, made up of peculiar murmurs, where signification is lost: phonemes thicken there, to which meaning is no longer attributable. They are no longer understood but only heard as, for enlightened reason, they progressively become the other.

A *mode of hearing* becomes discernible within the terms of the science of language, thanks to the role it attributes to the vowel. As it takes up the categories created by the grammarians and the philosophers, our corpus testifies to their re-employment according to another order of perception. Whereas in Paris a *visual* sensibility to the countryside is developing (nature is a "spectacle," the "simple life" is a "scene"),[19] the correspondents of Grégoire can *hear* the organs of the body and the local "singularities." It seems that, while writing is for them a "depiction" which refers to ideas, they do not classify the orality of patois among a set of documents (soon "popular" movements would be writings and depictions shut up in books or museums). It is still heard as a concert of vowels or "sounds."[20] To what is *said* and can be translated into the language of Paris, they add what is untranslatable – a "manner of speaking." The voice sings something other than the meaning which can be transported from one idiom to the next and thus reduced to the same. *Poutel* or *poutou*, according to Chabod, "signifies a kiss, but in a more tender and more vigorous manner" (Aveyron, G. 59). The "manner" of pronunciation overflows the "signified." Elocution is an excess – an addition or a waste product – in relation to semantic identity, which can be stated in French just as it can in the Languedoc language of Rouergue. Signification designates the "same thing" beneath linguistic metamorphoses, but it leaves outside its field plurality, difference, and particularity: the music of the earth, the body, and the passions.

Passions and Passivity

Patois suffers. It reveals "natural" seductions and fits of emotion which determine it just as much as changes in climate or the movements of bodily organs. It also suffers history. It is marked by the actions of foreigners and other societies, just as it is destined for the work of authors who, coming from outside, are the agents of the national language. In these various aspects, shown already in its tendency toward an "ease" of pronunciation, it is opposed to an ethic of the Enlightenment – that of effort. It does not control things any more than it controls itself. In the logic of Grégoire's correspondents, it appears to be both without power and "without rules" (Lyons, B.N. 22; cf. Bresse, B.N. 54; etc.), as though it were the reverse image of a society in which work acquires its productive capacity through conformity to laws.

Passion thus comprises a double form of passivity, with regard both to the "affections of the soul" and to history. But only the first element answers the question present in almost all the texts and nevertheless absent from the questionnaire:[21] what does patois have that is "proper" [*propre*] to it? For what is it "proper"? The word brings into focus a reaction before an empty space. Just what might it contain, this peculiar "property" that is idiom, prone as it is perpetually to vanish? Since the autonomy of patois (what is "proper" to it) is measured by a specific utility (to be "proper for" something) – that is to say, by what it "serves to express"[22] – it is characterized by its "abundance" for love, tenderness, friendship (this is the dominant series), and also (but this remains a subsidiary series) for anger, hate, etc.[23] This description indicates not so much what patois does or produces as what grows there. Admittedly, it mentions also its "richness" concerning "work on the land" and "countryside occupations,"[24] or its aptitude either for comedy, satire, and gaiety, or for "tragic scenes."[25] But on the whole, these characteristics remain secondary in relation to the "fertility" of patois when it comes to passions, which are here for the most part simple (Bordeaux, G. 138) and non-violent (Bresse, B.N. 51), associated with naivety (Périgord, B.N. 44), good-heartedness (Lot-et-Garonne, G. 118), and good sense (Saint-Claude, G. 210), and which contrast with the corruption and "artificial needs" of towns. The two terms "strength" and "softness" reappear constantly to depict the local idiom. But the second term dominates. It casts a nostalgic veil over the picture of a repertory of the heart which distance transforms into a shadowy paradise. This place is haunted by softened passions and calm virtues. Already they are conjugated in the past tense: "The customs of our good ancestors were simple like their patois, and this seemed made to depict simplicity and good-heartedness" (Lot-et-Garonne, G. 118). A "dire change" dooms the lost world of childhood to idealization. "The village where my father lived, and where I spent the early days of my youth, was a haven of happiness, simplicity and virtue. Today it is a vile cesspit" (Lorraine, B.N. 38).[26]

The calm which extends over this region whose "naivety is very pleasing" (Périgord, B.N. 44) or whose vocabulary represents the legend of an "erstwhile simplicity" (Lot-et-Garonne, G. 118) no doubt gives their significance to the responses which relate the "vigor" of patois to "what is lacking in French." The questionnaire asked about the existence of "very vigorous sayings and even any which are lacking in the French idiom."[27] But vigor here, linked by Court de Gébelin to the "passions one wishes to depict" and based on the "relations of words with Nature,"[28] corresponds precisely in patois to what is missing in the "national idiom": nature, still close to the former, is becoming absent from the latter. Harshness, coarseness, heaviness, strength, abundance, originality, picturesqueness, "voluptuous" expressions, "allegorical terms," "bold metaphors," "titillating forms": these qualifiers refer explicitly to the vigor which almost all the correspondents recognize as belonging to patois.[29] In fact, they have in mind less a virtue which might be proper to it than the virtue with which it is endowed by that nature which it offers up to view. It is therefore said everywhere to be "expressive" – whence the contrast between a vocabulary often held to be very "limited" and a "vigor" which, as soon as it is specified, is characterized rather by a "manner of speaking." The vocabulary is scarce, but it is spoken by nature, which can be gentle or violent, and which the notables perceive in the speech of the countryfolk. Thus in moments of emotion: "The peasant expresses his fits of anger in a more vigorous manner than in any language. Commonly, he swoops without reflection and like a falcon on his antagonist, which would seem to prove that he is very close to nature" (Gers, G. 89). This observation can turn into a confession: "Our ignorance is extreme; our education, worthless. We are men of nature and, like them, we are bold and impetuous" (Gers, G. 85).

"Slaves" (G. 89) or "savages" (G. 288), these "men of nature" are the echoes of nature, which is the true speaker of their patois. Bound to the earth, "rarely using the organ of speech, and endlessly busy providing for themselves the bare necessities of life," they respond to animals more than to men. "Our laborers talk almost continually to their oxen (*o! o!* – go; *jâ jâ* – stop), and the shepherdess to her dog: *A l'auveillas, baraca, à l'auveillas; vei la lai; o lo dorei, baraca, o lo dorei*" (Limagne, G. 166). This communication with "beasts," a common theme of the literature on peasants,[30] has as its converse the "line of demarcation" which patois draws up "between the inhabitants of the towns and the countryside" (Bresse, B.N. 54). The communion with nature and the absence of relations with men work together to create an isolate. "Anywhere where a modicum of communication has not been established with those living nearby, patois regins almost alone, and it is always the same" (Gers, G. 90). In the absence of travel and exchanges, we have here the immobile underside of commerce and of a social history. Behind their Wall of China (gradually crumbling away before the invasion of French and the "contagion of the age"), countryfolk form an "isolated and separate caste which does not communicate with the town" (Mâconnais, G. 222). They are there like the "cedars of Mount Lebanon" (Bresse, B.N. 51). They live in a park in which the murmur of nature can be heard everywhere. According to the Abbot Rolland, the "climate," the "air," temperament or "character" give "birth to the vigorous expressions of their language" (Provence, B.N. 99). Between the elements, the beasts and these "men of nature," harmonies – alternately violent and sweet, though in the end more "naive" than fearsome – compose the poem, which is "always the same," singing down there in the vigor of patois.

An "abundance" surfaces between consonants and rises right up into depictions of ideas to change them into vocalizations. But this force is not exploited. It is waiting for the labor which will make it productive. For patois really to become a language [*langue*], agents must intervene – that is to say, "authors." That is how it happened in the past. "Italian and Spanish only really became languages once they were set down by good authors" (Lot-et-Garonne, G. 107). In the same way, Languedocian owed its progress to academies, the *Puys d'amour* (Lyon, B.N. 28). Patois asks to be "civilized" (Gers, G. 86) and "cultivated" (Carcassonne, G. 15). Like its speaker, the man from Languedoc of whom "one might think that he has just been created in the same way as a donkey or a calf" (Gers, G. 85), patois is a wild filly, a "natural beauty"; it must be "exercised by skilful writers," "handled with an expert, graceful and philosophical touch," as Gascon was "in the hands of Montaigne, of Malherbe" (Mont-de-Marsan, G. 149). Otherwise, language remains "crude," as the Friends of the Constitution in Auch observe in the case of Armagnac: "Today, the patois in this region is what the French language was in its beginnings. . . . Since the English ceased to be masters of these regions, nothing has happened there which might electrify the workers on the land" (Gers, G. 86 and 85).

Without a master of the language and the country, nothing moves there. These inert resources thus call for a proprietor who might "enrich" patois-speaking nature by putting it to work. Already Grégoire's correspondents discern in this passive land the traces of what foreigners have made of it as they occupied or moved across it. One can find in it "several terms derived from Spanish, from the time when the Spanish owned the Netherlands" (Bouillon, 1, B.N. 63). "The Roman colonies created something of a revolution in our language" (Aveyron, G. 53). Patois does no work of its own. What happens there comes from others. In this respect, it is the complete opposite of a tool and of what, for Condillac, was already the ideal for a language: "Languages are simply methods, and methods are simply languages."[31] With these unregulated, unproductive idioms, enlightened notables had beside them the equivalent of what Africa would be for the bourgeois of the nineteenth century: an immobile continent, whose natural resources had to be possessed by the fatherland, put at the disposition of progress, made profitable, and "cultivated." A specific policy was thus being drawn up and justified in advance.

Notes

Translator's note: I am grateful to Luce Giard for her suggestions in the preparation of this translation.

1 [*Translator's note*] Certeau is referring to the questionnaire sent by the Abbot Grégoire in August 1790 to a number of provincial contacts throughout France, concerning the patois of their respective regions (see above, p. 000). The collected responses to this enquiry constitute the "corpus" to which Certeau refers intermittently throughout this chapter. It is worth including here an extract from the note which Certeau provides on his sources in the introduction to *Une politique de la langue*: "A part of this enquiry has been published in *Lettres à Grégoire sur les patois de France* . . . , ed. and introd. A. Gazier (Paris: Pedone, 1880; re-ed. Geneva: Slatkine, 1969). One must add to this publication the [following] manuscript dossiers . . .: the Bibliothèque de la Société de Port-Royal, mss REV. 222 and 223; the Bibliothèque

Nationale, mss NAF 27 98. Henceforth the letters published by Gazier will be designated by the letter G, the manuscript collection of the library of Port-Royal by the initials P.R., and the collection of the Bibliothèque Nationale by the initials B.N. The reference to the source will be followed by the number of the page or folio" (*Une politique de la langue*, p. 11, n. 3).

2 [*Translator's note*] French contains two words, *le langage* and *la langue*, which correspond to the single English word "language." The distinction between the two words, when it is significant, depends somewhat on the system of reference in play. As a rule, *le langage* is the more general term, referring to the function or human faculty of language as a means of communication and expression, whereas *la langue* refers to particular languages or linguistic systems. In the present context, the most appropriate translation for *la langue* will often be "the national language" (which the agents involved tended to oppose, as a coherent and rational system, to the disorganized flux of patois). In other instances where the choice of this term carries a significance which may not be apparent in the English, the French term will be indicated in square brackets.

3 J.-J. Rousseau, "Prononciation," in *Oeuvres complètes* (Pléiade, 1961), vol. II, p. 1251. He adds: "As each province and each canton adopts a particular pronunciation, it turns the common written language into its own language as it speaks" (ibid.). A re-edition of the text can be found as an appendix to *Essai sur l'origine des langues*, ed. C. Porset (Bordeaux: Ducros, 1968), pp. 216–21.

4 "Writing is only the representation of the word, it is bizarre that more care is taken to determine the image than the object" (ibid., p. 1252). "Since it is therefore the spoken word which is the most commonly used part of language [*la langue*], the greatest care of the Grammarians ought to be to establish clearly the nature of its modifications, but on the contrary they concern themselves almost exclusively with writing" (ibid., p. 1249). For Jean-Jacques, the spoken word comes first, and "writing, which appears as though it ought to fix language securely, is precisely what alters it" (*Essai sur l'origine des langues*, ch. V, p. 67).

5 Cf. Jean Starobinski, *J.-J. Rousseau. La transparence et l'obstacle* (Paris: Gallimard, 1971), 2nd edn, p. 359.

6 J.-J. Rousseau, "Prononciation", p. 1250.

7 J.-J. Rousseau, *Essai sur l'origine des langues*, ch. V, p. 67.

8 Cf., for example, Abbot Grégoire, *Promenade dans les Vosges* (Epinal, 1895), p. 23, etc..

9 Question 13.

10 According to the responses, the word-endings are "commonly consonants" in Aveyron (G. 57), Jura (G. 209), Bergues (B.N. 18), and Britanny (G. 282 and 287). These are exceptions. Moreover, with respect to the same regions, other responses affirm that the opposite is the case: in Agen (G. 113), in Jura (B.N. 53, G. 202 and 204), etc. As far as word-endings are concerned, there is pressure at work in favour of the vowel.

11 See above, notes 2 and 3.

12 Jérémie-Jacques Oberlin, *Essai sur le patois lorrain des environs du comté du Ban de la Roche* (Strasbourg: J.-F. Stein, 1775). He proposed this programme for an "Academy" which would "consist of scholars from each province, together at the same time with people of the meanest and common extraction." This is an analogous program to that drawn up by J.-J. Rousseau, in his *Essai sur l'origine des langues*, but this text, written between 1756 and 1761, only appeared in 1781 in the *Traités sur la musique*.

13 J.-J. Rousseau, "Prononciation," p. 1249 (or in C. Porset (ed.), *Essai sur l'origine des langues*, p. 217).

14 Mont-de-Marsan, G. 150; Lyons, B.N. 30.

15 Thus in Mâconnais: "This patois varies from one village to the next with regard to accent, pronunciation, and word-endings" (G. 222). In every case, it is a question of the vowel. Cf. Aveyron, G. 54; Bergues, B.N. 18; Berry, G. 269; Bouillon 1, B.N. 63; Britanny, G. 287; Lorraine, B.N. 37; etc.

16 Thus in Lyons, "the only difference we see [between French and patois] is that which comes from the peasants' pronunciation, from the substitution of vowels for each other, and from their word-endings" (B.N. 29). Cf. Périgord, G. 154; etc.

17 Britanny, G. 287. Cf. Agen, G. 110; Auch 1, G. 84; Lorraine, B.N. 37, etc. It is a leitmotif of the responses.

18 Cf. Agen, G. 110; Mâconnais, G. 221; etc..

19 This is already apparent, for example, in the numerous texts cited by Geoffroy Atkinson, *Le Sentiment de la nature et le retour à la vie simple* (Geneva: Droz, 1960).

20 By "sounds" [*sons*], Court de Gébelin designates vowels (Antoine Court de Gébelin, *Monde primitif analysé et comparé avec le monde moderne, considéré dans l'histoire naturelle de la parole, ou Origine du langage et de l'écriture* (Paris, 1775), p. 284). For him, however, the vowel remains "depiction and language," but of sensations and of "what moves the soul" (ibid.); cf. M. de Certeau et al., *Une politique de la langue* . . . , p. 98. He produces, moreover, a quite remarkable table of correspondences between the "sounds" (A, E, I, O, U) and sensorial perceptions (*Monde primitif . . . ou Origine du langage* . . . , pp. 289–90).

21 However, question 8 did ask "for what kinds of things, occupations, passions is this patois more abundant in terms?"

22 Everywhere the form of the response is of the type: "proper for expressing," "abundant in terms for expressing," "fertile in terms for depicting," etc.

23 Cf. Artois, G. 257; Aveyron, G. 56; Bouillon 2, G. 232; Britanny, G. 287; Carcassonne, G. 16; Gers, G. 89; Hautes-Pyrénées, B.N. 67; Lorraine, B.N. 41; Lyons, B.N. 29; Mont-de-Marsan, G. 150; Perpignan, G. 80; Provence, B.N. 99; Saint-Claude, G. 208; etc.

24 Hautes-Pyrénées, B.N. 67; Provence, B.N. 99; etc. The "richness" in this area is often very specialized. Thus Chabot specifies that "it is for agriculture and the making of small pieces of textile called *serges* and *cadis* . . . that we are reasonably rich in this domain" (Aveyron, G. 56). On this subject, see M. de Certeau et al., *Une politique de la langue*, p. 130ff.

25 Thus if one takes two neighbouring regions, Liège and Bouillon, the first has a patois which is "proper for comedy," while the second has a patois "proper for expressing . . . pathos and tragic scenes" (G. 232–3). One can note too an aptitude for "gaiety" (Bresse, B.N. 51), an "abundance in rhymes and jokes" (Britanny, G. 281) or in "satire and gaiety" (Saint-Claude, G. 208), etc.

26 Some years previously, the image presented by Rétif de la Bretonne of his native village in Lower Burgundy had not been effaced by this more mental than physical distance. See Emmanuel Le Roy Ladurie, "Ethnologie rurale du XVIIIe siècle: Rétif, à la Bretonne," in *Ethnologie française*, vol. 2, 1972 (1974), pp. 215–52.

27 Question 12.

28 Court de Gébelin, *Monde primitif . . . ou Origine du langage . . .*, pp. 103 and 277. Cf. ibid., "Discours préliminaire," p. XVI, on "the vigor which poetry and eloquence owe to the relation of words with Nature." What interest Gébelin are the "causes which produce the vigor of words," beneath the diversities of form (op. cit., p. 281).

29 There are some exceptions. "There exist almost no vigorous expressions. The language of slaves must not and cannot be vigorous," say the Friends of the Constitution in Auch with regard to the patois of Armagnac (G. 89). And Cherval says of Bressan that "it has no vigor" (B.N. 51). In general, it can be noted instead that the loss of vigor is measured by the advance of French: "The patois of the Ardennes, as it comes closer to the French language, becomes visibly impoverished as it rejects a large number of very vigorous words and expressions which are only imperfectly replaced by the words and terms drawn from French" (Bouillon 2, G. 234). "Vigor" is, moreover, an obligatory qualifier of patois. Thus, in the Breton translation of the *Almanach du Père Gérard* (1792), the Popular Society of Hennebont naturally finds the "vigorous and naive expression of the celtic idiom" (cited in Ferdinand Brunot, *Histoire de la langue française*, vol. IX, I (Paris: Armand Colin, 1927), p. 45).

30 Among others, though better than others, Nicolas Rétif recounts how his father Edme would speak to the horses, the dogs and the bulls. See E. Le Roy Ladurie, "Ethnologie rurale du XVIIIe siècle . . .," p. 218.

31 Condillac, *La Grammaire*, "Discours préliminaire," in *Oeuvres* (Paris: 1798), p. XLII.

15

Mystic Speech

A Locus of Speech

The mysticism of the sixteenth and seventeenth centuries proliferated in proximity to a loss. It is a historical trope for that loss. It renders the absence that multiplies the productions of desire readable. At the dawn of modernity, an end and a beginning – a departure – are thus marked. The literature of mysticism provides a path for those who "ask the way to get lost. No one knows." It teaches "how not to return." . . .

The texts of mysticism use the word "night" to describe their global situation, but they also apply it more particularly to ways of experiencing that situation as an existential question. The texts are tales of "passions" *of* and *in* history. The different mystic trends, confronted with hidden truths, opaque authorities, and divided or ailing institutions, did not basically set out to pioneer new systems of knowledge, topographies, or complementary or substitutive powers; rather, they defined a different *treatment* of the Christian tradition. The ways of the mystics were accused (with good reason) of being "new." Prisoners of circumstance ("another shall bind you"), yet grounded in their faith in a Beginning that still comes in the present, the mystics established a "style" in the form of *practices* defining a *modus loquendi* and/or a *modus agendi*. What is essential, then, is not a body of doctrines (which was on the contrary the effect of their practices, and, especially, the product of later theological interpretations), but the epistemic foundation of a domain within which specific procedures are followed: a new space, with new mechanisms. At the heart of the debate pitting the "theologians" or spiritual "examiners" of the age against the mystics, the theorists of the literature see either "mystical statements" ("figures of speech," "turns" of phrase, ways of "turning" words around) or "maxims" (rules of thought or action specific to the "saints," or mystics). The mystics' reinterpretation of the tradition is characterized by a set of procedures allowing a new treatment of language – of all contemporary language, not only the area delimited by theological knowledge or the corpus of patristic and scriptural works. It is ways of acting that guide the creation of a body of mystical writings.

We find, on the one hand, in the context of a degenerating tradition darkened by time, an effort to go beyond; and on the other hand, a progression from a cosmos of divine messages (or "mysteries") to be understood, to itinerant practices which trace in language the indeterminate path of a mode of writing: these two features characterize the modernity of the works which for over two centuries were called "mystic" by those who produced them and theorized about them. They suggest a way of entering those aging texts and surveying the movement of their modes of writing against the background of today's issues.

One last prefatory question: can we postulate, behind the document transmitted to us, the existence of a fixed referent (a fundamental experience or reality), the presence of which would be the test of a properly mystical text? All of these writings display a passion for what *is*, for the world as it "exists," for the thing itself (*das Ding*) – in other words, a passion for what is its own authority and depends on no outside guarantee.... An ab-solute (un-bound), in the mode of pain, pleasure, and a "letting-be" attitude (Meister Eckhart's *gelâzenheit*), inhabits the torture, ecstasy, or sacri-fice of a language that can *say* that ab-solute, endlessly, only by erasing itself. But what name or identity can be attached to this "thing," independent of the always localized labor of letting it come? The other that organizes the text is not the (t)exterior [*un hors-texte*]. It is not an (imaginary) object distinguishable from the movement by which it (*Es*) is traced. To set it apart, in isolation from the texts that exhaust themselves in the effort to say it, would be to exorcize it by furnishing it with a place of its own and a proper name; it would be to identify it with the residue of already constituted systems of rationality, or to equate the question asked under the figure of the limit with a particular religious representation (one excluded from all of the fields of science, or fetishized as the substitute for a lack). It would be tantamount to positing, behind the documents, the presence of a what-ever, an ineffability that could be twisted to any end, a "night in which all cats are black."

In the beginning, it is best to limit oneself to the consideration of what goes on in texts whose status is labeled "mystic," instead of wielding a ready-made definition (whether ideological or imaginary) of what it is that was inscribed in those texts by an operation of writing. The issues immediately at hand are the formal aspects of the discourse and the tracing movement (the roaming, *Wandern*) of the writing: the first circumscribes a locus, and the second displays a "style," a "walk" or gait. . . .

My purpose here is to pinpoint the locus established by mystic speech, leaving for the future a possible analysis of its walk, or the mystic "procedures" which produce endless narrativity. Only then will we have gained access to these writings, which found the subject on its own dissolution ("aphanisis") in that unreadable something other written in its body.

At the dawn of modernity, then, a new literary and epistemological "form" appears with texts labeled "mystic" in order to distinguish them from other past or contemporary texts (theological treatises, biblical commentaries, etc.). The problem is not to determine whether an exegetical treatise by Gregory of Nyssa, for example, is a product of the same experience as a discourse later termed "mystic," or whether both are constructed following roughly analogous rhetorical processes; it is, rather, to understand what happens inside the field delimited by a *proper name* ("mystic"), in which an operation regulated by an applicable set of *rules* is undertaken. A corpus can be considered the effect of this relation between a name (which symbolizes a circumscription) and rules (which specify a mode of production), even if, as is often the case, the name is used to add different or earlier productions to the constellation of texts it isolates (in the sixteenth and seventeenth centuries, already existing writings were termed "mystic," and a mystic tradition was fabricated), and even if the rules of "mystic" construction were already structuring texts well in advance of their group designation (it is often noted that procedures deemed "mystic" in modern times are regrouped under other labels in earlier or contemporary documents). At the outset of the analysis, we thus find, in the system of differentiation of discursive formations, the isolation of a "mystic" unity articulating a new space of knowledge. The right to exercise language *otherwise* is objectified in a set of circumscriptions and procedures. . . .

[Since] its historical boundaries are in constant flux, it seemed preferable to begin in the middle and study the field of mysticism at the height of its formalization – from Saint Teresa (1515–1582) to Angelus Silesius (the pseudonym of Johann Scheffler, 1624–1677). At this point, its modes of functioning are more legible, allowing us to define its *place*; a regressive history of its development and a study of its later incarnations are then made possible. . . .

A Site: the Tradition Humiliated

Mystic literature belongs first of all to a certain topography. In modern Europe, it has its privileged places: certain regions, social categories, group types, forms of labor, or, even more to the point, certain concrete modes of monetary relations (begging, communal holdings, trade, etc.), of sexual experiences (celibacy, widowhood, etc.), and power relations (allegiances to benefactors, ecclesiastical and political affiliations, etc.). We must first of all ask what constants can be extracted from the data furnished by the few analyses which depart from the "ahistorical" slumber of studies on mysticism. I will summarize some of the relevant information regarding the mystics' place, in particular, their social origins and situations.

During the sixteenth and seventeenth centuries the mystics were for the most part from regions or social categories which were in socio-economic recession, disadvantaged by change, marginalized by progress, or destroyed by war. The memory of past abundance survived in these conditions of impoverishment, but since the doors of social responsibility were closed, ambitions were redirected toward the open spaces of utopia, dream, and writing. Lucien Goldmann tried to explain the Jansenist spirituality of Port-Royal by the situation of its authors, who were members of the *noblesse de robe*, a class which was in the process of losing its former powers.[1] The case was similar (though this is actually not an explanation) for other French mystics of the same period. Many were connected through family ties to the decadence of the petty nobility of the southwest provinces, the misery of the country squires, the devaluation of parliamentary "offices," or, most of all, "to an entire stratum composed of the middle aristocracy, rich in vitality and spiritual needs, but of reduced social service or utility."[2] The same thing applies for the difficulties experienced earlier in the century by compromised Leaguers (such as the Acarie family) or émigrés (such as the Englishman Benoit of Canfeld). Among the religious hermits, we find the same geography of affiliations (minus the parliamentarians). Aside from a few mystics on the road to social promotion . . . , the majority of them . . . belonged to social milieux or "factions" in full retreat. Mysticism seems to emerge on beaches uncovered by the receding tide.

In sixteenth-century Spain, Saint Teresa belonged to a *hidalguía* (noble class) that had lost its duties and holdings; Saint John of the Cross, a nurse in the hospitals of Salamanca, came from a ruined and fallen aristocratic class, etc. But ethnic distinctions, *la raza*, counted more than position in the social hierarchy. The "new Christians," or converted Jews, in whose features their contemporaries saw only the mask of the Excluded, remained close in many ways to the Jewish tradition (the tradition of the *gespaltete Seelen*, divided souls, whose cleaved lives created a hidden interiority); they were prominent in the ranks of the *alumbrados* (illuminati). . . . Barred from certain Orders (such as the Hieronymites and Benedictines), suspected by the Dominicans, these "scorned ones" went on to become great spiritual leaders among the Franciscans (Diego de Estella), the Augustinians (Luis de León), the Jesuits (Lainez, Polanco), and the Carmelites (Saint Teresa's grandfather had himself converted to Judaism and was forced to abjure in 1485). From John of Ávila (who turned the University of Baeva into a sanctuary for the "new Christians") to Molinos, a strange alliance linked "mystic" speech and "impure" blood. In fact, their position midway between two religious traditions, one repressed and internalized, the other public but weighed down by success, allowed the new Christians to become the major initiators of a new mode of discourse freed from dogmatic redundancy – just as in the nineteenth century the widespread adoption of German culture by Jews led to theoretical innovation and exceptional intellectual productivity, the results of differences maintained in the use of a common language.

In Germany, seventeenth-century mysticism was similarly a product of an impoverished rural aristocracy . . . ,or of small-scale urban craftsmen . . . : in other words, they came from the classes most negatively affected by the progress made by other social categories (in particular, the urban bourgeoisie). The decline of their classes allowed for greater independence from religious authorities, and was accompanied by a refusal of the new order. In addition, Silesia, the privileged land of the mystics . . . , was the province in the eastern part of the Holy Roman Empire hardest hit by the Thirty Years' War (with losses of 60–70 percent); it was also burdened with the social deterioration of its peasantry, economic competition from Poland and Kurland, and the alienation of its political rights under Charles VI. Sects and schools of theosophy and mysticism abounded in this land forsaken by history.

This topography, which can neither be systematized nor generalized, has already pinpointed areas of particular instability or forms of social disinheritance. In a society based upon an ideology of stability, changing one's "station" in life is never good, and a lowering in social or family status is considered degeneration. Such a fall is an open wound in a social order that is viewed as a struggle against constant deterioration in relation to family origins. It constitutes an inability to protect the heritage against the inroads of time. The tradition is going away and turning into a past connection. That is what these groups, haunted by the certainty of extinction, experienced more deeply than any others. At the extremes, they vacillated between ecstasy and revolt – *mysticism and dissent*. The privileges they "held," handed down from preceding generations, started to fall away, leaving them alone, without inherited property, with no assurances for the future, reduced to a present wed to death. Contrary to what some have said, the dangers of the present were not dispelled by any expectations of future security or any past acquest; the present, for them, was the restricted scene upon which the drama of their doom was enacted, inscribed in facts (a law) and the possibility of a new beginning (a faith). They had nothing left but present exile.

If the mystics were locked within the confines of a "nothing" that could also be an "origin," it is because they were trapped there by a *radical* situation to which they responded with utmost seriousness. In their texts, this can be seen not only in the connection their innovative truth always has to pain, but, more explicitly, in the social figures that dominate their discourse – the madman, the child, the illiterate. An analogous situation today would be if the down-and-outs of our society, the fixed-income elderly or alien workers, were the eponymous heroes of knowledge.

In the minds of the religious believers of the sixteenth and seventeenth centuries, a second state of affairs was inseparable from the foregoing situation – the humiliation of the Christian tradition. They were experiencing, in their shattered Christendom, another fundamental decline: that of the institutions of meaning. They were experiencing the disintegration of a sacred world. In other words, they were leading lives of exile, hounded from their land by the defilements of history. *Super flumina Babylonis*: the theme of mourning, disconsolate despite the intoxication of new aspirations, was endlessly repeated. Here again, referential permanence is lacking. The Churches and the Scriptures were considered equally corrupt. Sullied by time, they obscure the Word whose presence they should be. Of course, they still mark its place, but only in the form of "ruins" – a word which haunted the writings of reformists. They also indicate the places where one should await, beginning *now*, the birth of God. God must be distinguished from His signs, which are subject to deterioration, whereas He, being already dead, is free from the erosion of time. Birth and death – the two poles of the mystics' evangelical meditations. They do not reject the ruins around them. They remain in them; they go to them. In a symbolic gesture, Saint Ignatius of Loyola, Saint Teresa of Avila and many other wished to enter a "corrupt" order, not out of any taste for decadence, but because those disorganized places represented in their minds the state of contemporary Christianity and, like the cave of rejection at Bethlehem, were *where* they were to seek a repetition of a founding surprise. More generally, their *solidarity* with the collective, historically based suffering – which was demanded by circumstances but also desired and sought after as a test of truth – indicates the place of mystic "agony," a "wound" inseparable from the social ill.

This religious and social experience should be seen in connection with the movement that led "spiritual" scholars and theologians to seek witness among people far below them in social status – maidservants, cowherds, villagers, etc.... Like Cardinal Bérulle climbing up to a maidservant's garret, these Magi go among the "little people" to hear that which still speaks. A field of knowledge takes leave of its textual "authorities" to turn to the exegesis of "wild" voices. Innumerable biographies of poor "girls" or "enlightened illiterates" were produced, and constitute an important part of the spiritual literature of the time. In these writings, a tradition, humiliated after having functioned as the court of reason, awaits and receives from its other the certitudes that escape it.

The Discourse on Utterance

To gain a perspective on the process which slowly replaced a divided Christianity with national *political* units, breaking down the social organization of universal belief into sects, "retreats," and "*spiritual*" communities, it is necessary to take a more general view that includes a recognition of the socio-political instability of the age and the fragmentation of its frames of reference. As a matter of fact, the "Machiavellian Moment"[3] and the "mystic invasion"[4] coincide. The project of constructing an order amid the contingencies of history (the problem of the reason of State) and the quest to discern in our earthly, fallen language the now inaudible Word of God (the problem of the spiritual subject) arose simultaneously from the dissociation of cosmic language and the Divine Speaker. In addition, these two complementary restoration projects have recourse to the same "ecclesial" heritage of a unifying whole, although they express it in henceforth specialized modes: for one, the reason of State, for the other, the "community of saints." . . .

Becoming separate from one another was not an aim of these various projects. It was, on the contrary, a necessity imposed by the disorder around them, from which they were obliged to distinguish themselves in order to mark the place of a new beginning. A multitude of microcosms appear, as reductions and replacements for the previous dismembered macrocosm. Two biblical images obsess them – the mythic image of paradise lost, and the eschatological or apocalyptic image of the New Jerusalem.[5] From this point of view, rational (political or scientific) production and irrational (spiritual or poetic) ones are inspired by the same utopian vision, the goal of which is a "great instauration"; though *compartmentalized* in various sectors (the division of the world is the fundamental experience of the age), this shared vision centers all of these recapitulatory attempts on a *unitary* reference: a common origin of history, a general law of the heavenly bodies, and a sacral hierarchy of power, of which the king remains the symbol. The mystics, too, were responding to the desire to "reduce all to one";[6] that desire continued to underlie their "experimental" inquiries long after the ebb of Neoplatonism. Like other sciences, even more so, the "science of the saints" is confronted by the necessity of reconciling a central contradiction: between the *particularity* of the place it delimits (the subject) and the *universality* it strives for (the absolute). Perhaps it is defined by this very tension, which is played out in the opposition between *all* and *nothing*, or between "*notizia*" ("universal and vague") and "understanding" [*l'entendement*] (which can only know the particular). . . . It is the search for a common language, after language has been shattered. It is the invention of a "language of the angels" because that of man has been disseminated.

Speaking-hearing[7] – such is the problem circumscribing the particular locus at which the universal project of the "saints" develops. The objects of the mystics' discourse have the status of symptoms; essentially, they are prayer (from meditation to contemplation) and the "spiritual" relation (in the form of communal exchanges and "spiritual guidance"). "Communication" (communications from God or those established among the saints) is everywhere a void to be filled, and forms the focal point of mystical accounts and treatises. They are writings produced from this lack. The rupture, ambiguity, and falsity that plurality spreads throughout the world creates the need to restore a *dialogue*. This *colloquium* would take place under the sign of the *Spirit* since the "letter" no longer allows it. How can one *hear*, through signs transformed into things, that which flows from a unique and divine *will to speak*? How can this desire in search of a *thou* cross through a language that betrays it by sending the addressee a different message, or by replacing the statement of an idea with utterance by an "I"? "It is a difficult and troublesome thing for a soul not to understand [*entender*] itself or to find none who understand it":[8] like *The Ascent of Mount Carmel*, all mystic texts are born of this "trouble," this distress in expectation of a dialogue. They reach their highest point with the poem driving away any messenger who is not *thou*:

> Surrender thou thyself completely.
> From today do thou send me now no other messenger,
> For they cannot tell me what I wish.[9]

In the work of Angelus Silesius, this corresponds to the "invocating drive" which casts aside the opaque positivity of the Holy Writ as a "nothing," and reclaims the "essential" – *thy* Word, in *me*:

> The [Divine] Writing is writing, nothing more. My consolation
> is essentiality,
> And that God speaks in me the Word of Eternity.[10]

Of course, the *invocatio* has long been the first moment of religious knowledge. It is the initial step in St Anselm's *Proslogion*, and the field in which a noetic, then a rationality of faith, develop. But from this time onward, the *invocatio* and the *auditio fidei* become isolated from the Christian scriptural corpus, which recedes and is read and experienced "from a distance," and turned into the object either of logical treatment by scholastic theology or historical treatment by positive theology; from language, from which the nominalists' God has been "unbound" . . . and which he no longer guarantees; and from the cosmos, which becomes infinitely diversified and ceases to be a network of analogies referring to a single referent and speaker. *Invocatio* and *auditio fidei* define something "essential" that is no longer a step on an itinerary of learning, but has been set outside the realm of knowledge. The act of *utterance* becomes separated from the objective organization of statements. And it lends mysticism its formal characteristics – it is defined by the establishment of a place (the "*I*") and by transactions (*spirit*); that is, by the necessary relation between the subject and messages. The term "experience" connotes this relation. Contemporaneous to the act of creation, outside an unreadable history, . . . a mystic space is constituted, outside the fields of knowledge. It is there that the labor of writing which is given birth through the animation of language by the desire of the other takes place.

This new space does not initially add another domain to the configuration of theological disciplines. Only later, beginning at the end of the seventeenth century, after the texts had allowed the questioning that produced them to be forgotten, were these writings transformed into an "applied" (or "practical") science of theological "speculation." The distancing that constitutes the no-place of allocution on the margins of objective contents does indeed involve a distinction between theory and practice; but the issue is how, or if, one can put into practice a language that is free in theory. In other words, if one can: address *to* God . . . the statements that concern Him; be in inter-course . . . *from thee* to *me*, with the Other or with others; hear and understand . . . those statements considered inspired. The tradition's ancient cosmological account is set on a new foundation, built upon a few strategic points: the present ability to speak (the *speech-act* in the here and now); the *I* that addresses a *thou* (the allocutionary relation[11]); the *conventions* to be established between the speaker and the allocutor[12] (the presuppositions and contracts of discourse); and the linguistic manifestation of the *allocutionary act* (the basis of the privilege accorded "indexes," i.e., the pragmatic or subjective elements of language, in mystic texts). These points fall within the province of utterance.[13] Moreover, the "experience" by which mystic writings define themselves has as its essential elements the *ego*, the "center of utterance," and the *present*, the "source of time," the "presence in the world that the act of utterance alone makes possible."[14]

For mysticism, unlike theology, it is not a matter of constructing a particular, coherent set of statements organized according to "truth" criteria; and, unlike theosophy, there is no interest in letting the violent order of the world reveal itself in the form of a general account (which makes personal experience irrelevant), but it is a matter of dealing with ordinary language (not the technical sectors) from an inquiry that questions the possibility of transforming that language into a network of allocutions and present alliances. A double cleavage. The initial division separates the *said* (what has been or is stated) from the *saying* (the act of speaking [*l'acte de se parler*]). The second, produced by "spiritual" labor, cuts into the density of the world to make of it a *dialogic* discourse: *I* and *thou* seeking one another in the thickness of the same languages.... *I* and *thou*: two terms whose difference, regained and maintained, will be lost in the relation that posits them.

A certain number of mechanisms necessarily follow. Analogous to the linguistic signs of utterance, these terms do not refer to an object or entity (they are not referential or denominative), but to the agency of discourse itself. "I" is an "empty"[15] from that simply announces the speaker. It is a "siteless site" related to the fragility of social position or the uncertainty of institutional referents. The question addressed is not one of "competence." It targets the *exercise* of language, performance, and thus, in the strictest sense, the "reestablishment of language within the context of discourse."[16] Of the elements in mystic texts related to utterance, I will cite only three – decisive – examples. They concern the precondition of discourse (a division that establishes contractual relations), the status of discourse (a locus where the Spirit speaks), and the figuration of discourse as a content (an image of the "I"). In these three modes – conventions to be established, a place of locution to circumscribe, and a representation on which to base a narrative – the relation of a traditional language to the possibility of its being spoken is renewed. More fundamentally still, what is renewed is the relation between the signifier and the constitution of the subject: do we exist to speak to the other, or be spoken by him?

A Contract ("Volo"), a Subject ("I"), a Figure (the Island)

The first of the three modes outlined above is the effort to determine a course of action to make "utterance contracts" possible once again. Since it was no longer possible to presuppose the same cosmos that was experienced in times past as a (linguistic) encounter between the Divine Speaker and His faithful respondents, it was necessary to *produce* the conventions needed to circumscribe the places where one can "hear" [*entendre*] and where one can "come to an understanding with" others [*s'entendre*]. An essential sector of mystic thought attempts to explain and obtain the conditions allowing one to "speak to" [*parler à*] or "speak with" [*se parler*].[17] It is necessary to compile a "circumstantial" range of possibilities. Mystics are engaged in a politics of utterance – they are comparable to lawyers who make the most complete list possible of the situations and addresses apt to lead a proceeding to a "felicitous" conclusion. This kind of "politics," . . . sets forth operational rules determining the relational usage of a language that has become uncertain of the real. It *reconstructs*, where the *ontological* relation between words and things has come undone, *loci* of *social* communication. Of course, this is not dictated by a political "will to persuade," but has to do instead with a spiritual "will to hear" (a distinction which is not all that clear). In any case, a multiplication of "methods" produces and guarantees certain kinds of exchange, such as, in the example of St Teresa, the community or *compañía*, the relation to authority or "spiritual guidance," and prayer or the "*colloquium*" with God. Other practices construct places of utterance ("foundations" or "retreats").

The establishment of these dialogic spaces is accomplished under the auspices of an essential, fundamental rule which has the status of their condition of possibility. It has the form of an exclusive structure (*only*): the relation tolerates *only* people who are unshakably resolved. Everything hinges on a *volo*, without which there would be no speech. This prerequisite designates the summoned addressee: "I *only* address those who . . . ," says the mystic. Or, "God *only* speaks to those who . . ." Everywhere, from St John of the Cross to Surin, this is a necessary "convention." It operates a closure: it delimits in language a path of circulation and a circumscription. It is the opposite of apologetic or predictive discourse based on the convention (for it is one also) of according statements an autonomous status allowing them to cross boundaries between groups. The threshold created by this stricture is expressed in a performative verb: *volo*. "Do not say 'I would' . . . but say 'I will,'" cautions Meister Eckhart.[18] . . . This *volo* does not imply any particular object; it is at the same time *nihil volo* ("I want *nothing*") and "I only want *God*" (that is, "God must will for me").[19] In other words, "it is necessary to give form to the desire,"[20] a desire "tied to nothing."

With this founding act, the subject enters a retreat, it goes where the world's objects are absent. The subject is born of an exile and a disappearance. The "I" is "formed" – by its act of willing *nothing* or by (forever) *being incapable of doing* what it wills – as a "desire" bound only to the supposed desire of a Deity. It is created by the state of being nothing but the affirmation of a will. Aside from what it can do or be, it also functions as a linguistic convention; for by centering on "God," it sticks to a religious language in its very focus. It completes a contract with the interlocutor which goes beyond the uncertain range of particular statements to make a general affirmation: "I place my stakes in language," or "you can be certain that my desire awaits you in words." That is the assurance every addressee is given. It is what, in the vocabulary of the time, was termed "intention" or, in Surin, the "formal aspect" of communication. In this respect, the *volo* manifests and founds what no longer comes naturally – a contract of language which, because it has no property, takes the form of the lack and the desire of the other.

Corresponding to the establishment by a *volo* of a "convention" among addressees that functions to set them apart from non-addressees, there is a need on the part of the addresser (or the author) to found the place at which he speaks. The mystic text does not rely on statements authorized elsewhere, which it might repeat/comment in the name of the very institution that "uttered" them. It does, however, presuppose a "command" (like the one St Teresa obeys by writing the *Libro de la Vida*), a request (for example, Anne of Jesus' to St John of the Cross to write his commentary, the *Cántico*), or an apostolic mission (Surin, Angelus Silesius); but these "authorizations" resolve only one question, To whom should I write? and not that other, more fundamental question, Where should I write? That is the question the organization of every mystic text strives to answer: the truth value of the discourse does not depend on the truth value of its propositions, but on the fact of its being in the very place at which the Speaker speaks (the Spirit, "el que habla"). The texts always define themselves as being entirely a product of inspiration, though that inspiration may operate in very different modes. In every case, though, divine utterance is both what founds the text, and what it must make manifest. That is why the text is destabilized: it is at the same time *beside* the authorized institution, but outside it and *in* what authorizes that institution, i.e., the Word of God. In such a discourse, which claims to speak on behalf of the Holy Spirit and attempts to impose that convention on the addressee, a particular assertion is at work, affirming that what is said in this *place*, different from the one of magisterium language, is the *same* as what is said in the tradition, or else that these two places amount to the same.

Right from its Introït (Prologue, Preface, or Introduction), the text indicates its status by assigning its contracting parties their reciprocal places. A topography of personal pronouns suffices to effect this distribution of positions . . . A commonplace (the text begins with the words, "one can take two paths to knowledge . . . ") lays out from the very start the disjunction around which the text is organized: *either* "faith" (the "common path") *or* "experience" ("for the few"). On one side, there is "knowledge by hearsay," originating with the "preaching of the Apostles" – that's "*us*," all of us. The other side is defined by quotations in Latin from the New Testament, "quod vidimus, quod audivimus, quod manus nostrae contractaverunt . . . annuntiamus vobis" – that's "*them*," the Apostles who, from a distance, contrast their *nos* to the *vobis* that "we" are. This opening places the author and reader on the same footing ("we"), based on a likelihood ("One can . . . ") and something already well known (that there is a present *we* opposed to a past *they*). The second paragraph shifts the scene and actualizes it. The Ancients' "experience" becomes contemporary ("In our own age," "in the middle of France") and the Apostles' experience ("them") becomes "our," although it remains reserved for the few and is always termed "extraordinary." The same passage functions as a transition. Switching back to French, it makes the speaker's "we" coincide with the Apostles' "we" ("we can also volunteer these words: that which we have seen . . . "), thus attributing to the author the "experience" and "extraordinary things" that justified the Apostles' writing ("that is why we have taken pen in hand"). Another "we" has appeared, in league with the Apostles, apart from the readers. A third action then strengthens the assent the "you" (readers) give the "we" (author), by making it hinge on "the faith *you* have in the words of the prophets" and "to which *we* are committed through our adherence to the Catholic religion." This knot ties "you" ("attentive" readers) to "we" (the author of "this discourse") by using the collective *we* ("you" plus "we") of shared belief. Then, gradually extracted from the initial "one" by a series of displacements, set apart from "all those to whom *we* speak in this book," there finally appears the "I" who "would like to do a service for eternity." In apostolic utterance, a subtle gradation of personal pronouns gives the "I" the right to address its readers. This convention puts the "I" *in the place* of the Apostles; the "I" speaks the language of the *other*. After this has been accomplished, it is possible to constitute a "science . . . of the things of the other life" – a heterology. But an "experimental" one, uttered by the "I" in *the present*, far removed from the common faith that has been subjugated by authority, in other words, by a "memory" which articulates the other of *the past*.

The presence of the subject as a speaker in the text he constructs is not a new thing. . . . What is important here is the fact that the "I" in this case plays the role of a "shifter."[21] On the one hand, it confirms the "objectivity of the text," since the author (the subject of the utterance), the narrator (of the text), and the actor (the hero of the story) are bound together in a single "I," and since the "I" is by convention identical to a proper name. Thanks to this "referential pact," it bolsters the traditional syntagm with new reliability (saying "I believe that . . . " assumes that the subordinate proposition is not, or is no longer, self-evident). On the other hand, it designates both the reason for and the content of the discourse: *why* one writes and *what* one writes. In this way, it compensates for the lack of an ecclesial mission. The need to give personal witness intervenes when Church predication loses its value, when the delegating, missionary institution loses its credibility or neglects its duties. The "I" replaces the world as speaker (and the institution that is supposed to make it speak).

This accounts for the success enjoyed in the sixteenth century by autobiographies of spiritual leaders (but also of poets and memorialists) . . . The autobiographical *I* is the (empty) space in which the discourse of subjectivity and individuality is constructed. It is defined on the basis of a signifier as a (proper) name, ab-solute, un-bound from the world which no longer supports it, and as the reciprocal term of God, ab-solute, un-bound from the world He no longer supported as his language. This is the *mythos* (that which founds speech) our civilization substitutes for the discourse of the cosmos; it is a "full" discourse spoken/produced by its speaker.

In this autobiographical literature, the *I* is both figurative and a figure, a symbolic representation. The figure, the third and last element to be discussed, is not utterative, except disguised as an image. It is, rather, an organizing factor. It marks *in* the text the *empty* place (empty of world) where the *other* speaks, following a process the discourse describes by *recounting its own production*. The opening chapter of St Teresa's *Interior Castle*[22] illustrates the imaginary, formal schema that is common to so many mystics. Since she "could find nothing to say and had no idea how to begin," she beseeched "Our Lord today that He would speak through me": this discourse is *nothing* if it is not the *other* speaking. . . . The scriptural experience of letting the other write is not an affair of theory, but takes place "today." But where will the other come from, in what space? At this point a "foundation" "offers itself." It is analogous to the dreams (*sueños*) from which St Teresa's writing constantly departs. It is fiction, a nothing that causes one to speak and write, but it is also something "there is no point in fatiguing ourselves over by attempting to understand" or verify. It is not something true, it is only a thing of beauty (*hermosura*): "a castle made of a single diamond or of very clear crystal." Like Duchamp's "glass," it is a transparent, finite space that has no place of its own, yet includes "many dwellings." The models of the celestial Jerusalem (an apocalyptic image), of "paradise" (and image of the origin), and of "Heaven" (a cosmological image) become miniaturized and combine in a translucent gem where "He takes His delights."[23] Such is the "soul of the just." This beautiful object immediately unites opposites: it combines unity and a plurality of "dwellings" (*Moradas* [translated in English as "mansions]) which permit an itinerary to be drawn up; it is a strict delimitation of a space one must "enter when one is in it already," a place where one dwells without dwelling there – and whose center is also exteriority (God). The coinciding of these opposites organizes the entire discursive formation devoted to the "interior castle" where, as Carmelite addressees are told, despite "how strictly cloistered you are," "you will take your delight" (*deleitaros*), "for you can enter it and walk about in it at any time without asking leave from your superiors."[24] That is exactly what St Teresa does.

To what does this dream refer – this dream that opens up for her a free space in which to write (walk about), a space she can enter without permission (*sin licencia*), where she can find so many "treats" (*regalos*)? The subject, the garden of the other, expresses itself in dreams. . . . There is a triple relation of the "I" to an imaginary *nothing*, an isolated (and atopic) locus outlined by the dream, and a *pleasure* [*jouissance*] which comes to the subject from the other. The subject is compared to "a person holding the candle in his hand, who is soon to die a death that he longs for; and in agony . . . is rejoicing with ineffable joy" – an erotic agony, "a glorious folly," a "heavenly madness" . . . [25]

It is in this place that St Teresa's *Life* is written, as a journey to the center. It is a journey whose itinerary combines the normality of an *order* imposed from without, by history ("commands," missions, a series of institutional and rational dependencies), and the *gaps* created in it by irruptions of "folly" (coming from within, from the other, in the form of fictions, dreams, and apparitions). It is built out of this mixture. *Libro de la Vida*: St Teresa's title already expresses the tension that makes her in-between place a mystic trace. The task of writing consists for her in "ordering," it consists of a chronological and didactic progression, a teaching through prayer requested by "them." But in spite of that, her "life" goes the way of dreams (*sueños*) and "follies" (*desatinos*), "surprises" that "lead her astray" and "ravish" her; it is a nostalgia (*tristezza*) that comes of not being unbound yet, of not being hidden at last by that elsewhere and other given only in fiction; it is to "die from not dying." It is also a nostalgia for an internal transparence that is impossible to achieve within existing relations, even religious ones. That nostalgia led Teresa to construct two transitory avatars of the "castle" – the book and the convent, her two consolations, her two strategies. The *book*: because it articulates dreams and desire in the common language and because that labor of articulation creates a poetic place. The *community* (or *buena compañía*): because it produces a shared speech (the *conversación*) among those who desire, and who agree on a common *volo*. The text (*libro*) and the convent (*fundación*) combine in the "constitution," the contract founding an island of utterance. . . .

One may legitimately ask whether the psychological person, far from expressing itself in the personal pronoun, is not rather an effect of utterance." However that may be, it remains to be known *who* or *what* says "I." Is the "I" a fiction of the other, which offers itself in its place? St Teresa, when discussing the crystal-castle that is the soul, speaks of a disappearance (ecstasy) or death that constitutes the subject as *pleasure* [*jouissance*] in the other. . . . In a different mode, Angelus Silesius, in his role as the subject of a poetic work, expects his creation to be the "son" (or "daughter") of the word of the Other. At the heart of mystic writing, there is something other that comes without reason: the poem and, secondarily, the dream. A "there is" – "es gibst," it gives (Heidegger) – is the beginning.

. . . An approaching strangeness arrives, with an inevitability it founds and names at the same time; there is nothing outside it (not even meaning, for it comes from beyond) to confirm or authorize it. The poet, merely the utterer of this founding act of nomination, bends to its inevitability. . . . The poem does what it says; it itself creates what it makes space for. But like the musician in Bosch's *Garden of Earthly Delights*, who is caught in his harp, his arms outstretched as though dead or passed out, played by the song that sends him into ecstasy, insane from being imprisoned in his instrument, that is, in the body of the voice of the other – the poet, too, is *robbed* by that excess which names but remains unnamable. . . .

This kind of poetry is not what the mystics say they "write," a term reserved for commentaries or treatises. It writes itself. It was for a long time, up to St Teresa, called "the music of the angel". . . . It arrives *before* the hour of labor, "at the time of the rising dawn."[26] The "música callada," silent music, comes first. But from where? . . . St John of the Cross says that sometimes God would give him the words to his poems, and sometimes he would look for them, laboring to follow the track of the "given words." Therefore, he makes a distinction between the "canciones" and his commentary (or "declaración"), which is, strictly speaking, the only thing he writes. While all writing is a demand for love, the "dichos de amor" in particular partake of an unexpected, unexplainable "abundance and impetuousness." Without reason, the *too much* of a "plenitude" overflows the space in which it reveals itself. "What is explainable in it" (*declara*) is only the *least* of it, or the effect it produces in a particular field (of language, of exchanges, of questions), that is, in a mode of writing giving form to one of the possible "meanings" generated by the poem.[27] . . .

Where, then, is the poem? Where, by itself, without explanation, does it obtain the power "to produce love and affection in the soul"?[28] In what sense is it mystical? These three questions are answered in the writing of St John of the Cross.

For him, the "canciones" are of such "breadth and plenty" (*archura y copia*) that they "touch (*toca*: burn and penetrate) everything." An excess of fire, occurring at every possible turn in history. This *abundancia* is best guaranteed and most readable in the Scriptures, but it is not more real or efficient there than it is in the poem. *The same* abundance "touches" the poet today as touched the inspired writers of antiquity. There is certainly not the same Church recognition of both, but they share *the same* "impotence" to make that understood, except by using "strange figures and similitudes." Thus, the poem comes at the same place at which the Scriptures speak (more exactly, it is the place where what is said in the Scriptures can "be heard" [*s'entendre*]), but it does not enjoy the same status. It has not been granted a Church alliance, so even if there are no internal differences, in order to interpret (*declarar*) the poem in the Church, in order to teach and comment on it, it is nevertheless necessary for it to be "confirmed" by the "authority of the Divine Scriptures."[29]

It is in the form of interpretation in a didactic situation that discourse is committed to memory, that historical or institutional alterity. The poem as such does not depend on it any more than that other space, the castle or "garden of delights" St Teresa's readers may "walk about in at any time without asking leave" of their superiors. The poem has a radical autonomy. Did not St Ignatius of Loyola, speaking in the third person of his own visions, those unwritten poems, say that "if there were no Scriptures to teach us these matters of the faith, he would be resolved to die for them, only because of what he had seen"?[30] His is a more ambiguous statement, since it presupposes that what he "saw" and the "truths" of the faith are the same. For St John of the Cross, on the other hand, the Christian exegesis of a poem or vision is an effect of writing and didactics, and is just one of the traces and one of the "meanings" made possible by the "given words."

These "canciones," which are in principle separable from their "declaración" (even though the evolution of the commentary is undoubtedly associated with revisions of the *Cántico*), in addition seem like a love poem. Religious allusions are absent in their content: all proper names and references have been purged, undermining the "Christian" realist illusion. This indication of what makes the poem poetic refers to the form of the "canciones," or more precisely, to their phonetic body. Here, an organization of (erotic) *meaning* serves as the support for an organization of (musical) *sounds*. The *Cántico* is written in the tradition of the *cantar en romance*; using the rhythm of the *lira stanza* (strophes of five verses, two with eleven feet, three with seven), it abounds in rich rhyme patterns, internal assonance and phonic repetitions, all within a structure transferring the words, pronouns, and verbs of the one (*thee*) to the other (*me*): a music of echoes and minor images in which the *Amado* is doubled, bursts, and retrieves himself in the gaze and advent of the other – but which other? Saussure's anagram rule and Ruwet's rule of parallelism – both of which establish the primacy of the signifier over the signified – here seem to be confirmed by the play of nouns ("wound," "quest," etc.), which shift freely from one position to the other, thus destroying the stability of the characters to whom they are attached.

The poem – a cadenced repetition . . . – does not stop at deconstructing meaning and making it music: it is what allows the very production of meaning. The "taste for echoes" awakened by the poem leads one "to seek a semantic connection between elements nothing binds together semantically";[31] it makes possible the indefinite prolongation of this semantical research as an echo effect. It says nothing. It permits saying. For that reason, it is a true "beginning." It is a liberating space, where yesterday's readers – but "we" also – can find speech. The "canciones" did not lay down a meaning once and for all; they created a place of origin for "love effects."

In what sense is this "convulsive beauty," which is "erotic – veiled, exploding – stable, magical – circumstantial,"[32] also mystical? If the musical secret of its efficacy is not answer enough, one could advance some tentative hypothesis: it is possible that the "mystical" character of the poem is located at the meeting point of the poetic and the religious; it could simply be the walk of the "goddess" as she crosses (and leaves) the Christian realm. What would be mystical, then, is the disappearance of the actors (the lover and the loved one, God and man) whereas the transactions between them prevail: "God and I are one in the transaction."[33] The "canciones" inscribe the movement of these transformations of action and agony in the very words and characters they deprive both of meaning and a place to be. Mystical also would be the relation of the poem to the religious tradition whose statements it presupposes, but uses in order to make them say the absence of what they designate. It is by taking words seriously, a life and death game in the body of language, that the secret of what they give is torn from them – and, as St John of the Cross says in relation to the "holy *doctors*," to do that is to make them confess the secret of their "impotence," of what they cannot "give." One more thing, perhaps, is mystical: the establishment of a space where change serves as a foundation and saying loss is an other beginning. Because it is always *less* than what *comes* through it and allows a genesis, the mystic poem is connected to the *nothing* that opens the future, the time *to come*, and, more precisely, to that single work, "Yahweh," which forever makes possible the self-naming of that which induces departure.[34]

Notes

1 Lucien Goldmann, *The Hidden God*, tr. Philip Thody (London: Routledge and Kegan Paul, 1964), esp. pp. 103ff.

2 Alphonse Dupront, "Vie et création religieuses dans la France moderne," in *La France et les Français* (Paris: Gallimard, Pléiade, 1972), p. 535.

3 John G. A. Pocock, in *The Machiavellian Moment* (Princeton: Princeton University Press, 1975). . . .

4 Henri Bremond, *A Literary History of Religious Thought in France* (New York: Macmillan, 1926–36), Vol. 2 (The Coming of Mysticism: 1590–1620).

5 See Charles Webster, *The Great Instauration: Science, Medicine, and Reform, 1626–1660* (London: Duckworth, 1975), pp. 15–31.

6 John Wallis, *Truth Tried* (1643), p. 91, quoted by Webster, op. cit., p. 30.

7 *Entendre* is translated variously below as "to hear" or "to understand." Both connotations should be kept in mind in each instance. The archaic Spanish *entender* is similar – Tr.

8 St John of the Cross, *Vida y obras*, p. 509 (in *Complete Works of St John of the Cross*, tr. E. Allison Peers [London: Burns, Oates and Washbourne, 1934], Vol. I, p. 13.

9 St John of the Cross, *Complete Works*, Vol. II, p. 51.
10 Angelus Silesius, *Le Pèlerin chérubique*, tr. Eugène Susini (Paris: PUF, 1964), p. 170.
11 "Illocutionary" (one can also say "allocutionary" or "illocutory") is the term used by J. L. Austin, the pioneer of research on utterance, to designate the act of speaking and discuss what it changes in relationships among interlocutors.
12 "Allocution" is the utterance of a discourse addressed to someone; the "allocutor" the person to whom the discourse is addressed.
13 Cf. Tzvetan Todorov, "Problèmes de l'énonciation," *Languages*, no. 17 (1970), pp. 3–11.
14 Emile Benveniste, *Problèmes de linguistique générale* (Paris: Gallimard, 1974), Vol. II, p. 83.
15 Benveniste, *Problems in General Linguistics*, Vol. I, tr. Mary Meek (Coral Gables, Fla.: University of Miami Press, 1971), pp. 219, 227, etc.
16 "Discourse" is to be understood here according to Benveniste's definition: "language in so far as it is taken over by the man who is speaking and within the condition of intersubjectivity, which alone makes linguistic communication possible" (*Problems*, p. 230).
17 The most common meaning of *se parler* is to converse with someone else, but taken literally it means "to speak oneself"; similarly, *s'entendre* can mean to hear or understand oneself, to be heard, or to come to an understanding with another. – Tr.
18 *Meister Eckhart, a Modern Translation*, tr. Raymond Blackney (New York: Harper & Row, 1941), p. 13.
19 Ibid., p. 3.
20 Surin, *Correspondance*, ed. Michel de Certeau (Paris: DDB, 1966), p. 974.
21 The term *shifter* is borrowed from Roman Jakobson and designates a signifier that effects a shift (a passage/articulation) between different isotopics (or codes).
22 St Teresa, *Moradas del Castillo interior*, chap. 1, *Obras*, II, pp. 341–345 (*Complete Works*, II, pp. 201–205).
23 *El*, unspecified: "He," the Other.
24 Conclusion, *Moradas*, p. 494 (*Interior* in *Complete Works*, III, p. 350).
25 *Vida*, chap. 16, in *Obras*, I, p. 683 (*Complete Works*, I, p. 96).
26 St John of the Cross, *Cántico espirituel*, Stanza 13/14 (*Complete Works*, II, p. 87).
27 Prologue, *Cántico, Vida y Obras*, pp. 901–902 (*Complete Works*, I, p. 212).
28 St John of the Cross, Prologue, *Cántico* (*Complete Works*, II, p. 25).
29 Ibid.
30 *The Autobiography of St Ignatius Loyola*, tr. Joseph O'Callaghan (New York: Harper & Row, 1974), p. 39.
31 Ruwet, "Parallélismes," in *Langue, discours, société* (Paris: Seuil, 1975), p. 319.
32 André Breton, *Poésie et autre* (Paris: Club du meilleur livre, 1960), p. 174.
33 Meister Eckhart, Sermon "Justi vivent in aeternum," in *Deutsche Werke* (Stuttgart: W. Kohlhammer, 1936), Vol. I, pp. 114–115.
34 "I AM THAT I AM . . . I AM that hath sent me unto you" (*Exodus* 3.14). Cf. Jean-Louis Schefer, *L'invention du crops chrétien* (Paris: Galilée, 1975), pp. 107–108.

Part V

Other Beliefs: Theology

16

Introduction: Michel de Certeau, Theologian

Frederick Christian Bauerschmidt

On ne choisit pas d'être croyant.... Fondamentalement, *être croyant, c'est vouloir être croyant.*

("Du corps à l'écriture," p. 295)

The publication of *The Mystic Fable* in English translation has made abundantly clear for English-speaking readers both Certeau's massive erudition regarding religion and his passionate interest in religious phenomena. Still largely unrecognized are the specifically *theological* aspects of Certeau's work; that is, the way in which he works from *within* Christian discourse. Certeau's theology is marked both by the Christian and Jesuit tradition in which he had been formed and by those distinctive themes that one finds in other areas of his work – alterity, history, resistance, rupture. Indeed, it is in no small part through reflection on the Christian tradition that Certeau develops these themes. Most of all, Certeau's theological writings make it clear that he remained a passionate believer to the end of his days.

In speaking of the specifically theological in Certeau, I refer to something distinct (though not entirely separate) from forays into "religious studies." One might say that whereas religious studies is a discipline of (and disciplined by) the academy, theology is a discourse shaped by the distinctive traditions and practices of Christian communities. At the outset of his 1966 essay "Culture and Spiritual Experience" (see bibliography for details) Certeau notes something like this distinction, speaking of "those who are chiefly concerned with religion" (i.e. theologians) and "the historians who work along socio-cultural lines" (i.e. those who practice "religious studies") ("Culture and Spiritual Experience," p. 3). But he goes on to note that these two approaches are not easily separated. Certeau himself constitutes something of a hybrid in this regard because he believed that "the essential element in any spiritual experience is not some 'otherness' quite outside of language and time." Rather, it is precisely within the specificity of the believer's cultural situation "that his yearnings and his predicament 'take flesh'; it is through this medium that he finds God, yet ever seeks him, that he expresses his faith, that he carries on simultaneously experiments in colloquy with God and with his actual brothers" ("Culture," p. 9). This understanding of religious experience – shaped both by a postmodern, historicist perspective and by the Christian doctrine of the Incarnation – requires that Certeau take the task of the religious historian (in all its secularity) with absolute seriousness, precisely for theological reasons. Thus the hybrid character of Certeau's theological writings: on one side the perspective of the passionate believer, the member of a religious congregation, the one who seeks to make Christian faith credible; on the other side the skeptical if not jaundiced perspective of the historian who can see in Teresa of Avila's theology yet another example of the modern turn to subjectivity; the sociologist who can analyze power relations within French Catholicism; the cultural critic who unblinkingly recognizes the marginal status of the Church in modern intellectual and social life.

Those familiar with currents of Catholic theology in the 1950s and 1960s will recognize in an essay like "Culture and Spiritual Experience" the ways in which Certeau was a man of his day. In Certeau's theology we can hear resonances of two modern Jesuit theologians in particular. When Certeau speaks of "the God who always reveals his truth as a truth about man" one can hear the "anthropological turn" taken by Catholic theology in the middle of the twentieth century, perhaps best represented by the German Jesuit Karl Rahner (1904–84). Rahner, responding to the German Idealist tradition, sought to reconcile Catholic dogma with the Kantian "Copernican revolution." Likewise, in stressing the historical conditioning of religious language and experience, Certeau builds on the works of the French Jesuit Henri de Lubac (1896–1991), particularly his historical studies such as *Corpus Mysticum* (Paris, 1949), which show the intimate connection between changes in belief and changes in the language of belief.[1] Yet Certeau does not simply borrow from the theological currents of his day, but brings them together in quite original ways. In particular, he fundamentally transforms Rahner's anthropological starting point by bringing it into contact with a radicalized version of de Lubac's historicism. The human person with whom he begins is not, as in

Rahner, the ahistorical subject of German Idealism, but rather a subjectivity constructed within language and culture, a self that has no unchanging essence, that is constituted by a series of ruptures.

Thus, while much Catholic theology in the 1960s was caught up in trying to inhale the dying gasps of existentialism, Certeau's historicism led him to focus attention on the ways in which cultures and traditions shape and authorize belief. He shows early on – long before any other theologian – an appreciation of the work of Michel Foucault, in particular the way in which Foucault shows how even (or especially) the most sublime ideas can mask the workings of power.[2] But Certeau also shows a keen appreciation of the Christian community and tradition as the indispensable, though problematic, locus of Christian experience. Speaking of the "Presence" that reveals himself "as that without which life is impossible," Certeau cites chapter 6 of John's Gospel: "To whom then shall we go? For thou hast the words of eternal life." But he then goes on to say that, "however 'eternal' and unapproachable this 'life' may be, it is nonetheless brought to the believer by a tradition, a religious teaching, a Church – realities that are rooted in history and society" ("Culture," p. 22). If God is the one whom Christians are "not without," this is only because they are not without the communally borne tradition from which they receive their language and to which they are accountable for their use of that language.[3] As Certeau wrote, in order for theology to bear the name "Christian," it must be "recognized" by other Christians.[4]

However, this quest for recognition raises a host of questions. Certeau pointed out with great acuity how languages and the traditions and practices that authorize them are not nearly so stable as they pretend. Traditions appear as continuities because we *narrate* them that way and, as he showed with his analysis of everyday life, a plurality of meanings can be borne by a single practice. Who are the authorities to whom we may appeal for recognition? To which narrative of continuity do we look to identify authentic traditions? What discourse can tell us the meaning of our actions? Mining the interstices of various discourses, Certeau shows that any discourse, no matter how monolithic, is always marked by fissures that threaten to shatter it. Thus, "faith speaks prophetically of a Presence who is both immediately felt and yet still to come, who cannot be refused without a betrayal of all language, and yet who cannot be immediately grasped and held in the terms of any particular language" ("Culture," p. 22). The "truly 'spiritual' person" must therefore learn to live "the interior paradox of a *particular form* of faithfulness to *the Infinite*" ("Culture," p. 26).

For Certeau, there is built into Christian faith a series of tensions – between particularity and universality, between continuity and rupture, between tradition and innovation – that gives it its dynamism, but that also establishes the *risk* of faith. Emphasis on this risk seems to become clearer in Certeau's theological writings as we move from the 1960s into the 1970s. The disarray within the Christian tradition becomes ever clearer; the fragmentation of theological discourse in modernity is far advanced; the Church's status as an institution that can determine truth has become questionable. Indeed, one might claim that a chief hallmark of modernity is the eclipse of the Church by the state as the exemplary form of human community. In the revolutionary changes in Catholicism that followed the Second Vatican Council (1962–5), Certeau witnesses such typically modern features as appeals to individual conscience, demands for rights, and liturgies that prized spontaneity. The Church no longer serves as the site for the production of meaning; increasingly Christians borrow their values from the culture of modernity.

"From the Body to Writing, a Christian Transit" takes up the question of how one might think of Christian belief in such a context, after the demise of Christendom or "Christian society." Using the language employed in *The Practice of Everyday Life*, Certeau asks how – given that the determination of what is Christian is always relative to a "place" and given that that place, which formerly was "religious," is now "civil" – one can continue to be a believer in the absence of a distinctively Christian "place." Certeau explores several possibilities. One is that Church institutions could simply tighten their grasp, issuing ever stronger doctrinal and moral statements in an attempt to retain or reestablish their status as institutions with the power to "make believe." But such pronouncements would no longer be a voice issuing from a living body, but instead a bodiless discourse, an incantation desperately seeking to conjure a body. Alternatively, believers could accept that the "place" that determines them is now the thoroughly secularized modern world and seek their Christian identity in serving that world on its own terms. But of course, as Certeau points out, all that this would leave as a marker of Christian identity is the evanescent "motivation" of individuals. A third alternative would be that Christians might accept the secularization of the world, yet not simply serve it on its own terms. Rather, through a set of checks and excesses, Christian identity would be marked by a distinctive ethic (e.g. rejection of divorce, abortion, etc.). But such a solution begs the question of who would define and authorize such an ethic. The loss of a body from which such ethical discourse could issue is precisely the loss that such an ethic seeks to address.

Having mapped the difficulties with all these alternatives, Certeau looks deeper into the problem and discerns there a tension that is not newly sprung upon the believer with modernity, but rather an ancient Christian tension between discipleship and conversion, between "*Nachfolge* and *metanoia*." How does one adhere to a tradition while recognizing the genuine newness of every step forward; how does one both "follow" and "change"? Any answer to such a question is primarily a matter of lived practice, not theoretical construct. The call to follow has no "objective" statement, but is only embodied in the response, which is always different from the call. The call to follow is therefore an evanescent event. As a result of this, the discourse of the believer cannot claim the status of "truth" (only a discourse that originates from a "place" can do this) but is rather "fable" – language without power. Yet it is precisely in this "weakness" of the fable that its power lodges, as it calls into question the strategically defined "reality" of systems of meaning. The fabulous tale of the empty tomb introduces the non-site of difference into a system of places.

The u-topic "no place" of the empty tomb is the enacted space of the pilgrim city; the "new Israel" that now joins the "old Israel" in its diaspora wanderings. For Certeau, the fate of believers in modernity is to become wanderers, those who leave in answer to the call to follow, without the burden of "truth" or "power" or "authority" or even "identity." Leaving the security of its homeland (which actually was a place of captivity), the Church, like Israel carrying the Ark of the Covenant, bears its fabulous and disruptive tale of Christ as it journeys across always alien territory toward the unnameable. For Certeau, such an understanding of Christianity – one that risks the "weakness of faith" – offers the possibility of faith in a world from which God has become absent.[5]

Notes

1 The claim to Rahner's influence is conjectural, though given Rahner's stature in Catholic theology it is hard to imagine that he did *not* influence Certeau in his anthropological starting point. The influence of de Lubac is clearer. In addition to citing de Lubac's work in numerous places, Certeau contributed an essay on the term "mystique" to de Lubac's *Festschrift, L'homme devant Dieu* (Paris, 1964).

2 Note the citation of *The Birth of the Clinic* in "Culture and Spiritual Experience."

3 Here Certeau is developing his notion of God as the one whom we are "not without" – an appropriation of Heidegger's "*nicht ohne.*" See M. de Certeau, "How Is Christianity Thinkable Today?" in *The Postmodern God: a Theological Reader*, Graham Ward, ed., pp. 146–7.

4 See M. de Certeau, *La Faiblesse de croire*, p. 209.

5 For a fuller treatment of Certeau's theology, as well as some critical remarks, see F. C. Bauerschmidt, "The Abrahamic Voyage: Michel de Certeau and Theology," *Modern Theology*, 12 (1), January 1996, 1–26.

17

The Weakness of Believing

From the Body to Writing, a Christian Transit

In passing from the spoken to the written word, I am not attempting to "reinforce" the place which I was speaking from, amass proofs, or block up the openings which an evening's talk may have left here. I would not want the written version to call to order – or forget – the "slips" which arise in discussion, all that escapes one's control in spoken language, as though it were necessary to subject the chance advent of desire, which has its source in the other, to the legality of writing. On the contrary, these glimpses allow writing to begin again. A certain work therefore introduces into established systems the mobility which the spoken word already betrays. It traces on our maps the longer voyages generated by the momentary "sallies" of conversation. Instead of moving from the written to the spoken, from an orthodoxy to its verbal illustration (or to "unguarded" remarks which one can allow oneself because they are not serious and will not influence the writing, which remains intact), the process starts from the mobility of speech, porous and tendered, more easily altered than writing by what is still only half expressed within it, and proceeds to produce a language which is reorganized by these first avowals, thus producing a shift in the ranks of knowledge or reason. Here, this process bears on Christianity: in fact, on the relation between a question of truth and my own position. Any analysis of this problem consequently puts in question the place from which I discuss it. There can be no textual work until the postulates of the remarks I make on Christianity are unearthed from their silent opacity. It is the relation between these remarks and their site of production which is the real subject here. The movement which turns the object of the statement [*énoncé*] back towards the site of its utterance [*énonciation*] must moreover be situated in relation to a "way of proceeding" specific to Christianity, if one is to take the latter not solely as an object of study but also as an operation. The whole evangelical tradition makes of such a movement the condition of a practice: "conversion" is that without which no "work" or "logos" of faith may be produced. If the site from which I speak were above suspicion, were placed beyond question, my analysis would cease to be evangelical and would become the establishment of a "truth" with a religious content. In the light of this also, when the discussion is taken up again, one should try not to lose or forget the questions which the voice has introduced, letting them develop to the point where they touch the position of the speaker which, made fragile again, produces effects which may flow back into language and be marked there.

As for the possibility of a place from which to act and speak as a Christian, these questions, as I understood them, suggested two very different directions and swung from one to the other: on the one hand, the possibility of belonging to the ecclesial body which alone gives credence to a work or a discourse of truth, and, on the other hand, the production of a "writing" made possible by confronting the corpus of Christian rites and texts with contemporary practices. By "body" I mean the historical and social existence [*être-là*] of an organized site. In a very broad sense, I call "writing" the inscription of a desire into the system of a language (professional, political, scientific, etc., and not solely literary), and so, as one says in law, the "insinuation" into a body (a corpus of laws, a social body, the body of a language) of a movement which alters it.

Thus two divergent options are signaled here. One of them involves a Church which "authorizes" a truth and necessarily mediates it. The other involves the movement which an evangelical questioning produces in fields of social activity. In the first case, Christians have a site of sense: a body of truth(s). In the second case, across work and leisure activities, there are only signifying practices: "writings." When I caricature in this way the poles between which our remarks came and went, I am only sketching the outer limits of the space in which I am seeking an analytical procedure which may allow somewhat more clarity. But it is perhaps simpler to say that this text aims at an operation of which it is at once a particular instance and an experimental development: how do we produce a language of believers?

An Imaginary Body: the Discursive Product

Someone asked during a discussion: "Where are you speaking from?" In other words, "On what authority are you speaking?" The participant referred my words back to the site which was their condition of possibility. Which is, in fact, a prerequisite move and the first issue. For a discourse which does not have recourse to "authoritative instances" is not for that matter free from some authority which endorses it. Quite the reverse, the less it displays its credentials (that is, the less it can be verified by its readers or listeners), the more it supposes some validation, gained from some public image, academic acclaim or social position. Hence the mass media effectively increase the role of the personality while depriving the discourse of the means whereby it might be verified. The reduction in proofs is made up for by the mythologization of the speaker. The production and commercialization of "authorities" wins out over the economy of the discourse.

But in the marketplace of these theatrical positions, another form of attachment to a site comes into play. The articulation of a discourse with a socio-economic body imposes limits on it. Even when treated as a star, the "specialist" remains controlled by the social body to which he belongs; he cannot do just anything. The better the body is organized, the more its discipline marks out a bone structure in the discourse. That is how speech is retained and at the same time sustained by professional, political, or scientific groups. The (secret) law of discourse is the (powerful) institution. The relation to the real is introduced into discourse through what the social body supporting it allows or disallows. What first and foremost allows one to adopt a medical,[1] academic, or indeed psychoanalytic[2] discourse is belonging to a body. Similarly, it is social initiation and selection alone which, in every society, give access to the place from which a certain discourse may be proferred. Social belonging founds linguistic "competence."[3] This does not mean that the rigor of research is invalidated, but rather that it evolves in a limited space inscribed within a field of forces and sustained by prior historical, economic, and political determinations. Research is indissociable from the violence of a body. Every discursive field is relative to a set of possibilities and impossibilities which are not dependent on it and which link it to historical determinations, in a relation to the real. In principle, Christian discourse is supported by a relation to a group: traditionally, the logos or discourse is authorized by an *ekklesia* or community. But what becomes of this language when the body with which it is articulated is disseminated? It cannot survive this disconnection intact. The first sign of this is that the discourse covers up either its site of production or the changes affecting this site when it is transformed into an imaginary object. It conceals what otherwise enables it to function.

In the past, classical theology legitimately armed itself with references to "authorities" which had "truth" value (canonical texts, definitions of a doctrinal authority, "Fathers" of the Church, etc.); that is how theology explained its dependence on ecclesial society, which was, in the last instance, the only body capable of conferring authorization. But now theology tends to efface these marks, claiming to be the bearer of messages validated by an evangelical "consciousness" or "spirit": a discourse determined by a social body gives way to a body defined by theology. This effacement of the authorities which until then had organized the text (and which are henceforth reduced to the Bible, an object of exegesis) does not imply that Christian discourse is uprooted from a specific place, but rather that it has changed places. The issue is no longer a doubtful ecclesial reality which may be recovered through the texts, but the production of a representation by the discourse. There is always a site of production, but a discourse which aspires to be theological can no longer admit to this. It is still a question of the Church, but henceforth as a represented body, a discursive product.[4]

Our discussion was an indication of this new mode of functioning. No conferred honour gave authority to my statements. I was simply trying to formulate a personal conviction from my various studies and experiences. Actually, I was validated by a public image, the religious "role" I was playing. Unknown to me or despite myself, my speech relied upon the social position which was imputed to me; it owed its credibility to the fact that I was functioning within the system of a collective imaginary, as theologian, member of a religious order, etc. I was holding a discourse of opinion in this place authorized by the religious beliefs of the public; and this departure from tacit convention could therefore only elicit aggression from the audience, or more sophisticated forms of pleasure. But what resistance did it meet with on the part of a reality other than that of the public? Whereas a medical discourse, even when introduced into the system of opinion, comes up against the limits which a body sets on it, religious discourse spreads out, slips away, proliferates, stopped by nothing and hiding just about anything. It resides idly in a realm of "illusionism" and pleasures, borne along by the play of appearances, caught in the witchcraft of language. It determines, or thinks it determines, the body of which it speaks. In escaping from the constraints of a real body, it enters a logic of perversion. And if deception is not of the same order as lying or error, but is of the order of illusion, then it is a question here of deception. Sincerity is not at issue. It is a question of the functioning which a structural change engenders, what happens when a language is no longer articulated with a body, is no longer supported and held by it.

From this point of view, explicit didactic references, in ecclesiastical circles, to received "authorities" only give another version of the same situation. Through texts, this version intends the better to hide what the body has become: manipulable by powers of another order. What is essential is not that texts should survive; it is that a Christian social body, the Church, should remain capable of determining the practice of these texts, itself a necessary condition for discourses issuing from this practice to relate to the *ekklesia* which "authorizes" them. For the ecclesial body no longer organizes operations which call themselves Christian, whether textual practices (readings of the Bible) or ethical conduct (sexual morality, for example).[5] It is therefore no longer what animates discourses but rather the object which these discourses represent. Hence the Church has ceased to be a site of production, becoming instead a product, an imaginary object of discourse. It would be easy to identify, in Christian language, the effects of this new economy which governs its production. The first signs to note are the changes occurring in the very representation of the body, social or individual: a reference all the more imaginary for being the more unitary. But I will retain only one point (albeit an essential one) concerning the possibility of constructing a language from an ecclesial site. This "site" no longer functions as an institution which founds a sense, capable of organizing a representation according to the limits of a body and hence supplying criteria for selection within evangelical strictures. On the contrary, it has transformed itself into an unlimited representation, indefinite. The Church, an ideological object, can go wherever there is need and claim to fill all the voids in society. Its discourse is fabricated with all the "off-cuts" of regional rationalities which formerly occupied the terrain of religion; its function is fictionally to overcome the limits which every effective practice [*pratique effective*] necessarily encounters: in whatever fashion these reappear, it names them always in the same language. The ecclesial vocabulary is therefore just a symptom of the limits proper to any technical activity. The same signifiers can cover all sorts of finitude since in fact they recognize none.

Whereas one can take seriously a discourse which formulates economic, financial, or political operations because it obeys rules and resistances imposed by a field which is proper to it, religious discourse is never falsifiable: it cannot be caught in the act of error because it has eliminated this possibility; it lacks weight because it is not within history. It has escaped from it. It increasingly hides what makes it work and still talks of "totality" or the "universal," because it can be anything at all. The same metaphor, lacking a relation to a body, can designate everywhere what is lacking in each body; hence the difficulty of finding a site from which one can seriously pronounce a language of believers at present.

A Body Undone: Vanishing Expressions and Anonymous Practices

In order to make up for the progressive loss of the ecclesial body and to find a real site again, people thought for a time that it was possible to preserve the unitary and globalizing form of the Church while finding a different social content for it. Hence, in the trend influenced by the "Worker Priest" movement, the Church remained in principle the only site where the sense of history could be spoken, but in fact its norms and its power to organize practices derived from the social field where it had to establish itself: namely from the working classes, which in effect imposed ways of thinking and choices of action. It is indeed the true site of history, but it is not Christian. That such effective action [*effectivité*] could be attributed to the Church was credible only by virtue of a play on the word "the poor." So a metaphor allowed the fiction to be maintained that history is made in one place alone (no longer the Church but the "world of work"), and that it has only one sense. But this quest for another space[6] already signaled that one fact was being taken seriously – the impossibility of the Church constituting a real place from which to speak – as well as the substitution of hard labor, limited and historical, for the officialese of a "universal" language. What Christians have learnt since then begins with this founding experiment. As it developed, this experiment could not but demystify the unitary ideology whose principle it had initially preserved. The concern for real action, on the part of Christians, involved them in activities and choices where differences were insurmountable, short of holding on to the increasingly abstract, and, in the end result, an unworkable "mandate" received from the hierarchy, or else the increasingly metaphorical and diversely interpreted language of dogmatic statements. At the same time, the divisions between militants or between effective involvements became stronger than the Christian label which they had in common. If Christian groupings were made at that time under the sign of individual affinities of a cultural, social, economic, political, or simply amicable nature, they responded to divisions which themselves were no longer Christian.

In the face of this destructuring of the Church, doctrine in turn adapted, by defending "individual Churches," "grass-roots communities," or "pluralism." Paradoxically, this redeployment made plurality, normally discouraged, into the index of a new unitary language. But do these sites of community provide operative criteria for the production of a Christian language? As soon as the community[7] seeks to express a Christian identity, it presents uniform features. It aims to establish for Christians a space of utterance proper to them, which is made necessary by the impossibility of self-expression in the language of work.

But it also excludes, in fact if not in principle, the goal of integration into the organization of social tasks, in order to play its part effectively there. Unlike in the case of "missions" (movements, etc.), this horizon has no place in an ecclesial politics; the latter is "prophetic" and marginal. Christian experience seems to find in this a "stopping" point, a sort of threshold before a change of state. The production of a space of speech compensates for the erasure of the actualization of faith in history, and this is expressed through a critical or prophetic distance from existing institutions.

In many ways, through this space, the community is continuing the eremetical and charismatic traditions of yesterday (disseminated prophetic sites), but without a relation to the constituted Church which used to be the premise, the referent, and the check on these "spiritual" groups. The community is propped up, without mediation, against the social organization which has replaced the Church in its function of being the referent of critique or prophetism, and which increasingly renounces the role of "stating meaning."[8] With these groups, it is as though all that remained of the Church were its marginal movements, testifying to a Christian radicalism which is always necessary and suspect, and as though the renewed questioning which they embody could be related only to civil, economic, and political society. Hence these communities bring back the problematics inherent to the spiritual movements, but now the ground which they presupposed is lacking. The institutions which the groups refer to are no longer religious and are less and less ideological. There remains the gesture of taking a distance from institutions, but without the ground which it was related to; an instrument adapted to work on one system survives the corpus which it has traversed. The function can no longer find the place where it used to be applied.

The progressive disappearance of the ground which had given rise to it doubtless explains the distortions which are introduced into community prophetism as soon as it functions in isolation, without the (sacerdotal, sacramental, social) institution which gave it a basis and provided it with statements from which it could derive effects of divergence. Prophetism, thrown out of itself, is abandoned to the internal logic of utterance. Since it is not linked to present organizations around work, culture, or politics either (unlike small non-religious groups), no monitoring and no content can localize it; it moves toward a saying [*un dire*] which is increasingly rarefied and empty, toward a pure utterance. Or else, in order to survive, the community alienates itself in a domestic activity ("familial," economic, etc.), of obvious legitimacy and necessity, but which reduces Christian prophetism, initially posited as the rationale of the group, to the role of façade, memory, or metaphor.

When describing the possibilities, as they appear to me today, open to the Christian community – either its emptying out if it means to adhere to its initial project, or its transformation into a group without any Christian marker, or else its fragmentation into transitory disseminated operations – I also ask myself what I am doing. Many meetings, friendships, and personal experiences confirm my analysis, but should also preclude it. It also runs counter to my desire, which for a long time held sway over me, to find a solution precisely in this – the lost Jerusalem, a "Refuge," as Christian heroes setting out on founding voyages for the borders of the Western world would say.[9] The longed-for land dissolving on approach or definitively lacking, such are the experiences which should lead us not to place within our real history, whether laborious or jubilant, but always limited, the poetic signs of a kingdom or a community. We cannot assume that the "Poem of Christ"[10] constitutes or creates an effective space in society, nor can we confuse a mythic site with a social place. The Christian community, by contrast, is founded on their identity, believing that it can define a group through myth. But experience shows that in wanting to hold on to the myth, the group vanishes, or else that in wanting to act and live, it destroys, in fact if not in principle, its definition as Christian and often any Christian reference. In circumscribing this alternative and the rarefaction which the logic of expression brings with it, the conditions of Christian production will emerge with greater sharpness: Christianity can no longer be taken as a place from which to speak when it becomes the object of work to be undertaken from the place (henceforth neither religious nor Christian) where we are situated in our present society.

At heart, Christian community expression is born of a demand for nomination. It constitutes itself socially because there is something else to say. Also, while not reducible to the fact of being marginal (situated outside of the fields of work), it does marginalize itself. Some rupture is essential to it. In order for an expression to be possible, a space of speech must be opened and, in order to do so, a break must be made in the social body. In this respect, the Feast of Fools is not the opposite of The Secular City,[11] but its corollary. When the organization of practices is exclusively "secular," how does one mark out one's difference other than through "madness"? Christian specificity can now be signaled only by a break in operative rationalities or social formations: madness is made of fractured logic and domains cut across.

An act, called forth and marked out by the "proper" name (of Jesus Christ or Christians), creates the differentiation which generates the community. It founds an "emancipated space" devoted to Christian (critical, prophetic, etc.) utterance. But, tacitly, this space is analogous to the one organized by utopian writing, which has as explicit premise an absence of referent, a non-site. In fact, here, the necessity of speaking combines with the impossibility of determining specific practices. What can therefore be marked in the composition of social sites is the act of differentiation. Taken to its limit, this utterance severs any statement from its meaning; never posited here or there, this utterance ceaselessly refers to "something else." The meaning-intention [*vouloir-dire*] speaks without speaking about something. It speaks about nothing except the proper name which marks it out. A rhetoric corresponds to it: it multiplies statements in order to mark them, through negation, with the act of saying themselves; it cultivates confession, autobiography, or testimony; it multiplies figures of style (paradox, oxymoron, etc.) which aim to ruin the discourse from within and thus make it own up to the ineffability of the subject[12] saying itself. The community exhausts the signs which it initially gave itself; it devours its own formulations one after the other. The voracity of utterance: before it no statement holds. It can tolerate only the proper name (a demonstrative of existence) which gives rise to it.

How many communities seem to put forward modes of expression (liturgies, communal readings, critical examinations, silent prayers) only to deny them subsequently, and thus designate the act of self-expression. The break through which these communities were born, by distinguishing themselves from an objective exteriority, multiplies within them and strikes every objective affirmation in turn. In certain cases, this internal logic stops at the limit, when the group uses discourses (psychosociological, political, etc.) which it knows to be foreign to what it means, but which remain the way for it to trace, negatively, the ineffable place of a Christian "saying." In certain respects, in many Western "spiritual" or "charismatic" groups, glossolalia or "speaking in tongues" brings with it a similar hollowing out of objective contents and the same absence of referent. The signifiers disappear from the discourse, which is transformed into singing and moaning, pure voice in the ecstasy and fervor of saying oneself in the vanishing of sense. There is an erosion of statement by utterance.[13] Social structures and structures of sense endorse each other mutually. Here, the disintegration of an ecclesial base throws the group which initially wanted to be bearer of the proper name off course, leading to a reduction in its statements. But, in evacuating sense, the community in turn vanishes. If it allows utterance for a while, it is nevertheless itself emptied by the work of erosion which it temporarily enables. Hence it oscillates between the desire which undermines it and social activities which give it a base while making it forget its own project. It pursues a question which, since it no longer has a social site, can create only scriptural sites; or else it takes up some occupation in the network of social practices. It seems to me that the two terms of the alternative point to the fragmentation which this community is destined to and the splitting of its elements, which, for a short period of unstable equilibrium, it claimed to reconcile.[14]

On the one hand, this community utterance reintroduces a repressed question under a Christian label, the question of the ecstasy which the symbolic of transparency or salvation bears with it, and which has come to seem increasingly out of place in our technocratic universe filled with statements and signifiers. This incongruity is immediately translated into scientific discourse: when confronted with sufferings in search of happiness, medicine and even psychoanalysis replace these "ineffable" demands with procedures aimed at rescuing and developing a language. From the relations out of which these procedures are born, in the opacity of medical or psychoanalytic proximity, only a few bubbles manage to reach the surface and burst into their discourses. Hence, by contrast with the therapeutic institutions which "possess" these discourses and which make them productive on condition that they efface the trace of the speaker from them, the subject cannot return into community speech except as some sort of savage. The subject reappears in the form of a pathos, necessarily a stranger to systems of statements. The discourse of science, which, if it means to be rigorous, must be able to be adopted by just about anybody, corresponds to the discourse of the subject, which seems to be becoming just about anything. Exiled and exiling itself from the social disciplines of knowledge, the language of desire tends toward a confusion of instituted languages – either the speaking in tongues which charismatic or pentecostal groups practice or the paroxysmal rarefaction which conscious operations force on any statement by pushing it to its "breaking point" of confusion and loss.[15] Excess, fusion, and finally absence of language are the successive moments which draw utterance toward voice and gestural language, sites from which this ghost which is the subject speaks; or else toward the work of erosion and deconstruction which is carried out on objective discourses. This is a questioning produced by the body itself or by a writing. It supposes a social place, it cannot constitute one. It is fundamentally utopian. Hence the communities which think that they can sustain this questioning by defining themselves through it are destined to disappear or to seek social practices which situate them elsewhere.

The practices which are closest to the initial project are the ones which involve a mode of communication, a style of relation. The project of a "way of living together" in effect gives rise to numerous little testing grounds which today try out and correct new social models. This ambition is, in fact, absorbed into the legitimate and necessary activities of a domestic economy. The group of friends or companions holds together thanks to the organization of an "intimacy" which is all their own and which links up, on the inside, with the structures of family, conjugal, amorous, or parental relations and, on the outside, with those of work, leisure, and politics. If the group wants to practice insularity, it becomes a phalanstery. If it wants to introduce its models into society, the community becomes a political group. In any case, it provides diverse responses to the question of the relation between the "domestic" and the social, but this operation is no longer, as such, "Christian." The problem of Christianity is therefore displaced towards practices, but these could be anybody's, anonymous, stripped of distinctive rules or marks. Since the community is not defined by a Christian utterance, it will be "Christian" only if, in the "domestic" sphere, activities which can be qualified as Christian are carried out. The site ceases to be relevant, and instead what matters is the possibility of an operation determined by Christian criteria.

The Work of an "Excess"

In fact, in order to protect the ideological reference to an ecclesial "body" (reduced to a private group), the community conceals the problem which these practices pose. For a time, it can make sure it is forgotten. But the community still refers back to it: all the activities which allow it to maintain the fiction of a site of expression proper to it are inscribed within the network of work or leisure activities, whether public or private, which take their norms, their limits, their possibilities, and their analytical instruments from the social life of today. How can a Christian reference be marked in social practices, since, for Christians, there are no longer any sites of production which are properly their own? That is the question. If one accepts that there is no longer any Christian place, and hence neither are there any tasks which are proper to it, then Christian experience can no longer be a system or a language, but it can introduce changes within the social sites where it intervenes. This makes of it a particularity. Hence the type of problems which it poses. The individual can be understood only as a variant in relation to laws or models.[16] Christian practices today, disseminated in accordance with the rules of the tasks performed and of the sites where they are performed, can be understood as "singularities"; that is to say, variants which are always relative to the norms of differentiated spheres. Are there shared, recognizable, and relevant reference points or criteria for the different operations which produce these variants? It is clear that were the reply to be in the negative the term Christian would be nothing short of mysterious; it would refer solely to the corpus (the material) on which heteronomic operations are carried out.

In so far as Christians are active in social life, a Christian "spirit," considered first of all descriptively, makes itself felt in work, either through the motivation governing it (militancy, testimony, etc.), or through moral conduct (dedication, generosity, pardon, etc.), or else again through choosing specific tasks (it would be possible to produce a topography of Christian militancy in teaching, journalism, cultural activities, social or medical work, etc.). These diverse elements constitute a "style." There is a Christian "profile." It is certainly not specific. Many others can have the same intentions and ethical behavior and occupy the same professional domains. But these psychological traits are frequently found in Christians as the already mute but still visible mark of the institutions which previously organized ways of life and structured needs. Hence the work which guarantees a pedagogical, philanthropic, or militant place in society takes over from the missions or priestly vocations of yesterday. That is why tasks which more or less surreptitiously restore a "global vision" or a "discourse of sense" are seductive: culture, political ideology, teaching, writing (whether popularizing or encyclopedic), etc.

So certain structures outlive the effacement of their religious determination. Former architectural constructions remain identifiable in the new geographies of our societies. Similarly, it seems that Christians gather in regions where the present society's past is most visible. Demographically, through where they are and who they associate with, they sketch its archeology. But in doing this, does the Christian "style" indicate anything other than a history which is still linked into the present, an effect of the latencies which characterize every society, a resistance from the past with respect to developments which change it? What are at stake are cultural, social, and psychological determinations: for each one of these moments, a society's continuation in time takes the form of stratified systems which can in principle be dissociated and are in fact increasingly dissociated from the act of belief. Christians are also active in other domains. Even if displayed mostly by Christians, these psychosociological "marks" do not constitute the criteria for a practice of belief. They can do so, for subjective reasons, because they are experienced as Christian determinations (and, historically, this is what they have been), but they do not show how faith may create a Christian variant of social practices.

There exists another path, a traditional one this time. A Christian variant can be the effect of restrictions, bans, and additions, due to ecclesiastical intervention or reflexion on evangelical texts. A "Christian ethics" would be characterized by the limits or additions which it would mark out in public and private activities. It would be the Christian who, in his tasks, would remain on this side of certain thresholds or, on the contrary, would go beyond the statutory normal requirements through additional contributions, codicils and excesses. A set of checks and excesses would result from Christian interventions, which could then be characterized as work carried out on a limit – a way of displacing the units defined by a society. Simple examples of checks: rest on Sunday; tolerance with regard to contraception, but rejection of abortion; political "pluralism," but the banning (in fact if not in principle) of communism; the condemnation of revenge, stealing, divorce, etc. Examples of excesses: militancy within professional positions, movement toward social milieus other than one's own, breaking away from (even "betraying") political orthodoxies, and, lastly, the constant marking of an alterity within established positions.

It has to be admitted, though, that there is hardly any agreement as to the content of these measures. One can, of course – and it is also useful – gather statistics as to their occurrence in "Christian milieus." But what is a "Christian milieu"? Statistics is guilty of a circular argument because it takes as relevant ("Christian") those very features by which it defines the milieu as "Christian."[17] If one moves from facts to doctrine, no greater unanimity exists there, for where could it come from? Not from the hierarchy, which is more concerned with language than with practices and where the decisions, if they are not the outcome of political games,[18] no longer represent or determine the actual behavior of believers. At least this negative aspect of things is clearly apparent in sociological studies.[19] Christian conduct varies, as does its relation to the official line. Should one therefore appeal to the ethical corpus which has constituted Christianity's intentionality over the past centuries? It has created a set of "normative contents." But it is not possible for Christians to reproduce it. One can never "reproduce" the past. The question which returns is therefore: who will select or "authorize" innovations, and in the name of what criteria?

Of the measures which seemed to characterize Christian intervention in practices, there consequently remains a corpus where the living and inert parts vary from individual to individual and which suggests, or just illustrates, two formal aspects of this intervention: on the one hand, it plays on the limits of the given which it receives from society, it displaces frontiers; on the other hand, there must be, today as yesterday, an "effective history [*Wirkungsgeschichte*] of the Gospels";[20] that is to say, a relation between the evangelical tradition and effective action. A praxis. No "faith" without "works." But nothing any longer lays down the objective content of these two necessities. In a first instance, civil society replaced the Church in the role of defining tasks and positions, leaving the Church with only a marginal possibility of correcting or going beyond the delimitation of domains. Today, the ecclesial site from which a coherent strategy around these border-lines[21] might be decided is, in turn, dissolving, which leaves every Christian with the risk of defining them for himself. What survives this progressive collapse of the "body" – a central problem for all present developments – is the formal relation between going beyond a situation and the decision to "do" faith. It is for the believer to take this on and fill it out with a "content." As the ecclesial "body of sense" loses its effectivity, it is for Christians themselves to assure the articulation of this "model" with actual situations. This "model" refers to the New Testament combination of "following [Jesus]" and "conversion" – of *Nachfolge* and *metanoia*: the first term indicates a going beyond which the name of Jesus opens up, the other a corresponding transformation of consciousness and of conduct. An excess which in history is named Jesus calls forth a decision which is inscribed as renewing in objective situations. The call to "follow" and the possibility of "change" entertain a formal relation which finds its truth in no single concrete expression.

Indeed, the call which is the principle of this relation cannot be known outside of the response which it receives. It has no expression of its own. We have access to Jesus only through texts which, in talking of him, narrate what he awakened and hence describe only their own status as writings of belief or of those who have turned round to respond. Jesus can only be identified in his concrete responses. We have only variants of the relation between the call and the decision, and never a statement which would lend the response an exemplary and authentic formulation by assigning to the call a site which might be proper to it. No text, whether "primary" or "apostolic," represents anything other than a "modification" (a writing) made possible by a call which cannot objectively be uttered in its own terms and which is recognized only gradually through successive conversions. The "follow me" comes from a voice which has been effaced, forever irrecuperable, vanished into the changes which echo it back, drowned in the throng of its respondents. It has nothing which is proper to it, no concrete place and no abstract expression. It is no longer anything except the tracing of a passage – made possible by it – a relation between an arrival (birth) and a departure (death), then between a return (resurrection) and a disappearance (ascension), indefinitely. Nothing but a name without a site. Writings which initially set out to respond, then, themselves develop as a series of "listening – following – changing," already inflected in a hundred different ways, and never with a stable term before them. The Name which institutes this series designates at once (and only) the different elements which it allows to emerge after it and whatever refers it to its other[22] in a movement of listening to and following the Father. Jesus is the vanishing unknown factor of this relation "call-conversion" which he names. He himself enters into this relation which posits terms which are indeterminate: he is yes (2 Corinthians 1:19), a response relative to an Unnameable who calls, and he is the continually "converted" son of the inaccessible Father who says to him "come."

The Christian movement[23] organizes an operation of which, even in the evangelical text, we have only the effect or the product, never the principle. This principle is in fact an evanescent event. It is "mythical" in a double sense: this event has no site, except for the writings which narrate it, and it generates speech and action and yet more "writings,"[24] while remaining itself unobjectifiable. This beginning point is a vanishing point. That which opens possibility is also that which goes beyond, withdraws or escapes. This event functions in the order of narration (and hence of operations) like "God" in the order of reasons (and hence of concepts and beings). It is a "fable" in the same way that God "is only a word."[25] The instituting and going beyond which this event names are signified only by the relations between writings (or operations) which are not finite in number. It seems to me that this movement is not compromised by the weakening, dissemination and even disappearance of the (ecclesial) sites. which it has traversed. They only constituted a space for its development, which can continue further. Evangelical sense (direction) is not fundamentally a site, but it expresses itself in terms of instituting and going beyond, relative to the effective sites of our history which yesterday were religious, today civil. Hence one cannot properly localize it, or seek new and specific expression for it. These projects are condemned to fail because they confuse the place where we are with the principle which creates trajectories of belief there.[26] Sense is always lost at the same time as posited in the objectivity of tasks which it does not define. All in all, it is no more sociological than ontological. It "converts," but it creates neither a place nor a being. It presupposes a world, it does not make one. Indeed, it can never be identified with the production which it renders possible. The response which it allows cannot remain moored, tied to a delimited space of the call, nor can it be confined to a (social or historical) site of the event. Practice, always relative to a site, is indefinitely "responsive" and believing, on the move, like Jacob who "went on his journey" after having erected a stele at Bethel, the unexpected and awesome place of his vision (Genesis 28:18 to 29:1). It always has to take risks further on, always uncertain and fragmentary.

For centuries the Church presented its geography of side aisles, transepts, and ambulatories to this step; that is how it constituted dogmatic, liturgical, and ethical topographies. Today there passes beyond it what first of all passed within it. Hence it is led to mark out the nature of sense through its own death as site, and thus achieve self-realization by itself reproducing the evangelical message which it was bearing: time must perish and solely the death of the body authorizes the signifying and journeying practice which is "speech." The message[27] which articulates the life of "speech" with the death of Jesus, destined to unpredictable trajectories as a spirit of which "you know neither whence it comes nor whither it goes" (John 3:8), has long since gone beyond the limits of the social body which was its underpinning and ground. Always on the move, in practices of reading which are increasingly heterogeneous and distant from any ecclesial orthodoxy, it announced the disappearance of the site. Having passed by that way, it left, as at Bethel, only the trace of stones erected into stelae and consecrated with oil – with our gratitude – before departing without return.

We can already sketch the conditions under which the "excesses" of this belief which has been cut loose from its moorings work on social practices.

First of all, Christian experience will be designated as private, whereas the determination of tasks will be public or private. There no longer seems to be room for a function which publicly combines these – that is, for a Church – even if the institution which played the role of the Church continues in the form of pressure groups, sociocultural associations, or groupings according to mentalities and property. This transformation, moreover, fits into a broader development which removes from public bodies the function of attributing sense to the existence of their members and which hands this issue over to the domain of personal risk, elucidated thanks to private (friends, family, collegiate) encounters. What disappears is therefore the possibility for Christian experience to unify itself as one body [*faire corps elle-même*]. But the necessity – and desire – is consequently reinforced of uniting with history as one body [*de faire corps avec l'histoire*]. There is no ground other than social places and tasks, interwoven, limited, and impossible to totalize. A telluric, political, and social experience is substituted for the protection afforded by the "body of sense" which guaranteed a "universe without refutation":[28] as though it had fallen from the sinking ecclesial ship, Christian experience is lost in the vast and uncertain poem of an anonymous reality which comes and goes; it renounces the appropriation of a sense which the hull and portholes conditioned, and instead receives from this indeterminate history a life which fulfills everyone by going beyond them. There is no body other than the body of the world and the mortal body. In the austerity of objective labors, there is proffered the grace of being altered by what comes, from ahead or from the side, and which goes on further – in the same way that the individual is reborn through being altered by the body of an other, and makes space for an existence of risk, both foreign to him and his own, which he makes possible by effacing himself. Concealed in the submission to the rules of a task and in the regular response to objective demands which have not been freely chosen, there can be an eroticization of history – an altering and altered passion, I would even go so far as to say being mad about loving. It is attentive, in any operation, to all the "calls" to which it may reply by turning round, discrete invitations to excesses which punctuate normal procedures with risk and which, without having a proper name or any corporate markers, manage to introduce everywhere ways of gaining by losing. It is analogous to what, since Ruysbroeck, mystics have called a "life common to all."[29] We have an image of it in Jesus swamped in the crowd like, at the end of *Children of Paradise*,[30] the clown lost in the flow of the street and gradually disappearing, "taken" – at last – by real history which until then he had merely represented.

Relegated to the private sphere and destined to lose itself in history, Christian experience must also situate itself in relation to a corpus and reread it. Past Christian experiences have given rise to countless "inscriptions" – institutional or textual. Of course the spirit which breathes life into them is not itself disclosed anywhere. Whatever production may result today from their reinterpretation is therefore not ratified by any institution or document: the divergence between "inscriptions," the un-doing of any organic connection between them, the heterogeneity of the present practices which determine their redeployment imply equally that it is impossible to identify belief and reconstitute a unity on the basis of the products of interpretative work. Designating belief is a private risk. In any discursive or socioeconomic site, it will be an effect of the questioning which I hear in these documents when I respond to them, and of the resistance which they offer to present social practices of reading. The establishment of criteria is itself only a particular element in this set of operations; it neither supervises nor dominates these. There are no stable principles which may escape the effects of interpretative operations. Practices are determined by the non-Christian conditions of their production, regardless of whether their object is Christian or not. The "excess" of belief is only traced in sites and behavior which are not proper to it. It is a writing – professional or familial, political or literary – where the relation to other Christian writings remains to be defined.

A Make-belief Fable

Feeling the Christian ground on which I thought I was walking disappear, seeing the messengers of an ending, long time under way, approach, recognizing in this my relation to history as a death with no proper future of its own, and a belief stripped of any secure site, I discover a violence of the instant. A poetic necessity (I would go so far as to say a "fervor," with all the force of that old word) is born of the loss which in fact opens onto a weakness. As if, for having glimpsed the signs of what we lacked, there gradually emerged the grace of being touched by what was most fragile and fundamental in it. The

joie impénitente
d'avoir aimé des choses ressemblantes
à ces absences qui nous font vivre

[impenitent joy
at having loved things resembling
those absences which make us live][31]

accompanies the return and "invention" of an in-fancy [*en-fance*]. What comes from elsewhere and goes further is nowhere to be found. Whatever altered or altering movement happens in us has the form of silence and beginning (*in-fans*). Something indefinitely originary, which the prose of Merleau-Ponty evoked discreetly: "It might even be the case . . . that we find in it [experience] a movement toward that which cannot possibly be present to us in the original and whose irremediable absence could therefore count as one of our originary experiences."[32] But, as far as belief is concerned, this "irremediable absence" is, in the everyday, the dissemination of an advent. The *in-fans* is an event in the turning round or alteration which responds to it. This "event," which has no social or rational place, can be expressed only in dream. Hence the biblical "stories" mingled with "dreams": "And Joseph dreamed a dream and he told it his brethren" (Genesis 37:5); "And the chief butler told his dream to Joseph" (Genesis 40:9); "Pharoah dreamed" (Genesis 41:1). Independently of the excesses which effectively trace this event within practices which lack a proper (Christian) name, the event is recounted in dream. It figures as a fable.

This sign of an innovatory non-site refers back to a will. It is a metaphor for a question of the subject which cannot, as such, be introduced into the rationalities or organizations of a society. Moreover, this metaphor remains in the interrogative; like dream, it has no sense except for what comes to it from elsewhere and from an other, as a response which one must believe in order to understand: "We have dreamed a dream and there is no interpreter of it" (Genesis 40:8); "I have dreamed a dream and there is no one that can interpret it" (Genesis 41:15), etc. Dream is unknown to the will; it passes without one being able to take it (in) [*sans qu'on le (com)prenne*]. The language of desire is at once the stranger who "troubles"[33] the place (the thief in the house) and is itself estranged from what it says (it remains masked in metaphor); more significantly still, this alterity internal to the dream (something other occurs) combines with the alterity of the speaker-interpreter (someone from outside comes, a stranger who repeats the enigma and whom one has to believe in order to give sense to the dream). Hence, in the interweaving of these alterities (the fable of the dreamer and the fiction of the interpreter), a will emerges which is difference. This will cannot therefore be confused with a choice. One does not choose to be a believer. It is a will which cuts across possibilities, these being only its symptoms. Fundamentally, being a believer is wanting to be a believer [*être croyant, c'est vouloir être croyant*]. Thérèse de Lisieux, attempting, at the end of her life, to account for her faith, declared herself a Christian because she "wanted to believe," a term which she emphasized as essential.[34] A formulation close to that of Derrida on Descartes: "To be Cartesian, . . . is to attempt to be Cartesian [*Etre cartésien, c'est . . . vouloir être cartésien*]. That is to say, . . . to-attempt-to-say-the-demonic-hyperbole from whose heights thought is announced to itself, frightens itself, and reassures itself against being annihilated or wrecked in madness or in death. At its height hyperbole, the absolute opening, the uneconomic expenditure, is always reembraced by an economy and is overcome by economy."[35] This will is not linked to a voluntarism, but to a "first passion" which is narrated in dreams.

This "first passion," marked out in practices by an excess which has no proper name, site, or sense, expresses itself in language through writings which originate in dreams. A Christian tradition of voices and visions which to us appear distant brings to us the "troubling familiarity" ("*inquiétante familiarité*")[36] of these dreams where the sense, at first absent (these "dreams" symbolize with a will), is an interpretative effect produced by the advent of another time. From this relation between fables (which desire recognizes well before they are "explained") and the determination of a sense through a history which is foreign to them (invention at a distance) is born writing. Writing is a textual site of the non-site, it weaves alterities. This "interpretation of dreams," which is what our exegesis is, states what exists only in movement. It is a literary "machine"[37] which produces, from fragments of fable, a converted and convertible language. There is a continual play between the two terms around which writing is constructed – an imaginary and an erotics of the "will." The text of belief is the result of an operation with respect to the fables which enable it. Since the institutional underpinning is lacking, since it has ceased to have an all-embracing role in relation to experience (in the past, each singular faith was formed within a Church) or to function as a referent (a reality was indistinctly presented, concealed in the life of the body), the "evangelical" corpus has become the only landmark. Since biblical discourse is no longer uttered by a Church, the former has been transformed into a discourse of a non-site. And the relation which it entertains with the act of belief is henceforth fundamentally different:

1. Instead of the expression of belief being an exposition of the (biblical) revelation which states the present truth in the historical density of an institutional and sacramental body, it is now a production which a reading operation generates from a text.
2. Instead of being a partial representation of a totality lived and given by a Church which determines theological or ethical systems, it is, alongside the fable, a divergence which responds to it while maintaining its distance, and hence it is a relation of other to other.
3. Instead of having the form of an authorized commentary which fills the biblical text with dogmatic or historical notes, and hence anchors it in an exteriority which would be its truth, provided by a wealth of theological or exegetical knowledge which would be the basis for its establishment and presentation, it is a risky proliferation, but controlled by procedures proper to this or that textual practice.

Hence the Bible passes by like a convoy of representations. Nowadays the Bible circulates in bookshops (editions of the Bible are on the increase and have good sales), in our streets and houses, and these processions of dreams come from afar, are recognizable, although they speak a language which is foreign to the languages of the sites where our knowledge is held. As Virgil said: "And in her step she was revealed, a very goddess."[38] A "manner," a procedure, a style offer the possibility of an echo – a response of gratitude – which precedes the production of what one can call sense (this echo resounding in the receptive region). In itself, fiction does not have a sense. It generates a movement. Since the Platonic division between appearance and reality, and hence between opinion and science or between fictional discourse and the discourse of truth, fiction is the language without force,[39] deprived equally of the privilege of stating being and of the power to organize practices (including the practice of its own reading). Its saying does not depend on anything which is external to it (even if a history was its condition of possibility). In the fable, "reality" is abolished. So one must forget oneself in order to reply to it, relinquish, as in sleep, the concern to secure a site or a truth (even a "historical" one), accept losing time and experience, "risk reality for appearance,"[40] and give space to a difference, to a "strength of weakness,"[41] to a fictional text; that is, to "that truth which seems a lie."[42] Thus a movement starts up. From the sign (or text) to the production of a sense (and of an other text) which traces a gesture of belief in another space, a whole activity develops, regulated at once by the resistances of the corpus (plural and mobile, relative to trajectories and methods) and by the determinations (scientific or general, at all events social) of practices of reading and writing. That is when an interpretation is made. It is constructed as a function of a depropriation, if it is true that "the near is the proper"[43] we must accept the distance which separates us from writers and speakers no longer living and, even more so, from a past Word.

As with Joseph, the one who interprets in the present is not the dreamer. He is the stranger to whom a story is offered. From his place he responds to a text (a narrated dream) and not to someone. Even less does he pride himself on being where the speakers speak from – the (historical) authors, or God – in order to explain what they "wanted to say." He is not in the same place as them, but is distant and different. He does not assign himself the place of the subject, contrary to what the theologian had to assume, through the mediation of the Church, in order to claim to say the same thing as the author better or differently. Neither is he obliged to take the Bible as a relic, an object "having belonged" to the dead person, the remains of someone no longer living, an object made "sacred" for being what was last visible before its extinction, the point where mourning is suspended and arrested by the disavowal (*Verleugnung*) of loss, already known elsewhere.[44] This will to "preserve" what one knows nevertheless to be well and truly "lost" makes the Bible function as a fetish.[45] It transforms the text into a substitute for the theologian of yesteryear. It denies the fact that the Word is no longer heard. Far from being this sort of anxious preservation of an identity, a task which is everywhere contradicted by the very methods which are put at its disposal,[46] Christian interpretation will be a process of work of the self on the self, responding from a distance to texts encountered on the way, dispersed, without any unity which one might grasp or seek, but nevertheless productive, because of the "turmoil" or (to take a more evangelical term) the "crisis" which, like dreams, they first provoke in us. If they allow sense to be constructed in this way, it is not at all a question of a sense which would state their being or truth. Here, on the contrary, throughout the operation of production, sense is predicated on the absence of truth, essence of author–subject which might be retrieved through the text. A distance between the site of production and the site of the text sets up an unbridgeable difference between the two. There is no "we" between them ("our" writing or "our" faith), for a death separates them, that of Jesus, that of his ecclesial body. The writing of belief therefore risks a sense, a traversal in its own space, "on the basis of a 'formal' organization which in itself has no meaning."[47] Hence its status as external to languages which organize social practices and its content as a difference in relation to the present, since the "meaning" which it produces is either beyond the present (teleological) or on this side of it (historical) or elsewhere with respect to the present (poetic and "fictional"). It too is of the order of a fable. However much it may be an interpretation, it nonetheless repeats at least the salient features of the evangelical fable, a language without force, structured by the absence of a body, the renunciation of proximity, and the obliteration of the proper.

From this perspective, it remains relevant – and necessary, for those who "forget themselves" when reading the first writings of belief – to explain the evangelical texts from a distance. Their content anyway corresponds to their status. Something of what they say is therefore true of all writing of belief. In this writing, an initial non-site (the empty tomb) in a sense gives rise to the function of the text (it articulates the belief which it results from with the belief of the addressees, which it makes possible), and gives rise to its content (it is the staging of this function, but according to the laws which govern a narrative). Hence the narrated story refers back to the workings which generate it. Instead of analyzing the text as a fable and recognizing in it a way of saying [*dire*], one can start from what it says [*dit*]. The two will be homologous, but the nature of the writing of belief will thereby be elucidated. Some sign will indicate how this said (the story) is characterized by a system of references to the other. The evangelical narrative is constructed by developing – unfolding and modulating – the formal relation which, in its totality, it entertains with the past (absent) object which it talks about and the future addressees (equally absent) which it is aimed at. Hence it deploys itself as a putting into relation in and through separation.

The evangelical play of *Nachfolge* and metanoia revealed the reciprocity between the gesture of Jesus – turning round in order to call – and that of the disciple – turning round in order to respond. On both sides their relation produces an act which "signals" ["*fait signe*"]. But what on both sides specifies and makes possible this signaling is a rupture of continuity: turning round. It qualifies the conduct of the disciple: breaking, abandoning, departing, renouncing, leaving, etc. And it qualifies the behavior of Jesus also. He left the Father, renounced his privileges, interrupted the genealogical line, broke his alliances, etc. His history is a series of departures, of "crises," divisions, and separations, until death, which will allow the whole corpus of his *verba et gesta* to "signal" – to become "evangelical." The very details of the text repeat this premise of signification: in Luke, Jesus is always turning round"[48] in order to speak. The advent of Jesus (the call) and the departure of his disciples (the response) suppose, in the first case, that he separates himself off in order to come and, in the second case, that they leave everything in order to follow him. A signifying practice intervenes in received identities (and in this way the streak of a difference appears in the unity of God) and in contractual stabilities (the opening of a movement toward the "Gentiles" emerges in the covenant between God and His people), as a break which institutes a relation which is not defined by conformity to a Law, but by conversion toward the other, no longer a "fidelity" but a "faith." Instead of a sacred "existence" ["*être-là*"] as principle and domain of just actions, there is the act of "coming" or "following," which makes for trust in the other, signals to him and "makes truth" [*qui fait confiance á l'autre, lui fait signe et "fait la vérité"*]. But it functions in a necessary relation to institutions and received forms which in principle are maintained.[49] The eruption of Jesus does not found a new site – a Testament, a religion – which would have a different content but the same form as the preceding one. It introduces the non-site of a difference into a system of sites. The caesura is at work everywhere, from the birth which upsets a whole genealogy to the death which disjoins the covenant between an elect people and the one God, from the word which rings false through to the miracle which resolves. In line with the signifying practice which organizes the text, everything splits, the homogeneity of traditions, the coherence of belongings, the unity of a people or of a public of listeners, the relation of authorities to their authoritative sources, etc. What the name "Jesus" signs in this text (premise of the work by which the entire text establishes this name in the spoken word and produces the name "Christ") is the sharpness, the *nettezza*,[50] the bone structure, as if the rest were secondary and were to follow – as effects of difference in an unforeseeable plurality of systems.

The relation which this break marks out in the site (that of the Covenant) where it is produced is called faith. It has many modulated forms within the general line of the narrative which the relation between an itinerancy and a communication still constructs, from birth to ascension. Believing is "coming" or "following" (a gesture marked by a separation), leaving one's place, being disarmed by this exile out of identity and contract, and thus renouncing possession and heritage so as to be delivered to the voice of the other and dependent on his coming or response.[51] Waiting in this way for death or life from the other, hoping that his voice will ceaselessly alter the body itself, making one's temple out of the effect in the house of a distancing of the self through a turning round which "signals," these are without doubt what the break of belief introduces within or in the space of play of any system, what faith and charity imply or what the figure of Jesus represents, itinerant, naked, and abandoned; that is, without a site, without power and, like H. Miller's clown, "forever outside"[52] of himself, wounded by the stranger, converted to the other without being held by him. But this does not constitute a site – be it institutional, dogmatic, historical, or psychological. The fable does not give an identity. It would still be a deception to take expenditure, waste or pauperization as the sites which this text might define and which a practice of the break might guarantee. The temptation of the "spiritual" is to constitute the act of difference as a site, to transform the conversion into an establishment, to replace the "poem" which states the hyperbole with the strength to make history or to be the truth which takes history's place, or, lastly, as in evangelical transfiguration (a metaphoric movement), to take the "vision" as a "tent" and the word as a new land. In its countless writings along many different trajectories, Christian spirituality offers a huge inventory of difference, and ceaselessly criticizes this trap; it has insisted particularly on the impossibility for the believer of stopping on the "moment" of the break – a practice, a departure, a work, an ecstasy – and of identifying faith with a site. Today we are even more radically obliged, due to history, to take this lesson seriously. It concerns the Church itself, which is losing its property. The Christian "new Israel" seems to rejoin the old Israel in exile and in the diaspora. Just as, after the destruction of the Temple, the Jews were deprived of a country, with no proper place and hence without history (there is history only where there is a site), so believers are abandoned to the road with only texts for luggage. The two thousand years necessary for this second exile can be seen as having resulted in the transfiguration of the "letter" of the Law into a "poem" of difference. Throughout this time, Christian work can be seen as producing this conversion of the legality of the text – that is, its remaining strength – into the weakness of a fable; the alphabet of divine wisdoms into the writing of a "madness"; the truth of thoughts and practices given by the Book into that of a "dream" which cuts into thoughts and practices. What from now on is essential is not what remains of ecclesial property – sites which henceforth function as financial associations, which have cultural prestige or are historically latent – nor is it the ideological substitutes for this body of sense – communities of utterance, historical facts, "anthropological" positivities. It is, rather, the operation which is traced in the effective sites of our social belonging when these sites are put into relation with the break of which the condition of possibility is the evangelical fable, throughout its present and past versions. No site can guarantee their connection. The fable remains always in the distance, as the poetic other of historical effectivity, as a utopia which articulates with social topographies only through private risk. There is no in-between or mediation except, ephemerally and never guaranteed, the act of belief, which is inscribed sometimes in practices without a proper name, sometimes in Christian fictions devoid of operative force. Thus trajectories of belief come and go, broken into narratives without power and stories without words, still made possible by the name of Jesus, this "significant passer-by" ["*passant considérable*"].[53]

Like a Drop in the Ocean

A transitory and local reflexion is incapable of stating Christianity's situation. It is only the narrative of a belief, as it is written from a place, from within solidarities and friendships, scientific and social practices. It is also yet another "dream" which a Christian break marks in my imaginary topography of water and stones, liquids and solids. A fragile and floating text, witness to itself alone, yet lost in the innumerable murmur of language, and hence perishable. But this fable heralds the joy of obliterating itself in what it figures, of returning to the anonymous work out of which it was born, of converting itself to this other which it is not. The writing of belief, in its weakness, appears on the ocean of language only to disappear, taken up into the work of uncovering, in other writings, the movement by which, ceaselessly, they "come" and "go." According to an expression of the mystics, it is a "drop in the ocean."[54]

This scriptural work has no respectability in itself, nor any truth in itself. It traverses the vocabulary of a space. It is orientated toward other work. It is a fleeting and rapid operation. Its "evangelical" mark would be the wound which the angel at Yabbok (Genesis 32:23–32), the night-time thief of the parable,[55] the uncanny familiarity of the dream produces by day in a territory or an activity. And since, by contrast, a signature is, in this, the sign of the locality where this work is carried out, the mark of the proper altered already by the effacement which it is destined for, I readily come back to the esoteric tradition according to which everyone spends his time, throughout his life, seeking out the sense – the direction – of which his proper name is the enigma. This text is in fact a stage in the itinerancy produced by the quest for the proper name; that is to say, the name which comes to us always from an other. "Michel" is "Who is like El?" – who is like the Unnameable, God? This word says the opposite of the proper. In the (fearful? respectful? retiring?) mode of the question, it calls for its erasure.

Notes

1 Who is "qualified" to pronounce a medical discourse? "What is the status of the individuals who – alone – have the right, sanctioned by law or tradition, juridically defined or spontaneously accepted, to proffer such a discourse?" Indeed, "medical statements cannot come from anybody" (Michel Foucault, *The Archeology of Knowledge*, trans. A. M. Sheridan Smith; London: Tavistock Books, 1972, pp. 50, 51).

2 Hence the related question of the "accreditation for the practice of psychoanalysis." See Jacques Lacan, *Ecrits* (Paris: Le Seuil, 1966), p. 230.

3 The two uses of the word "competence" communicate here: the sociological use refers to the relation which knowledge entertains with a social site (within one's "competence"); the other, linguistic, denotes the fact of knowing a language well enough to construct or understand sentences.

4 During the second third of the twentieth century (from 1933 to 1966 – as a reminder, Henri de Lubac's *Catholicisme* dates from 1938 and the Second Vatican Council lasted from 1962 to 1965), the internal shake-up of the Church finds expression in an "ecclesiological" overproduction: the object produced by the discourse slowly takes over from the body which produces it. But it still has the form of what is missing. Subsequently, a "pluralist" representation replaces a unitary one.

5 It is understandable that the hierarchy should set "checks," retreating from the open-handed reformist "adaptation" of previous years in order to mark limits in the dispersed proliferation of Christian "expressions." Any institution which refused this course of action would be suicidal. The "reaction" which at present prevails in the Church is, in this light, perfectly explicable: the refusal to vanish into the just about anything. Unfortunately, these gestures arrive too late. The restrictive measures no longer work. They do not change practices. In fact, the ambition behind these "checks" is generally of a more modest nature: they seek solely to preserve a language. The hierarchy is too cautious to ask for anything other than for principles to be upheld in statements, regardless of what the actual practice of Christians is, which is not addressed, as though it had no relevance for official discourses. Already sketched here are the preoccupations of the future curator of the cultural treasure produced by Christianity. No longer a body [*corps*] but a corpus [*corpus*].

6 This transit in search of a "working-class" land is in line with a series of "departures" over four centuries. An elsewhere becomes necessary to the Church as soon as it has difficulty finding a place of its own in the culture. Since the seventeenth

century, "missions" have tried to establish in other domains (the savage, disadvantaged milieus, "refuges," etc.) the basis which was missing from their own internal identity. On this historical aspect, see Michel de Certeau, *The Writing of History*, chapter 4, "The Formality of Practices from Religious Systems to the Ethics of the Enlightenment (the 17th and 18th centuries)." But the more the internal "base" diminishes, the worse this movement of extraposition becomes, until today, when, for the mass media or for "unbelievers" concerned with "values," it is often the external effects of this exit out of itself which give credence to the existence of the Church. Like a star which, after its death, still emits light.

7 By "community," I do not particularly mean groups who live together and share activities, but any grouping which aims to provide a site for the expression of a Christian identity. It is no longer a Church, an institution which organizes religious practices in accordance with a received truth. And, even if made up exclusively of Christians, it is not yet a team which has as its goal a social activity or the expression of a friendship.

8 For a long time, political, economic, or civil society functioned as a substitute ecclesiology, and hence as a site of sense. From the political doctrines of the seventeenth century to the social philosophies or economic sciences of the nineteenth century, a whole tradition attributed the role of being the social site of sense for the entire population to a particular class in society (the bourgeois elite of the "Enlightenment" or the working classes of the nineteenth century), and moreover attributed to it pedagogical, sacramental, and missionary functions which replaced former ecclesial functions. Increasing technocracy progressively took away this role of "stating meaning" from economic, social, or political formations. Questioning the meaning of existence is no longer taken on by institutions, nor is the reply, assured by social groups. This questioning gives rise to communal elaborations in the private sphere, in the chinks of technocratic companies and public services. On this new social structuring, see Michel de Certeau, *Le Christianisme éclaté* (Paris: Le Seuil, 1974), p. 35.

9 See Michel de Certeau, "Ethno-Graphy: Speech, or the Space of the Other. Jean de Léry." [In this volume.]

10 On the "Poem of Christ," see, for example, Peter Kemp, *Théorie de l'engagement*, vol. 2, *Poétique de l'engagement* (Paris: Le Seuil, 1973), pp. 77–111.

11 See Harvey Cox, *The Secular City: Secularization and Urbanization in Theological Perspective* (New York: Macmillan, 1965/6) and *The Feast of Fools: a Theological Essay on Festivity and Fantasy* (Cambridge: Harvard University Press, 1969).

12 "Subject" should be understood here not in relation to the individual but to the site which spoken language refers back to: the speaker of the discourse, the addresser of the contract of utterance, the subject of the utterance.

13 In the American Jesus Freaks communities, the balance is different, because the ineffable experience of election or salvation is immediately translated into something objective: the ineffable grace of being "elect" or "saved" must be spelt out in the biblical text which speaks the truth on this and is received as a corpus which is literally revealed. The vanishing of sense in the ecstasy of saying oneself (saved) is

immediately linked back to the necessity of reading the true letter. This combination guarantees the transition from speech act to textual work, from an utterance to a system of statements, and hence also from a subjectivity to the social organization of a body of knowledge. Instead of demonstrating the very close link between saying and said, Catholic Christianity tends to show the opposite: a gradual dissociation of the unspeakable act of affirming one's Christianity (utterance) from the exegetical products of a historicizing or semantic practice carried out on Christian documents (statements); that is, the dissociation of an "aphasia" of believers from a knowledge of clerics.

14 The community really does represent the evangelical movement, but it mistakes it for something which should define a site: it perishes in the trap of this contradiction or else, in responding to the demand that it should define itself as a site, it ceases to be Christian.

15 See, for example, the reflexions of Paul M. van Buren, *The Edges of Language. An Essay in the Logic of a Religion* (New York: Macmillan, 1972), on the subject of the word God: "The logic of 'God' is the logic of the last limit of language..." (p. 132).

16 Likewise, the study of a particular literary text focuses on identifiable variants at the level of "expression," whereas the serial structural analysis of a "genre" (the folktale, the short story, etc.) defines general models which allow a multiplicity of literary productions to be generated. One could say, analogically, that Christian productions no longer make up a genre of their own, but represent possible variants, each one relative to the many "series" constituted by the social organization.

17 The instability of the relations between belief and behavior is a problem which dates back three centuries: see the reference in note 6 above.

18 Which they frequently are. Thus, in 1973, the support which a certain French political position expected from traditional "Christian milieus" on the subject of legislation on abortion produced a more hardline doctrine on the part of the hierarchy, which in turn allowed the "Church" to exert political pressure indirectly on this issue or on the subject of education. A system of alliances between social milieus and political powers orientated the "doctrinal" position. The traditional Christian position was the tool of a political game between pressure groups.

19 See, for example, the very precise studies, the best of their kind, carried out in Switzerland by the Institut für Ehe- und Familienwissenschaft in Zürich (*Situation und Bedürfnisse der Ehe-und Familienpastoral in der Diözese Chur...*, 1970), or in Germany (*Synode, Amtliche Mitteilungen der gemeinsamen Synode der Bistümer in der Bundesrepublik Deutschland*, ed. K. Forster, vol. 2, 1970, 19ff; vol. 1, 1971, pp. 21ff).

20 Franz Böckle, "La morale fondamentale," in *Recherches de science religieuse*, vol. 59, 1971, p. 363, note 85.

21 In English in the text. (Tr.)

22 "The Word was with God, and the Word was God" ["Le Verbe est à lui et vers lui"], John 1:1.

23 See Claude Chabrol and Louis Mann, *Le Récit évangélique* (Paris, Aubier Montaigne, coll. "Bibliothéque de sciences religieuses," 1974), pp. 91–161.

24 In the broad sense which I give to "writing."

25 See Emmanuel Levinas, *En découvrant l'existence avec Husserl et Heidegger*, 2nd edn (Paris: Vrin, 1967), pp. 217–36, "Language and proximity," especially the section entitled "It is only a word" (pp. 235–6).

26 The community really does represent the evangelical movement, but it mistakes it for something which should define a site: it perishes in the trap of this contradiction or else, in responding to the demand that it should define itself as a site, it ceases to be Christian.

27 Which is not solely the written text.

28 Raymond Aron, in Christian Chabanis, *Dieu existe-t-il? Non . . .* (Paris: Fayard, 1973).

29 For Ruysbroeck, the "life common to all" (*dat ghemeyne leven*) joins created beings to each other in the "service of all" and makes the "moments" of action and contemplation (initially distinct, successive, or antinomic) coincide. The "elevated" man is the "common man"; he "owes himself to all those who seek his help" and he shares the "life common to all" of God, eternally active and eternally at rest. See John of Ruysbroeck, *The Adornment of the Spiritual Marriage, The Sparkling Stone, The Book of Supreme Truth*, trans. C. A. Wynschenk Dom, ed. and int. Evelyn Underhill (Felinfarch: Llanerch, 1995, pp. 109–10); *Royaume des amants de Dieu, XXXV and XLIII*, etc. On *ghemeynheit* and the "life common to all," see, for example, Paul Henry, "La mystique trinitaire du bienheureux Jean Ruisbroec," in *Recherches de science religieuse*, vol. 41, 1953, pp. 63–75.

30 *Les enfants du paradis* (1945), a French film directed by Marcel Carné. (Tr.)

31 Rainer Maria Rilke, *Vergers*, 59 (Paris: Gallimard, 1926), p. 81. This poem was written directly in French. The German edition of Rilke's works (*Sämtliche Werke*, ed. Rilke-Archiv, II/2, Wiesbaden, 1957) and the most complete French collection (*Œuvres*, vol. 2, *Poésie*, ed. Paul de Man; Paris: Le Seuil, 1972, p. 500) give as the last word of the last line "act" [*agir*] rather than "live" [*vivre*].

32 See Maurice Merleau-Ponty, *Le Visible et l'Invisible* (Paris: Gallimard, 1964), p. 211.

33 In the story of Joseph, the eunchs are "sad" (Genesis 40:6–7), or the pharoah "troubled" (Genesis 41:8), because of the dream.

34 See Thérèse de l'Enfant-Jesus, *Ecrits autobiographiques* (Paris: Le Seuil, coll. "Livre de vie," 1957), pp. 247ff.

35 Jacques Derrida, *Writing and Difference*, trans. Alan Bass (Chicago: University of Chicago Press, 1978), pp. 61–2.

36 Freud's essay "The Uncanny" (*The Standard Edition of the Complete Psychological Works of Sigmund Freud*, trans. Alix and James Strachey, vol. XVII; London: Hogarth Press and the Institute of Psychoanalysis, 1955, pp. 217–56) is particularly concerned with literary fiction. See Jacques Derrida, *Dissemination*, trans. Barbara Johnson (Chicago: University of Chicago Press, 1981), p. 268; Michel de Certeau, *L'Absent de l'histoire*, "Alterations," pp. 176ff.

37 As we know, Pascalian dialectics designates its literary production as a "machine" capable of "turning statements in all senses" and of "varying the utterances": "ways of turning things are infinite." See "Traité des ordres numériques," in Pascal, *Œuvres complètes* (Paris: Le Seuil, 1963), p. 65. It is the logical form of an "infinite" movement of transformation or "conversion."

38 Virgil, *Aeneid*, I, 405: "Vera incessu patuit dea," Virgil in 2 volumes, trans. H. Rushton Fairclough (London: Heinemann, 1978, vol. 1), p. 269.

39 See Philippe Lacoue-Labarthe, "The Fable (Literature and Philosophy)," trans. Hugh Silverman, in *The Subject of Philosophy*, ed. Thomas Trezise (Minneapolis: University of Minnesota Press, 1993), pp. 1–13.

40 Schiller distinguished two stages in aesthetic education: "for a long time man just uses appearances for his own ends"; but a "total revolution" occurs when there appear in him "traces of a free and disinterested appreciation of pure appearance." "From the moment when man begins at all to prefer form to matter and to risk reality for appearance (which, in return, he therefore has to recognize), a breach is opened in the circle of his animal life and he finds himself on a path that has no end." See *On the Aesthetic Education of Man in a Series of Letters* (1794–5), trans. and int. Elizabeth M. Wilkinson and L. A. Willoughby (Oxford: Clarendon, 1982 (1967)), Letter 27.

41 Philippe Lacoue-Labarthe, op. cit., p. 12.

42 Dante, *Inferno*, XVI, 124: "Quel ver c'ha faccia di menzogna." *The Divine Comedy*, trans. Geoffrey L. Bickersteth (Oxford: Basil Blackwell, 1985), p. 116.

43 Jacques Derrida, *Margins of Philosophy*, trans. Alan Bass (Chicago: University of Chicago Press, 1982), p. 133.

44 See the remarks of Pierre Fédida, "La relique et le travail du deuil," in *Nouvelle Revue de psychanalyse*, no. 2, entitled "Objets du fétichisme," 1970, pp. 249–54.

45 See Octave Mannoni, *Clefs pour l'imaginaire ou l'Autre Scène* (Paris: Le Seuil, 1969), pp. 11ff: "I know, but still . . ."

46 The exegete is well aware that his technical apparatus, organized by literary and historical disciplines dating back to the beginning of the century, leads him far from the inspired site of speech from which the theologian claimed to talk in the name of the Church. He examines objects, using methods which are foreign to them. But he puts checks everywhere, due to the received ideology with which he covers his work, the dogmatic restrictions which suspend its logical developments, the "theological" isolation which sets the biblical corpus aside, etc. He is the man of the but still. He is functionally what remains of the theologian, linked to a text which is "held on to," as is the rest of the ecclesial body.

47 Jacques Derrida, *Margins*, p. 134.

48 Luke 7:9; 7:44; 9:55; 10:22–3; 14:25; 22:61; 23:28.

49 See, for example, Louis Mann's analyses of the "effacement" and "resurrection" of toponyms in the Gospels, a work of transformation while maintaining a network, in *Sémiotique de la Passion. Topiques et figures* (Paris: Aubier Montaigne, coll. "Bibliothèque de sciences religieuses," 1971), pp. 31–47.

Select Bibliography

hensive bibliography of Certeau's work compiled by Luce Giard. It
uce Giard (ed.), *Le voyage mystique. Michel de Certeau* (Paris: RSR/
91–243. Listed here are Certeau's books and translated articles. All
English will be indebted to Jeremy Ahearne's in *Michel de Certeau:*
ts Other (see below).

Books

re Favre, *Memorial*, trans., ed., and introduced by Michel de Certeau
de Brouwer, 1960).

, *Guide spirituel pour la perfection*, ed. and introduced by Michel de
Descleee de Brouwer, 1963).

Chardin, *Lettres a Leontine Zanta*, introduced by R. Garric and H. de
Michel de Certeau (Paris: Desclee de Brouwer, 1965).

, *Correspondence*, ed. and introduced by Michel de Certeau (Paris:
uwer, 1966).

autres écrits politiques (1968; Paris: Seuil, 1994); original title *Le prise de*
nouvelle culture. Translated as *The Capture of Speech and Other Political*
m Conley and introduced by Luce Giard (Minneapolis: University of
s, 1997).

on dans la différence (1969; Paris: Desclee de Brouwer, 1991).

Loudun (1970; Paris: Gallimard/Julliard, 1990). Michael B. Smith
translation of this through the University of Chicago Press in

ire, s.l., Mame, 1973.

50 Nettezza was already the wor
Léonce de Grandmaison came
Jesus-Christ (Paris: Beauchesne,
51 Thus, in the Transfiguration, li
and the voice of the cloud repl
parallels.
52 [In English in the text – Tr.].
(New York: New Directions E
process of becoming, always se
53 I take this word from Mallarmé
Mallarmé, *Œuvres complètes* (Pa
54 See Saint Bernard, *De diligendo*
33; Surin, *Guide spirituel*, VII,
chrétienne, in *Œuvres*, vol. 6, p
concept and its transformations,
55 Luke 12:39; Matthew 24:43; A

There is a compr
can be found in
Cerf, 1988), pp.
bibliographies in
Interpretation and

Bienheureux Pie
(Paris: Desclee
Jean-Joseph Suri
Certeau (Paris
Pierre Teilhard d
Lubac, ed. by
Jean-Joseph Suri
Desclee de Br
La prise de parole
parole. Pour un
Writings, by T
Minnesota Pr
L'Etranger ou l'u
La possession de
is publishing
1999.
L'Absent de l'hist

50 Nettezza was already the word – taken from Catherine de Gênes – by which Léonce de Grandmaison came to characterize the evangelical figure of Jesus, in *Jesus-Christ* (Paris: Beauchesne, 1928, vol. 2), p. 121.

51 Thus, in the Transfiguration, listening replaces inhabiting the holy site (the tent), and the voice of the cloud replaces the vision of "glory." See Luke 9:28–36 and parallels.

52 [In English in the text – Tr.]. Henry Miller, *The Smile at the Foot of the Ladder* (New York: New Directions Books, 1958), p. 48, Epilogue: "We are always in process of becoming, always separated and detached, forever outside."

53 I take this word from Mallarmé on Rimbaud in his letter to Harrison Rhodes. See Mallarmé, *Œuvres complètes* (Paris: Gallimard, coll. "Pléiade", 1945), p. 512.

54 See Saint Bernard, *De diligendo Deo*, §28; Harphius, *Theologia mystica*, II, 3, chap. 33; Surin, *Guide spirituel*, VII, 8; Fénelon, *Instructions sur la morale et la perfection chrétienne*, in *Œuvres*, vol. 6, p. 116, etc. On the significance of this symbolic concept and its transformations, see Michel de Certeau, *The Mystic Fable* I.

55 Luke 12:39; Matthew 24:43; Acts 16, 15, etc.

Translated by Saskia Brown

Select Bibliography

There is a comprehensive bibliography of Certeau's work compiled by Luce Giard. It can be found in Luce Giard (ed.), *Le voyage mystique. Michel de Certeau* (Paris: RSR/Cerf, 1988), pp. 191–243. Listed here are Certeau's books and translated articles. All bibliographies in English will be indebted to Jeremy Ahearne's in *Michel de Certeau: Interpretation and Its Other* (see below).

Books

Bienheureux Pierre Favre, *Memorial*, trans., ed., and introduced by Michel de Certeau (Paris: Desclee de Brouwer, 1960).

Jean-Joseph Surin, *Guide spirituel pour la perfection*, ed. and introduced by Michel de Certeau (Paris: Descleee de Brouwer, 1963).

Pierre Teilhard de Chardin, *Lettres a Leontine Zanta*, introduced by R. Garric and H. de Lubac, ed. by Michel de Certeau (Paris: Desclee de Brouwer, 1965).

Jean-Joseph Surin, *Correspondence*, ed. and introduced by Michel de Certeau (Paris: Desclee de Brouwer, 1966).

La prise de parole et autres écrits politiques (1968; Paris: Seuil, 1994); original title *Le prise de parole. Pour une nouvelle culture*. Translated as *The Capture of Speech and Other Political Writings*, by Tom Conley and introduced by Luce Giard (Minneapolis: University of Minnesota Press, 1997).

L'Etranger ou l'union dans la différence (1969; Paris: Desclee de Brouwer, 1991).

La possession de Loudun (1970; Paris: Gallimard/Julliard, 1990). Michael B. Smith is publishing a translation of this through the University of Chicago Press in 1999.

L'Absent de l'histoire, s.l., Mame, 1973.

La culture au pluriel (1974; Paris: Seuil, 1993). Translated as *Culture in the Plural*, by Tom Conley and introduced by Luce Giard (Minneapolis: University of Minnesota Press, 1997).

Le christianisme éclaté, with Jean-Marie Domenach (Paris: Seuil, 1974).

L'Ecriture de l'histoire (1975; Paris: Gallimard, 1984. Translated as *The Writing of History* by Tom Conley (New York: Columbia University Press, 1988).

Une politique de la langue. La Révolution française et les patois: l'enquête de Gregoire, with Dominique Julia and Jacques Revel (Paris: Gallimard, 1975). Chapters 2–7 are by Certeau.

L'Invention du quotidien, vol. 1: *Arts de faire* (1980; Paris: Gallimard, 1990). Translated as *The Practice of Everyday Life*, by Steven Rendall (Berkeley: University of California Press, 1984).

L'Invention du quotidien, vol. 2: *Habiter, cuisiner*, with Luce Giard and Pierre Mayol (1980; Paris: Gallimard, 1994); the 1980 edition is only prefaced by Certeau, the later edition has two chapters by him. Translated as *The Practice of Everyday Life*, vol. 2: *Living and Cooking*, by Timothy J. Tomasik (Minneapolis: University of Minnesota Press, 1998).

La fable mystique, vol. 1: *XVIe–XVIIe siècle* (1982; Paris: Gallimard, 1987). Translated as *The Mystic Fable*, vol. 1: *The Sixteenth and Seventeenth Centuries*, by Michael B. Smith (Chicago: University of Chicago Press, 1992).

L'Ordinaire de la communication, with Luce Giard et al. (Paris: Dalloz, 1983). The part written with Luce Giard constitutes part III of *La prise de parole et autres écrits politiques*, translated into English by Tom Conley.

Heterologies: Discourse on the Other, trans. Brian Massumi, foreword by Wlad Godzich (Minneapolis: University of Minnesota Press; Manchester: Manchester University Press, 1986).

Histoire et psychanalyse entre science et fiction, ed. Luce Giard (Paris: Gallimard, 1987).

La faiblesse de croire, ed. Luce Giard (Paris: Seuil, 1987).

Selected Articles in English

"Jean-Joseph Surin," in James Walsh (ed.), *Spirituality through the Centuries: Ascetics and Mystics of the Western Church* (London: Burns and Oates, 1964), pp. 293–306.

"Culture and Spiritual Experience," trans. J. E. Anderson, *Concilium*, 19 (1966), pp. 3–16.

"Power against the People," *New Blackfriars*, 51 (1970), pp. 338–44.

"Is There a Language of Unity?," trans. Lancelot Sheppard, *Concilium*, 51 (1970), pp. 79–93.

"On the Oppositional Practices of Everyday Life," trans. Fredric Jameson and Carl Lovitt, *Social Text. Theory/Culture/Ideology*, 3 (1980), pp. 3–43.

"Writing vs Time: History and Anthropology in the Works of Lafitav," *Yale French Studies*, 59 (1980), pp. 37–64.

"History: Ethics, Science and Fiction," in Norma Haan et al. (eds), *Social Science as Moral Inquiry* (New York: Columbia University Press, 1983), pp. 135–52.

"Lacan: an Ethics of Speech," *Representations*, 3 (1983), pp. 21–39.
"The Madness of Vision," trans. Michael B. Smith, *Enclitic*, 7(1) (1983), pp. 24–31.
"Pay Attention: to Make Art," in Helen Mayer Harrison and Newton Harrison, *The Lagoon Cycle* (Ithaca, NY: Cornell University Press, 1985), pp. 17–23.
"The Gaze: Nicholas of Cusa," trans. Catherine Porter, *Diacritics*, Fall (1987), pp. 2–38.
"Mystic," trans. Marsanne Brammer, *Diacritics*, 22(2) (1992), pp. 11–25.
"History Is Never Sure," trans. Michael B. Smith, in Ian Buchanan (ed.), *Social Semiotics*, 6(1) (1996), pp. 7–16. This is a translation of Certeau's introduction to *La possession de Loudun.*
"How is Christianity Thinkable Today?," in Graham Ward (ed.), *The Postmodern God* (Oxford: Blackwell, 1997), pp. 142–55.
"White Ecstasy," trans. Frederick Christian Bauerschmidt and Catriona Hanley, in Graham Ward (ed.), *The Postmodern God*, pp. 155–8.

Books on Certeau

Jeremy Ahearne, *Michel de Certeau: Interpretation and the Other* (Cambridge: Polity Press, 1995).
Claude Geifre (ed.), *Michel de Certeau ou la différence chrétienne* (Paris: Cerf, 1991).
Luce Giard (ed.), *Michel de Certeau* (Paris: Centre Georges Pompidou, 1987).
Luce Giard (ed.), *Le voyage mystique. Michel de Certeau* (Paris: RSR/Cerf, 1988). This volume also appears as two complete issues of *Recherches de Science Religieuse*, 73(2, 3) (1988).
Luce Giard, H. Martin and J. Revel, *Histoire, mystique et politique. Michel de Certeau* (Grenoble: Jerome Millon, 1991).

Special Issues of Journals on Certeau's Work

Diacritics, 22(2) (1992), ed. Tom Conley and Richard Terdiman, with articles by Roger Chartier, Tom Conley, François Hartog, Samuel Kinser, Richard Terdiman, Stephen Ungar, and Mark Poster, and Certeau's essay "Mystic."
Social Semiotics, 6(1) (1996), ed. Ian Buchanan, with articles by Ian Buchanan, Tom Conley, Tan See kam, Lois McNay, Susan Melrose, and Gail Reekie, and Certeau's "History Is Never Sure."
New Blackfriars, 77 (1996), ed. Graham Ward, with articles by Jeremy Ahearne, Frederick Christian Bauerschmidt, Ian Buchanan, Joseph Moingt, and Graham Ward, and a preface by Luce Giard.
South Atlantic Quarterly (1999), ed. Ian Buchanan, with articles by Frederick Christian Bauerschmidt, Ian Buchanan, Tom Conley, Verena Andermatt Conley, John Frow, Mark Poster, Richard Terdiman, and Graham Ward.

Other Articles in English on Certeau's Work

Frederick Christian Bauerschmidt, "The Abrahamic Voyage: Michel de Certeau and Theology," *Modern Theology*, 12(1) (1996), pp. 1–26.

Frederick Christian Bauerschmidt, "Introduction to Michel de Certeau," in Graham Ward (ed.), *The Postmodern God*, pp. 135–42.

Ian Buchanan, "Writing the Wrongs of History: de Certeau and Post-colonialism," *SPAN: Journal of South Pacific Association for Commonwealth Literature and Language Studies*, 33 (1992), pp. 39–46.

Jacques Derrida, "The Number of Yes," trans. Brian Holmes, *Qui Parle*, 2(2) (1991), pp. 120–33.

John Frow, "Michel de Certeau and the Practice of Representation," *Cultural Studies*, 5(1) (1991), pp. 52–60.

I. W. F. Maclean, "The Heterologies of Michel de Certeau," *Paragraph*, 9 (1987), pp. 83–7.

T. Schirato, "My Space or Yours? De Certeau, Frow and the Meanings of Popular Culture," *Cultural Studies*, 7(2) (1993), pp. 282–91.

R. Silverstone, "'Let us then Return to the Murmuring of Everyday Practices': a Note on Michel de Certeau, Television and Everyday Life," *Theory, Culture and Society*, 6(1) (1989), pp. 77–94.

Graham Ward, "Postmodern Theology," in David Ford (ed.), *Modern Theologians* (Oxford: Blackwell, 1996).

Graham Ward, "Certeau," in *Theology and Contemporary Critical Theory*, 2nd edn (London: Macmillan, 1999).

Index